Brute Force

THE SUNY SERIES

HORIZONS OF CINEMA

MURRAY POMERANCE | EDITOR

Brute Force

Animal Horror Movies

Dominic Lennard

Cover image: David Naughton (as David Kessler) in *An American Werewolf in London* (1981), directed by John Landis. Credit: Universal Pictures/Photofest.

Published by State University of New York Press, Albany

© 2019 State University of New York

All rights reserved

Printed in the United States of America

No part of this book may be used or reproduced in any manner whatsoever without written permission. No part of this book may be stored in a retrieval system or transmitted in any form or by any means including electronic, electrostatic, magnetic tape, mechanical, photocopying, recording, or otherwise without the prior permission in writing of the publisher.

For information, contact State University of New York Press, Albany, NY
www.sunypress.edu

Library of Congress Cataloging-in-Publication Data

Names: Lennard, Dominic, author.
Title: Brute force : animal horror movies / Dominic Lennard.
Description: Albany : State University of New York, [2019] | Series: SUNY series horizons of cinema | Includes bibliographical references and index.
Identifiers: LCCN 2018056834 | ISBN 9781438476612 (hardcover : alk. paper) | ISBN 9781438476605 (pbk. : alk. paper) | ISBN 9781438476629 (ebook)
Subjects: LCSH: Horror films—History and criticism. | Animals in motion pictures.
Classification: LCC PN1995.9.H6 L3853 2019 | DDC 791.43/6164—dc23
LC record available at https://lccn.loc.gov/2018056834

10 9 8 7 6 5 4 3 2 1

To my mother and father

Contents

List of Illustrations	ix
Acknowledgments	xvii
Introduction: Welcome (Back) to the Jungle	1
1 Going Ape: *King Kong*	21
2 Out of Our Depth: Surviving Marine Monsters	43
3 Man versus Wild: Bears, Wolves, and the Men Who Fight Them	69
4 Creepy Crawlies: Intelligent Ants, Sickening Spiders, and Other Ill-intentioned Invertebrates	89
5 Mad Science Makes for Cranky Creatures	113
6 In Their Sights: The Gaze of the Predator	137
7 Snakes Alive	153
8 Bad Dog! The Rogue Hounds of Horror	169
9 Beast Mode: Becoming the Wolf Man	187
Aftermath	213

Notes	217
Works Cited	237
Index	247

Illustrations

Figure I.1 Saber-tooth cat (*Smilodon fatalis*) skull cast with jaws open. These impressive predators were a fearsome hazard of the Pleistocene environment in North and South America. Other species of saber-tooth roamed Europe, Africa, Eurasia, and Indonesia. 3

Figure I.2 Famous cinematic snake-hater Indiana Jones (Harrison Ford) faces a cobra in *Raiders of the Lost Ark*. We are predisposed to fear snakes because of the threat they posed to our prehuman ancestors. 7

Figure I.3 Tim (Joseph Mazzello), hiding behind a log, is fascinated by the sight of the Tyrannosaurus devouring its prey in Steven Spielberg's *Jurassic Park*. The impulse to observe one's predators is reflected elsewhere in the animal kingdom. 9

Figure I.4 *Hercules and Iolaus slaying the Hydra* (1545), engraving by Sebald Beham. As well as its reptilian frame and multiple snake-necks, the hydra is depicted here with wolfish heads. Mythological traditions are filled with monsters that resemble, or combine features of, animals that would have presented real threats in our species' own natural history. 10

Figure 1.1 *Gorille enlevant une femme* by Emmanuel Frémiet. 22

Figure 1.2 A gorilla ominously approaches a bound beauty in *The Sign of the Cross*. 23

Figure 1.3 The captured king: the mighty Kong manacled for public amusement in *King Kong* (1933). 25

x   Illustrations

Figure 1.4   While acknowledging her beauty, Jack Driscoll
              (Bruce Cabot) is nevertheless initially unfriendly
              toward his lovely female shipmate, Ann (Fay Wray)
              in *King Kong*, wary that she'll generate intrasexual
              male rivalry. It won't be on the ship, but Jack will
              find a rival, all right.   28

Figure 1.5   The weary Kong, riddled with bullets, seconds before
              falling from his great height in a fate that also
              symbolizes his romantic rejection, in *King Kong*.   31

Figure 1.6   The beautiful and flirtatious Dwan (Jessica Lange)
              quickly becomes the center of attention upon
              awakening in *King Kong* (2005).   36

Figure 1.7   "You know how much an associate professor earns?"
              Despite the romantic setting, Jack (Jeff Bridges) begins
              to count himself out as a competitive mate for the
              high-maintenance starlet Dwan in *King Kong*.   37

Figure 1.8   Kong faces off against a Tyrannosaurus in Ann's
              (Naomi Watts's) defense, in Peter Jackson's *King Kong*.   39

Figure 1.9   Tough guy, soft heart: Ann (Naomi Watts) approaches
              Kong, gazing contemplatively over Skull Island at
              sunset, in *King Kong*.   39

Figure. 2.1   Mistaking the ocean for a domain of spirited leisure,
              Chrissie (Susan Backlinie) becomes herself the
              plaything of the predator in Steven Spielberg's *Jaws*.   46

Figure 2.2   Already psychologically consumed by his own animal
              aggression, Quint (Robert Shaw) is now literally
              consumed by the animal in *Jaws*.   48

Figure 2.3   A fatal attraction: the shark sails in to cause tourist
              terror in the SeaWorld lagoon in *Jaws 3-D*.   50

Figure 2.4   Facing judgment: Captain Nolan (Richard Harris)
              sails out to confront his nonhuman nemesis in
              Michael Anderson's *Orca*.   52

Figure 2.5   Susan (Blanchard Ryan) sorrowfully releases her
              dead lover, Daniel (Daniel Thomas), shortly before
              she too slips permanently under in *Open Water*.   54

Figure 2.6	Deli section: tidal wave survivors take refuge on the tops of shelves and refrigerators as a great white shark patrols the flooded supermarket in Kimble Rendall's *Bait 3D*.	56
Figure 2.7	A shark is lobbed through a California billboard in Anthony C. Ferrante's cult hit *Sharknado*.	58
Figure 2.8	Her surroundings seem tranquil, but journalist Sue Charlton (Linda Kozlowski) is poised to be prey for a saltwater croc as she refills her canteen from a pond in *Crocodile Dundee*.	60
Figure 2.9	Having gobbled a few of them by now, a giant African crocodile eyes off another appetizing teenage morsel (Caitlin Martin) in Tobe Hooper's *Crocodile*.	61
Figure 2.10	In Greg McLean's *Rogue*, a boat full of tourists cruises down a scenic waterway in the Kakadu region of Australia's Northern Territory before the wildlife makes the excursion a lot less agreeable.	63
Figure 2.11	"This is the island of the pregnant woman, no?" Nancy (Blake Lively) gestures to the formations beyond the water, in which she sees her mother symbolized, in *The Shallows*.	65
Figure 2.12	Trapped on a small rock after a shark attacks her, Nancy inspects her wound as a similarly stricken seagull looks on, in *The Shallows*.	67
Figure 2.13	Washed up on the shore and lucky to be alive, Nancy again looks to the mountains that remind her of her mother, having embraced her fighting example in *The Shallows*.	67
Figure 3.1	Both jaws and claws: the colossal carnivore of *Grizzly* closes in on its prey.	71
Figure 3.2	Jenson (Leslie Nielsen) grows increasingly bestial as he intimidates a young camper, Bob (Andrew Stevens), in *Day of the Animals*.	74
Figure 3.3	Eager to impress, the clean-cut engineer John Patterson (Val Kilmer) has little sense of the chaos that awaits in Africa in Stephen Hopkins's *The Ghost and the Darkness*.	75

Figure 3.4	"They are not lions—they are the ghost and the darkness": The twin man-eating terrors of the East African village of Tsavo in *The Ghost and the Darkness*.	77
Figure 3.5	The wild touch: Charles Remington (Michael Douglas) drinks the blood of a bull during a Masaai tribal ritual in *The Ghost and the Darkness*.	78
Figure 3.6	"So, how are you planning to kill me?": aging billionaire Charles Morse (Anthony Hopkins) calls Bob Green's (Alec Baldwin's) jealousy likes he sees it, moments before their plane crashes, plunging them into the wilderness, in *The Edge*.	80
Figure 3.7	John Ottway (Liam Neeson) tries to formulate a plan to escape certain death after a drilling crew's plane crashes in the Alaskan wilderness in Joe Carnahan's *The Grey*.	84
Figure 3.8	Man versus Wild: the alpha wolf, black as the death it brings, scatters its subordinates to face John Ottway alone in *The Grey*.	85
Figure 3.9	John Ottway of *The Grey* remembers himself as a child (Jonathan Bitonti), his perspective now aligned with that of his defiant father (James Bitonti): "Once more into the fray."	86
Figure 4.1	Dainty nightclub singer Willie Scott (Kate Capshaw) squeals in disgust under a virtual ecosystem of insects in *Indiana Jones and The Temple of Doom*.	90
Figure 4.2	Disease-threat: a spider emerges from the mouth of its infected host in *Spiders*.	93
Figure 4.3	An oversized flesh-eating ant makes a sensational first appearance in *Them!*	94
Figure 4.4	The chemically enhanced arachnid lumbers downtown in Jack Arnold's *Tarantula*.	96
Figure 4.5	Poor Carey (Grant Williams), dwarfed by the domestic in Jack Arnold's *The Incredible Shrinking Man*.	98
Figure 4.6	Carey battles the spider in *The Incredible Shrinking Man*.	99

Figure 4.7	An ant has arranged its dead in Saul Bass's *Phase IV*.	102
Figure 4.8	No room of one's own: with the door closed against them, the spiders begin trickling under it in Frank Marshall's *Arachnophobia*.	104
Figure 4.9	A spider slides down the soapy clean skin of teenage girl after it leaps on her in the shower in *Arachnophobia*.	105
Figure 4.10	Primal fear: the spider begins creeping up the leg of the arachnophobe Ross Jennings (Jeff Daniels), repeating his childhood trauma, in *Arachnophobia*.	107
Figure. 4.11	Sex pest: a spider backs the near-naked Ashley (Scarlett Johansson) against a wall and sprays her with web in *Eight Legged Freaks*.	109
Figure. 4.12	"Right there": Peter (Michael Shannon) tries to show Agnes (Ashley Judd) a nonexistent human-biting bug in William Friedkin's *Bug*.	110
Figure 5.1	Ready to bite the Big Apple: the Rhedosaurus clambers out of the Hudson River in *The Beast from 20,000 Fathoms*.	115
Figure 5.2	The eponymous amphibian giant of the original *Godzilla*, disturbed from his marine seclusion by thermonuclear bomb tests.	116
Figure 5.3	Professor Deemer (Leo G. Carroll) inspects the oversized arachnid he has created in his lab in Jack Arnold's *Tarantula*. Soon it will escape, its growth continuing unabated.	121
Figure 5.4	Fly in the face of reason: Hélène (Patricia Owens) shrieks in terror as she sees her husband André (David Hedison) in his mutated form in *The Fly*.	125
Figure 5.5	Ambitious young inventor Seth Brundle (Jeff Goldblum) tries to woo science journalist Ronnie Quaife (Geena Davis) by boasting of his big discovery in David Cronenberg's *The Fly*.	126
Figure 5.6	"You have to leave now, and never come back here": Seth Brundle, already substantially mutated, warns his	

	lover Ronnie away before he reaches the peak of his terrifying transformation in *The Fly*.	128
Figure 5.7	"Welcome to Jurassic Park": having revealed a majestic brachiosaurus to his guests, John Hammond (Richard Attenborough) proudly announces his creation in Steven Spielberg's *Jurassic Park*.	129
Figure 5.8	What might have been: with the survivors ferried out of harm's way in *Jurassic Park*, thankful for their safety, Hammond rests his eyes sadly on the genesis of his now-botched dream of Creation.	132
Figure 5.9	Having vanquished the cruel and freakish Indominus rex, a concoction of mad science and marketing, the Tyrannosaurus rules again in Colin Trevorrow's *Jurassic World*.	134
Figure 6.1	Peeping Kong: Jack Driscoll (Bruce Cabot) assures Ann Darrow (Fay Wray) of her safety in her upstairs apartment in *King Kong* (1933). But Kong, by peering through windows, has located her almost immediately.	138
Figure 6.2	John Patterson (Val Kilmer) tries to aim his rifle atop a hunting platform at night in *The Ghost and the Darkness*. The human can't see his prey, but we know the lion can as the film immerses us in its night vision.	140
Figure 6.3	A gull careens down on Melanie Daniels (Tippi Hedren), scratching her forehead in the first move by the eponymous antagonists of *The Birds*.	143
Figure 6.4	Don't look now: erratic cutting allows us only a quick yet gruesome glance at the corpse of the Brenner family's neighbor, found with his eyes pecked out, in *The Birds*.	144
Figure 6.5	The Tyrannosaurus rex refused to make an appearance during the park tour, but, having escaped its enclosure, it looks directly into one of the cars at the human within (Ariana Richards), in *Jurassic Park*.	150
Figure 6.6	Dennis Nedry (Wayne Knight) is blinded by the venom of the seemingly cute Dilophosaurus in *Jurassic Park*.	151

Figure 7.1	An oversexed serpent glides up the naked Georgie's (Mercedes McNab's) leg in *Vipers*.	156
Figure 7.2	Trouser snake: a black mamba wriggles toward the sensitive flesh of criminal Steve (Oliver Reed), in *Venom*.	159
Figure 7.3	The snake-like Sarone (Jon Voight) openly eyes-off Terri (Jennifer Lopez) in *Anaconda*.	161
Figure 7.4	The snake devours its human double, Sarone, in *Anaconda*.	162
Figure 7.5	A snake prepares to strike a nude couple (Samantha McLeod and Taylor Kitsch) having sex in the plane's bathroom in *Snakes on a Plane*.	165
Figure 8.1	When good boys turn bad: the deranged dog of *Cujo*.	170
Figure 8.2	As Father Merrin (Max von Sydow) faces the looming status of the demon Pazuzu in *The Exorcist*, we see two feral dogs fighting viciously on the ground below.	178
Figure 8.3	No ordinary mutt: the calculating and uncanny dog-Thing in John Carpenter's *The Thing*.	180
Figure 8.4	Sticking your nose where it doesn't belong: the playful Saint Bernard is contaminated by the dark side of the wilderness he enjoys in *Cujo*.	183
Figure 9.1	Detail from *Werewolf* (1512), woodcut by Lucas Cranach the Elder.	188
Figure 9.2	Wilfred Glendon (Henry Hull) lurks in his laboratory as his change takes hold in *Werewolf of London*.	190
Figure 9.3	Lisa Glendon (Valerie Hobson) introduces her suspicious husband Wilfred to her former lover Paul (Lester Matthews), of whom Wilfred is correct to be suspicious, in *Werewolf of London*.	191
Figure 9.4	Kill what he loves best: Wilfred, having broken into his own house, reaches for his wife Lisa at the climax of *Werewolf of London*.	194
Figure 9.5	On an evening walk in *The Wolf Man*, Gwen Conliffe (Evelyn Ankers) admits to her admirer Larry Talbot	

	(Lon Chaney Jr.) that her heart belongs to another: "I really shouldn't be here." "Oh, but you are here," Larry responds.	197
Figure 9.6	Lawrence Talbot (Benicio del Toro) begins busting through his restraints as terrified doctors flee the lecture theater in Joe Johnston's *The Wolfman*.	199
Figure 9.7	Bill Neill (Christopher Stone) sprouts fangs during a moonlight tryst with werewolf Marsha (Elisabeth Brooks) in *The Howling*.	201
Figure 9.8	Bodily dysfunction: the naked David (David Naughton) begins to transform in *An American Werewolf in London*.	203
Figure 9.9	Jack Nicholson as the (almost) obsolete literary editor Will Randall in Mike Nichols's *Wolf*.	203
Figure 9.10	Will Randall, bloodied but unbowed, faces his younger challenger in *Wolf*.	205
Figure 9.11	Thor the Alsatian warily surveils the werewolf Ted (Michael Paré) as he steps from his trailer in *Bad Moon*.	206
Figure 9.12	Oliver (Kent Smith) tries to comfort his reluctant lover, Irena (Simone Simon), who's sexually hindered by knowledge of her occult werecat lineage in Jacques Tourneur's *Cat People*.	207
Figure 9.13	Alice (Jane Randolph), all alone in the pool, flounders and shrieks as her mate-rival, Irena—in the form of a snarling black panther—stalks the room around her in *Cat People*.	209
Figure 9.14	Animal magnetism: Ginger Fitzgerald (Katharine Isabelle) enjoys her newfound allure as she strides down the high-school corridor in John Fawcett's *Ginger Snaps*.	211

Acknowledgments

Throughout the writing of this book I was encouraged and enlivened by the conversation and support of several friends and colleagues, among them Glenn Fraser, Tara Lomax, Elizabeth Pearce, and Monica Koehn. Special thanks are due to Stephanie Eslake for her expert and eagle-eyed suggestions on draft material. I'd also like to acknowledge the interest and advice of James Peltz and Rafael Chaiken at SUNY Press, and of my dear friend Murray Pomerance. Further, my warm thanks to Eileen Nizer (production), Michael Campochiaro (marketing), and John Wentworth (copy editing). I'm grateful for the love and encouragement of my parents, Tony and Lee-Anne Lennard, to whom this book is dedicated, as well as the support of my wonderful wife Dongqin "Genghis" Ruan (my favorite fierce creature). Last, not least: thanks also to my faithful dog, Ahab, who kept me company at every stage and growled protectively throughout many of these films. You're a good boy.

Introduction

Welcome (Back) to the Jungle

YOU HAVE NOT, I HOPE, FELT THE jaws of an animal rend flesh from your bones, or seize your head in an oversized maw; or drag you into the marine deep, wondering whether you will die first of drowning or dismemberment, but likely not thinking much at all—your panic response overwhelming everything. I hope you haven't had some creature sting you into anaphylaxis; or sink its fangs into you, flooding your circulatory system with venom; or even coil around you until you hear your own bones crack. You mostly likely haven't been dragged into the wilderness and mauled by lions, or savaged by a pack of wolves, or caught in the death-roll of a crocodile. I can be sure that you haven't been stamped into the ground by a gigantic primate or torn apart by a Tyrannosaur. Probably you have little desire to have such experiences, knowing already that any one of them would be unpleasant. Yet through horror movies we have been visualizing these scenarios for decades. In films such as *King Kong* (1933), *Jaws* (1975), *Arachnophobia* (1990), *Anaconda* (1997), *Jurassic Park* (1993), *The Edge* (1997), and *Snakes on a Plane* (2006) we see situations in which animals bite, sting, squash, swallow, and generally get the better of us humans. We might imagine ourselves atop a hierarchy of creation, or at least ruling comfortably over our nonhuman brethren; yet animal horror hits us with a radical demotion—with scenarios in which we find our power not nearly as entrenched as we're used to. As paleoanthropologists Donna Hart and Robert Sussman summarize, "the bizarre realization that humans get eaten comes hard to the Western mind."[1] The realization might come hard, but it obviously holds considerable dramatic interest, and it's these strangely alluring cinematic scenarios, and the animal aggressors that perpetrate them, that this book is devoted to exploring.

Try to imagine yourself in the Pleistocene. It's the period between 2.6 million and twelve thousand years ago. You are aware of yourself as capable of hunting, but also as liable to being hunted. Being away from your tribal group is dangerous; moving around after dark is dangerous. The hominin reading these words likely has little need to fear the kind of predation described in this book, but that wasn't the case for his or her distant ancestors. As Hart and Sussman's influential book *Man the Hunted* (2005) has described in considerable detail, until relatively recently we have been not only predators but also a prey species. We've gradually gained the upper hand over those who'd gladly have us for lunch, even taking down animals larger than ourselves, but as Barbara Ehrenreich points out, "well into the epoch of man-the-hunter, humans still had good reason to fear the tall grass, the forests, and the night."[2] Zoologist Hans Kruuk informs us that as humans entered the ecosystem there were a greater number of carnivorous species than there are today,[3] and that "man must have been a welcome addition to the prey spectrum of many carnivores, and there are no reasons to assume that maneating was not a normal aspect of day-to-day predation during the Pliocene and Pleistocene."[4]

Crime scene evidence from so long ago is naturally tricky to come by, but what has been found supports Kruuk's hypothesis: our human and protohuman ancestors were prey for prehistoric predators. We walked through a world with numerous species of ancestral lion, and leopard— the latter hunters of incredible stealth who appear even to have crept into the caves where our forebears slept to strike.[5] Fossil hominid skulls have been found with puncture marks that match the tooth profiles of the big cats with which these early humans shared their wild world.[6] The genus Homo emerged at around the same time as the Smilodon, the saber-tooth cat armed with canine teeth over six inches in length (Fig. I.1). These ferocious felines lived in North and South America but hung around long enough to see the arrival of ancestral humans.[7]

In Africa and Asia, hominins nervously coexisted with numerous extinct species of giant hyena, as well as forerunners of the current crop, which are formidable hunters today. One of the earlier incarnations was the 440-pound short-faced hyena, which preyed on early hominins. Through careful examination of skeletal damage, and with reference to the eating habits of modern-day hyenas, scientists have even been able to describe the sequence of being eaten by one of these creatures:

> First step: strip off the edible facial muscles causing subsequent damage to cheek bones and upper jaw. Second step: crack the centre of the jaw open to reach the tongue. Third step: crush

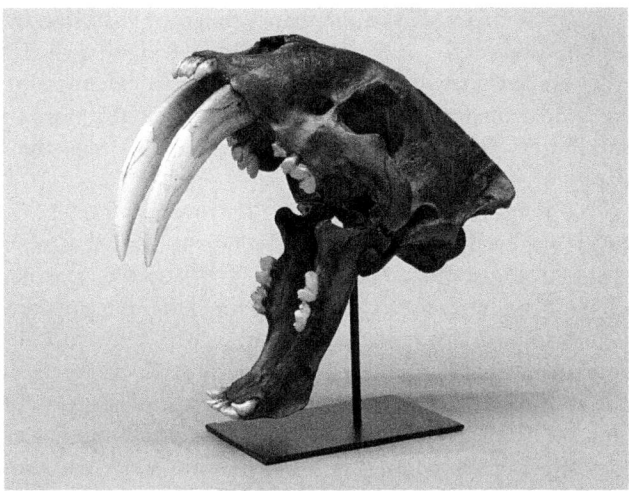

Figure I.1. Saber-tooth cat (*Smilodon fatalis*) skull cast with jaws open. These impressive predators were a fearsome hazard of the Pleistocene environment in North and South America. Other species of saber-tooth roamed Europe, Africa, Eurasia, and Indonesia. Photograph: Bone Clones.

the facial skeleton to obtain marrow. Fourth step: break open the cranial vault to expose the brain, an organ that is prized by hyenas for its plentiful lipid content.[8]

A horror scene if ever there was one. There were also 250-pound wild dogs, which could hunt alone or in packs. And of course there would have been snakes, for which our living primate relatives share our aversion. Luis Llosa's film *Anaconda* notwithstanding, the fossil record on snakes eating early humans is less clear,[9] although if size ratios are any indication, our fairly small-statured Australopithecine cousins were definitely in trouble[10]; and there are numerous instances of large snakes seizing infants for consumption even today.[11] Depending on their location, our ancestors may also have encountered the short-faced bear Arctodus, which weighed a metric ton and stood six-foot high while still on all-fours[12]; Arctodus lived alongside protohumans until the end of the Pleistocene eleven thousand years ago. In addition to the enormous saltwater crocodiles that still inhabit the continent, early residents of Australia likely encountered Megalania, a twenty-three-foot Komodo dragon whose bite, like that of today's Komodos, would induce prolonged and shock-inducing blood loss.[13] And of course we could venture further into the past, finding other threats for earlier ancestors: creodonts, for example, were an order of mammalian predators that became extinct eleven million years ago, and which likely preyed on primates.[14] The focus of this book isn't wide enough to include an exhaustive catalogue of age-old animal anxieties, but it's fair to say that the noble image of "Man the Hunter" has been much exaggerated, and must be balanced with evidence of our prey-status.

"Try to imagine yourself in the Pleistocene": movie-lovers may have noticed my earlier allusion to a scene in *Jurassic Park*, in which grouchy paleontologist Alan Grant (Sam Neill) tries to persuade a boy of around ten that he isn't so clever for mocking the appearance of a fossilized velociraptor skeleton that Grant's crew have just discovered. "Try to imagine yourself in the Cretaceous period," Grant says, urging this kid to envision himself eviscerated by a pack of raptors. Obviously, humans did not coexist with dinosaurs, but we know our ancestors still had big, toothy problems. In films like *Jurassic Park* we can imagine ourselves suddenly slotted back into a matrix of predation that we have only recently (for the most part) escaped. Predation by animals is hardly unique for the majority of the animal kingdom, and cinema's animal attackers, as Michael Fuchs recognizes, "are remnants of a past state in humanity's relatively brief existence in which human beings were pitted against nature's forces on a daily basis."[15] Such films provide us with a sense of ourselves in alarming ecological context, reminding us that our current power is far from unquestionable.

Of course, despite our dominance today, prehistoric perils sometimes arise in the modern era. British hunter Jim Corbett, who lived in India in the early 1900s, reported that one female tiger had managed to kill 436 people, and two other tigers had killed 64 and 150, respectively. Similarly, government statistics listed reported tiger kills for the whole of India in 1902 at as many as 1,046 people—and that's only the kills that were reported.[16] Hart and Sussman note that 425 people were killed by tigers between 1975 and 1985 on the Indian side of the Sundarbans delta (shared with Bangladesh).[17] Indian authorities in the area have distributed plastic facemasks to be worn on the back of one's head to deter tigers (tigers prefer to stalk oblivious prey), and dummy humans have been rigged to deliver electric shocks to condition the tigers to consider humans an unappetizing meal.[18] Leopard attacks are rarer, but in the Garhwal region of Northern India, seventeen people were reported killed in 1996, and nineteen the following year.[19] The attacks may be rarer but often involve a leopard actually breaking into a victim's house to carry him or her away.[20]

Predators remain a problem elsewhere. As Hart and Sussman point out, "Deaths from polar bears have always been a part of Inuit life, with several attacks per year even as populations decline from climate change"[21] Among the Aché, a Paraguayan forager society, being eaten by a leopard accounts for an alarming 8 percent of all male deaths.[22] Australia is a developed country, but it's also home to a virtual living dinosaur, the saltwater crocodile, which reaches between fifteen and twenty feet in length and weighs up to 2,600 pounds—the world's largest living reptile. This brute has a bite force of 3,700 pounds per square inch: greater than that of bears and estimated to be at the low-end of what a Tyrannosaurus would have possessed.[23] And they'll eat humans when they can, with one or two unlucky or foolhardy folks being snatched up per year. Inhabitants of industrialized societies are largely spared such incidents, yet when stories emerge they run through the media like wildfire, their interest-value grossly disproportionate to virtually all other kinds of death. Such fatal animal attacks carry explosive conceptual power. They startle us with the reminder of our capacity to be mere meat for something else, a reminder which, as Fuchs puts it, "implies a questioning of mankind's self-aggrandizing notion as the centre of the universe."[24]

Once Bitten, Twice Shy

I have not evoked our history as prey in the context of animal horror movies for the trivial symmetry of it: that history is very much with us. So powerful and important is the human legacy of being prey that we continue a fascination with its possibility. As we know, while you may not be under threat from predators, your distant ancestors were. And whatever your position in life now, you're part of a long and unbroken line of "winners" in evolutionary terms. You're here because your genetic relatives survived long enough to reproduce in a world in which they could have been just a protein source for something else. You're a winner, but over hundreds of thousands—millions—of years, those successes in survival and reproduction were hard-won, and you retain the ancestral knowledge to "know better" than those who perished. Throughout evolutionary time, precautionary behavior has paid off. Giving a start at the sound of a rustle in the bushes, even if it turned out to be nothing, was a small "cost" if it helped protect us against getting wiped out. This biases our development toward an optimal level of anxiety, including fearful but biologically cheap "false positives," like flinching. In excess amounts, anxiety becomes maladaptive, but when it comes to serious threats, being scared kept us safe. Serious threats would often have been animals—and we're still ready for them. As Jeffrey Lockwood explains,

> Our evolutionary history as soft, slow sources of protein and vulnerable targets of venom quite reasonably accounts for our tendency to be alarmed by creatures that can eat, sting, or bite us. Cultural and technological changes happen much

faster than genetic change, so we are left with minds and bodies poised for dangers on the savanna while we try to stay safe on the freeway.[25]

It doesn't matter that guns or fast cars are now more likely to kill us than big cats; adaptation doesn't happen that quickly, and we're still equipped with nervous systems tuned for a world of animal violence. For the most part we have long since escaped these primal terrors, but as far as our psychology is concerned we're not out of the woods yet. As Ian Tattersall writes, "Insulated as most of us are today from the practical dangers of predation, we are nonetheless (often) meat-eaters who are still haunted by atavistic fears."[26] It wasn't arbitrarily that I mentioned the Pleistocene (although we might have gone further back): this is the period in which humans reached their anatomically modern state, and the selection pressures placed on our ancestors by animal predators throughout that era helped shape who we are today.[27]

Predator evasion is a fundamental adaptive problem. Just as the emotion of disgust has its origins in the threat of bacteria and parasites, and worked to keep us safe long before the germ theory of disease came along,[28] we also retain the psychological residue of our interactions with predators. We can see easily that other animals have formed behavioral adaptations in response to the pressures of predation. After gull chicks hatch, their parents will carry their eggshells away from the nest, innately aware that the presence of the eggs makes their nest stand out to predators.[29] Other animals may display mimicry, play dead, or may, like zebras, be aware that blending in with the herd makes identification and pursuit of a single target confusing. They already know to do this: they don't have to be taught—selection has molded it into instinct. Obviously, the role of social learning is much higher in the case of humans than for other animals: our sense of sources of danger is not only "instinct"; nevertheless, some basic principles still apply. H. Clark Barrett points out that

> [o]ur ancestors faced the risk of predator attack since well before they were human, stretching back to our most ancient mammalian ancestors. Pursuit of prey, too, stretches back to the earliest insectivorous primates and crescendos in the big game hunting of our own hominin lineage. Few things seem more Darwinian than predator-prey interactions, so it is hard to imagine such encounters not shaping our evolution.[30]

We certainly owe numerous features of our psychology and physiology to the selection pressures of predation. Barrett suggests that animal predators probably drove us toward increased sociality;[31] indeed, we'll see that throughout many horror films, such as *Jaws*, *Rogue* (2007), *The Edge*, and *The Grey* (2011) animal predators repeatedly have the narrative effect of compelling the unity of otherwise disparate characters. Only through cooperation and strength in numbers do such characters stand a chance, and those who chose to remain antipathetic to their fellow humans become easy prey. It's also thought that fear of the dark, a phenomenon deeply intertwined with horror as a genre, is an adapted response linked to the weakness of our night vision relative to that of large carnivores that hunt at night. Packer and colleagues have demonstrated that man-eating lions will not only choose overwhelmingly to attack after dark but also time their attacks toward the darkest parts of the night, in fact preferring to strike in total darkness.[32] Barrett even suggests that "it is plausible that the proper domain of our ability to detect motion—on which nearly all social perception and cognition depends—is predator–prey interactions, and that social-action processing evolved on top of these ancient mechanisms."[33]

By now, it is highly unlikely that we need to be taught from a null starting-point that large, fast-moving carnivorous creatures present a threat to us, just as young children don't need to be taught apprehension around great heights. This doesn't mean we're born with a specific "template" for lions that gets "matched" when we see one, but it's clear that we do have ingrained fear responses and that we come into the world biologically primed to learn some fears more easily, and deeply, than others (what psychologists call "biological preparedness"). In the case of some co-evolutionary animal threats, biologically prepared fear is now beyond question: snakes, for instance, of great concern in numerous films (Fig. I.2), gave our primate

Figure I.2. Famous cinematic snake-hater Indiana Jones (Harrison Ford) faces a cobra in *Raiders of the Lost Ark* (Steven Spielberg, Paramount, 1981). We are predisposed to fear snakes because of the threat they posed to our prehuman ancestors. Digital frame enlargement.

ancestors such a hard time that we do appear to have a specific "template," triggered by curvilinear snake shapes, designed to zero in on serpents and prioritize them in our attention above other stimuli. Snakes don't just attract our curiosity, they override everything else: in psychological experiments they command attention with unrivalled urgency.[34]

Some adaptations stand out: freezing in fear ("attentive immobility") has evolved in numerous species. Freezing allows prey animals to assess a threat while temporarily delaying attack, given that sudden evasion triggers the chase impulse of predators such as wolves and big cats. Freezing may even cause an inattentive predator to pass its meal by.[35] Generally, what adaptations are specifically dedicated toward avoiding animal predation is less clear, and ripe for further research (and many are likely by now alloyed with other adaptations focused on personal defense). But one of the most fundamental of anti-predator behaviors is also the simplest: interest. As Hans Kruuk points out, bird and mammal prey species are frequently curious about their enemies, showing "a clear attraction . . . toward the most dangerous and effective predators."[36] What's more, they do not simply watch to ensure their own immediate safety: birds will fly long distances to observe the commotion of a predator in their colony, "long necking" as Kruuk puts it. "It seems likely," he indicates, "that this curiosity helps the birds to learn what kind of adversary they are facing," and given that they face a variety of threats, some potentially novel to them, this learning is useful.[37] Many African mammals are similarly possessed by curiosity about their predators. In the Serengeti, prey animals such as wildebeest and antelope, while keeping a minimum safe distance, will choose to approach predators to observe them. As Kruuk recounts, "it is an unforgettable scene to see whole herds of several different species all staring quietly at a walking large cat, like a lion or a cheetah. They may follow it, and one cannot help but compare such a herd to a crowd of people, gaping at somebody or something."[38] As he notes, such behavior carries a small risk, and it costs the animals the time they could spend grazing, but these appear to be outweighed by the information-gathering benefits of observation—there's an instinctively understood value to knowing more about your natural opponent.

Animal Attractions: The Spell of the Predator

Let's get back to *Jurassic Park* for a minute. "Look how it eats," Alan advises his young co-travelers as they watch a Tyrannosaurus from behind a log as it tears flesh from an ostrich-like Gallimimus—and having narrowly escaped becoming the same kind of meal themselves. Twelve-year-old Lex (Ariana Richards) obviously has a lower tolerance for anxiety, wants to hurry off—and that's probably smart. But she doesn't look away either. Young Tim (Joseph Mazzello), his head raised higher than the others', is obviously entranced: "Yes," he murmurs. A moment later: "Look how much blood . . ." The trio leaves, with Alan snatching the spellbound kid away before he cranes his head too high and risks becoming a target. Getting well clear of this reanimated super-predator is definitely a good idea, and yet (particularly as the camera positions us to share the humans' voyeuristic view), we understand that there's something worth seeing here (Fig. I.3).

There are clear symmetries between our own interest in nature's brutal beasts and that of our brethren throughout the animal kingdom: our curiosity around impressive carnivores, Kruuk writes, "is comparable to the curiosity aspect of anti-predator behaviour in animals. We are interested in the mechanisms of danger and the fate of the attacked."[39] The kind of large carnivores that preyed on us throughout deep history and occasionally still do today are especially alluring: "The appeal and attraction of carnivore danger is obvious . . . in a zoo," writes Kruuk, "where children and adults are drawn to the lions, tigers and wolves as to a magnet."[40] Our fascination certainly stems from a deep need to monitor and assess threat. The evolution of more complex nervous systems allowed organisms to build on their goal of self-preservation through the inclusion of mechanisms beneficial in their flexibility, like conditioning, instrumental learning, and conscious deliberation and threat-assessment,[41] hence the utility of our curiosity around dangerous animals. We know

Figure I.3. Tim (Joseph Mazzello, lower-right foreground), hiding behind a log, is fascinated by the sight of the Tyrannosaurus devouring its prey in Steven Spielberg's *Jurassic Park* (Universal, 1993). The impulse to observe one's predators is reflected elsewhere in the animal kingdom. Digital frame enlargement.

enough to pay attention, but we don't know everything: information-gathering is important.

Unsurprisingly then, intimidating animal predators have been central to human stories since we began telling them. The great biologist Edward O. Wilson has noted that what is living, as a matter of visual preference, is inherently more interesting than what is not: "No one in his right mind looks at a pile of dead leaves in preference to the tree from which they fell," he writes. But he notes that some creatures "have more to offer because of their special impact on mental development,"[42] and even become channeled into cultural and religious forms. "In all cultures," he notes as an example, "serpents are prone to be mystically transfigured," and behind these archetypes are individuals whose minds are "primed to react emotionally to the sight of snakes, not just to fear them but to be aroused and absorbed in their details, to weave stories about them."[43] Fierce creatures stalk through or tower over too many mythological traditions to catalogue here, although we might mention briefly as examples the monster Leviathan of the Hebrew Bible, Christianity's beast of Revelation, the serpentine goddess Tiamat of Ancient Mesopotamian lore, or the monstrous wolf Fenrir of Norse mythology. The beasts of religious tradition are often to be confronted by a brave hero (Fig. I.4).

Figure I.4. *Hercules and Iolaus slaying the Hydra* (1545), engraving by Sebald Beham (1500–1550). As well as its reptilian frame and multiple snake-necks, the hydra is depicted here with wolfish heads. Mythological traditions are filled with monsters that resemble, or combine features of, animals that would have presented real threats in our species' own natural history.

As Barbara Ehrenreich notes, "If there is one central human mythological theme, from Gilgamesh to Beowulf, it is of the human-eating creature that ravages the countryside until someone—hero or god—successfully confronts it."[44] As Paul Trout puts it, "Wherever one looks, animal predators slither, run, and swoop their way through the mythic landscape in search of human flesh," reminding us that "humans are good to eat."[45] In hybrid creatures—mythical monsters—we see agglomerations of the scariest parts of animal predators: scales, fangs, claws, serpentine physiology, and so on. Trout's extensive 2011 study *Deadly Powers: Animal Predators and the Mythic Imagination* examines the extent to which these myths would have arisen from the animal threats of our ancestral landscape. As he notes, "storytelling is universal because it reflects an adaptation that helped humans survive," and deeply wrapped up in this was our need "to deal with our predicament as a prey species—to address our fear of being hunted, killed, and eaten by predators. . . . [W]e told stories to stay alive. And, in a figurative sense, we still do."[46]

Narrated encounters with lethal creatures engage our fear and fascination. While in our relatively secular age they may not be invested with the religious awe of earlier accounts, animal horror films tickle this age-old attraction. Why watch films in which human characters are chewed up by nonhuman foes? Why watch horror films at all, for that matter—a genre literally defined by fear and physical attack? Well, certainly, some of us don't watch them. But among those who do, I'd suggest a key reason is that the "cost" they impose on these viewers, in terms of exposure to stress, is somehow outweighed by the survival benefit we intuit in them. We know that things that are dangerous are worth paying attention to. Wilson writes that "fascination creates preparedness, and preparedness, survival."[47] Our response to animal predators is not entirely predetermined: it leaves room for reflection and decision making (and thus, in movies, engaging narrative action).[48] Animal horror films allow us to run simulations of hostile encounters. They show us scenarios, character traits, actions and reactions, some successful and others less so. To our deepest stone-age brains, they're an implicit learning opportunity. Through them we can gather information on the threat, learn its behavior, countenance strategies and precautions against it, and learn our own limits.

In light of the above, I haven't taken us through a blow-by-blow historical account of the development of animal horror cinema,[49] tracing its emergence as if it were a bounded artistic phenomenon, "movement," or cultural trend, because, as the above indicates, it isn't. Animal horror is more akin to an impulse. Dan Whitehead is almost certainly correct to suggest that "the very first horror stories ever told were about animals. Whether painted on cave walls or shared around a fire, our primitive ancestors first learned mortal fear from the predatory beasts that shared their domain. Such tales spoke to our need for survival, rather than entertainment."[50] But it probably runs deeper: it's likely the evolution of language itself was promoted by pressures to more effectively signal the existence of animal threats.[51] Certainly it is well documented that several types of nonhuman primate (e.g., vervet monkeys) will use distinct alarm calls for different types of predators, which we might see as a type of protolinguistic communication. Thinking more cinematically, anthropologist Lynne A. Isbell has explored how co-evolutionary threats were instrumental in the development of our impressive visual acuity: the benefit to watching out for predators goes back to the origins of human vision itself.[52] In short, while animal horror movies might not possess much cultural prestige, they undoubtedly represent the tail end of an almost inconceivably long and unbroken tradition, stretching deep into prehistory.

Getting a Closer Look

If our fear and fascination with some animals—animals of the kind that appear in horror movies—is ingrained, then what is left to say about them? A lot, actually. While this book will sometimes consider the way our evolutionary inheritances affect what we see onscreen, we are complex mixtures of genetic and environmental influences: the way we view animals is obviously subject to cultural variation. Across a variety of cultural or historical contexts, particular animals may be ignored, disdained, petted, and revered; they may be attributed different personalities, or taken to symbolize different traits or values. We have recently seen in the humanities a rise in academic interest in our relationships with animals (sometimes termed the "animal turn"), including in film studies. As for animal horror specifically, Gregersdotter and colleagues observe, "with the exception of some notable classics, like *King Kong* (1933), *Jaws*, and *The Birds* (1963), animal horror cinema has long been seen as a low-budget, low-quality form of entertainment that is largely disconnected from serious cultural debates,"[53] but the climate is gradually changing, as their recent collection, *Animal Horror Cinema: Genre, History and Criticism* (2015) indicates. Charles Darwin's theory of evolution by natural selection, through which (in *The Descent of Man*) he linked human beings to apes via a common primate ancestor, remains the most significant and powerful theory in the life sciences. Yet still today a fundamental division between the "human" and the "animal" is deeply embedded in the vast majority of our cultures. As Gregersdotter and colleagues describe, central to approaching animal horror has been the importance of thinking about "how films rely on and simultaneously subvert and reinscribe the basic conceptual separation of the human and non-human animal."[54] Indeed, as we'll see, the tension of animal horror movies regularly arises from overlaps and collisions between these conceptual categories, and others that are closely aligned (e.g., civilization/wilderness), forcing us to consider that the templates we use to understand the world around us may be less reliable than we think.

The renewed academic interest in animals in the humanities has tended to cluster around various approaches inherited from postmodernist theory.[55] From these angles, attention to animals often becomes part of critiquing what are seen as dominant patriarchal, capitalist, and colonialist attitudes and social structures. Just as capitalism and patriarchy, for example, are thought to determine how humans are culturally valued, in order to maintain the dominance of their nefarious ideological programs, they also assign an exploitative place to animals toward that same goal. The vocabulary of animality, of course, is often mobilized in the oppression of humans. Referring to humans as in some way "like animals" ascribes to them the same negligible moral value attributed to nonhumans, therefore legitimating their oppression. Yet this process of 'dehumanization' also reinforces our disdain and moral distance from animals themselves, thus compounding their exploitation.[56] According to this perspective, then, our views of animals are intertwined in systems of both animal and human exploitation. Animals themselves, like socially disempowered humans, have projected onto them various meanings, and this categorizing activity plays a part in maintaining the various hierarchies of power that have been postmodernism's traditional critical focus. Emerging out of these perspectives has been a collection of positions loosely grouped as "posthumanist" for their rejection of the human exceptionalism associated with traditional humanism.[57] Posthumanism acknowledges that humans, rather than being elevated beyond nature, are a type of animal, and therefore regarding them as fundamentally different from the broader spectrum of creaturely life is philosophically unsupportable. We may wish to flatter ourselves that merely being human endows us with some unique moral specialness; but from a secular perspective, there can no longer be a divine or absolute line with homo sapiens on one side and the rest of the animal kingdom on the other.

Posthumanist scholarship correctly recognizes that (as Darwin canonized) humans are immersed in the same evolutionary narrative as all life. At the same time, it paradoxically clings to the postmodernist tenet that the "human" itself is historically defined and constructed[58]: that there is no underlying human nature or characteristic behavior, and what we think of as human nature is molded from historical, social, and cultural influences. As David Bordwell puts it, for the typical postmodernist scholar, "social structures superimpose historically defined categories upon human beings, thus 'constructing' subjects in representation and social practice."[59] Since postmodernism hit universities in the late 1970s and early 1980s, theoretical approaches to film and literature emphasizing human nature as culturally constructed to the exclusion of evolved biological influences have, as David Bordwell puts it, "saturate[d] the humanities."[60] However, this romantic tabula rasa view of human nature cannot be reconciled with evolutionary theory. We would all concede that a squirrel has what we might call a "squirrel nature," evolved in response to squirrel adaptive problems, forged from the pressures of its natural environment, and that an otter or eagle or chimpanzee has its own nature; however, various strands of academic postmodernism are united by their dismissal of any adapted nature for humankind.[61] Posthumanism's reverence for this extreme social constructionist premise means that despite its interest in biological context, this latest postmodernist iteration has missed chances to explore the wealth of scientific evidence from the behavioral sciences indicating that human nature is certainly not only the product of social and cultural power differentials. In other words, it has neglected ways in which humans are adapted animals. As posthumanism has largely persisted with postmodernist theory's assumption that humankind, unlike other species, is "beyond nature," it fosters human exceptionalism even as it claims to move beyond it. Despite a stated interest in eroding the boundaries between the human and animal, then, posthumanism seems to me somewhat ironically held back by postmodernism's traditional diehard social constructionism, as well as its skepticism of scientific thought.

In the humanities, postmodernist approaches that attribute any human "nature" to speak of as only the product of various types of social "power" and "discourse" may, according to literary scholars Brian Boyd and colleagues, by now have "hardened into habit or dogma." However, at the same time, they note that elsewhere, "the evolutionary analysis of human nature has been maturing."[62] As I have touched on in this introduction, we are far from "blank slates" to be arbitrarily inscribed by our parenting, culture, or society. Perhaps the most significant single work marshalling the evidence against the entire legacy of blank slate thinking is Harvard psychologist Steven Pinker's 2002 book *The Blank Slate: The Modern Denial of Human Nature*.[63] As Pinker demonstrates, research in areas such as neuroscience, behavior genetics, and cognitive and evolutionary psychology highlights the powerful influences of biology and genetic variability on who we are. Evolutionary psychology is invaluable for its project of identifying the adaptive functions of the mind, allowing us to better understand our psychology in the context of the evolutionary engineering that characterizes the rest of earthly life. As

Pinker explains, "We see these signs of engineering everywhere: in eyes that seem designed to form images, in hearts that seem designed to pump blood, in wings that seem designed to lift birds in flight [but] signs of design in human beings do not stop at the heart or eye."[64] A relatively young science, evolutionary psychology has grown rapidly because of the theoretical indispensability of its underlying appreciation that the brain, like any other organ, is an outcome of natural selection, optimized through inherited traits that maximize the survival and reproductive success of the organism for which it works. In short, evolution did not stop at the neck. And as Pinker describes, "Evolutionary psychology explains why the slate is not blank. The mind was forged by Darwinian competition, and an inert medium would have been outperformed by rivals outfitted with high technology—with acute perceptual systems, savvy problem-solvers, cunning strategists, and sensitive feedback circuits. . . ."[65] Accordingly, its work has focused on forwarding testable hypotheses concerning human nature based on evolutionary logic. Particularly important have been cross-cultural analyses that demonstrate shared human tendencies and behaviors regardless of culture; and studies of identical twins raised apart, which clarify relative genetic/environment influences. Collectively, the wealth of empirical evidence accumulated and replicated in the behavioral sciences more broadly makes very clear that the idea that human nature is the exclusive product of parenting, society, or culture (or "discourse") is unsupportable.

While the blank slate position has by now been thoroughly undermined within the sciences, it retains powerful cultural and political currency—as noted, including in segments of academia. I share Boyd and his colleagues' fear that "by insisting on the separateness of humanistic subjects and modes of inquiry, many in the humanities have deprived themselves of the resources discovered in other fields," and that for literary and film scholars, "acknowledging the reality of human evolution presents no serious dangers and offers immense opportunities."[66] Consequently, I count myself as one among a growing number who "distinguish ourselves from 'cultural constructivists,' who effectively attribute exclusive shaping power to culture."[67] Culture does surely shape us, as do historical circumstances. But these are far from the only shaping influences. Accordingly, this book regularly embraces both cultural and biological influences on behavior and its representation—an approach that, I feel, is particularly pertinent to examining our fear and fascination with such long-running co-evolutionary pressures as animal predators.

Despite their marginalization within literary and film studies, analytical approaches that acknowledge the relevance of our evolutionary heritage to artistic and cultural productions and the human behavior they depict are gaining ground. These are gestured to in the dissatisfactions with the abstractions of film theory articulated in Bordwell and Noël Carroll's 1996 anthology *Post-Theory: Reconstructing Film Studies*, with its focus on a more empirically grounded "cognitivism"[68] (Bordwell would delve further into evolutionary thinking in his own 2008 essay on cognition and emotion, "What Snakes, Eagles, and Rhesus Macaques Can Teach Us").[69] These approaches gathered further steam with the release of Boyd and colleagues' 2010 anthology *Evolution, Literature, and Film: A Reader*,[70] which placed the work of film scholars side by side with that of biologists and evolutionary psychologists, as well as further work by the pioneer of Darwinist literary studies Joseph Carroll, including *Reading Human Nature: Literary Darwinism in Theory and Practice* (2011) and more recently *Darwin's Bridge: Uniting the Humanities and Sciences* (2016). Further progress in this consilience of the humanities and sciences has been made through the inclusion of Carroll's work in the latest (2017) edition of Rivkin and Ryan's much-taught *Literary Theory: An Anthology*, in a newly added section, "Cognition, Emotion, Evolution, Science."[71]

Nevertheless, I appreciate that my approach may sometimes strike readers as unconventional. Like the scholars cited above, this book does not discount culture as a force in shaping of human behavior, but rather embraces a "biocultural" approach, which holds that "works of art are shaped by our evolved human nature, by culture, and by individual experience."[72] Truly considering ourselves as animals, with fears and inclinations forged from the pressures of our habitat and biological niche, allows us to view our numerous literary and filmic tales of nonhuman predators with new insight. As Boyd and colleagues put it, "Adopting an evolutionary perspective enables us to build theories of literature and film not from near the end of the story but from the start, from the ground up. By building in this way, we can ask altogether new questions and return to older questions with sharper eyes and surer hands."[73] My approach, then, is a little different from what might be expected, but I hope the reader will find it insightful in its analysis of both cultural contexts and the biological animals—human and nonhuman—that inhabit them.

Framing Animals?

I'm sympathetic to trends in human–animal studies scholarship that highlight and critique humans' brutality toward other species. This is a book about animals assaulting (and often chowing down on) humans, although we all know that the reality is overwhelmingly the reverse. There may be a temptation to think of animal horror, in its affront to human dominance, as a kind of "revenge" genre. However, given that it surely predates our own species' dominance, any broad version of that hypothesis runs into problems pretty fast. But animals don't make films directly, and there's much value in considering the meanings we attribute to them and how they might be framed. On the subject of ethics, Gregersdotter and colleagues note that while there's been long-running public concern around the treatment of animal performers, "the use of animals in films also raises questions of the ethics of representation of non-human creatures."[74] As they realize, this seems particularly pertinent to animal horror, given its focus on eliciting fear from and (narratively at least) opposition to animals.

Many of these films aren't great PR for animals—that much is obvious. And if our view of animals is subject to cultural influences, what does this mean for the real animals with which we interact? This is an exceptionally difficult question, and I hope that the reader isn't too disappointed that it isn't answered here. If at the most primal level our interest in such films stems from a desire to observe and learn from predators, it seems logical that we gain some "information" on them. But whether such knowledge, in a context we know is fictional, translates into attitudes toward real animals, and whether it is applied behaviorally in real life, is quite another question. It's worth noting that *Jaws* has been routinely linked to the demonization of sharks, with real consequences for conservation. Marine biologist George Burgess, thirty years after the film's release, tells us that "there was a collective testosterone rush that went through the U.S. in the years following *Jaws*, where guys just wanted to catch these sharks so they could have their pictures taken with their foot on the head of a man-eater and the jaws later displayed on their mantle."[75] Yet scientists in the field also attribute to the film a beneficial explosion of positive research interest in an animal that had been generally neglected; in other words, negative representations don't necessitate negative effects. We also need to bear in mind that claims of film and television's ability to negatively influence viewers' behavior have a long and sensational history but remarkable trouble holding up under honest scientific scrutiny.[76] Recently, psychological measures of "implicit" or "unconscious" bias related to other humans have fallen into controversy over what they actually measure,[77] and their failure to predict real-life discrimination.[78] It seems that the unconscious biases we hold do not necessarily manifest in behavior. Alternatively, it may also be true that *Jaws* is a very particular case; it's not at all clear that the extraordinary cultural resonance of Spielberg's film can be easily extrapolated to other films, or even to other types of animals. As we'll see, the animal attacker is virtually always vanquished in these films, and it may be that dramatizations of human triumph give implicit moral support to the anxieties around everyday animal exploitation. If animals in movies appear to oppose us, maybe it's easier to feel that they somehow "deserve" their fate, legitimizing our consumption of them as a spoil of conquest in a broader struggle for survival? Again, I remain agnostic. Even if we accept this (speculative) thesis, its behavioral consequences are also unclear. But it's something to think about. What I would say is that I hope this book's exploration of animals onscreen draws the reader into deeper contemplation of the cultural and emotional lenses through which we see animals, and fosters a respectfully refreshed view of the richness and wonder of animal life.

Into the Wild

This book isn't arranged as a chronology of cinematic animal horror, though the order of films within chapters is generally by year of release. Nor is it an exhaustive catalogue of every such movie,[79] which, given the size of the subgenre, would preclude deeper discussion. It's foremost an exploration of themes, patterns, tendencies, and preoccupations. I haven't covered every species or permutation of animal horror, but its significant trends (in both popularity and critical success) are represented. However, I have kept my focus mainly on the beasts of Western cinema, primarily in order to afford adequate attention to the (still diverse) cultural contexts in which these creatures are embedded. I regret this limitation, though I think readers will find that many of the observations herein will apply to the bad brutes of movies (fewer in number) in other filmic traditions. Indeed, the amphibian behemoth of the Japanese *Godzilla* (1954) is touched on as a point of subtextual overlap, since it shares with various Western productions (including an American remake) the era's cultural trepidation around atomic destruction.

Regarding the animals themselves, some may be thankful to hear that I stick to "true predators" in the zoological sense, so parasites aren't included (despite their occasional appearance in horror). The creature responsible for the most human deaths, the mosquito, is ironically neglected in movies, swatted aside in favor of its more physically impressive (or simply revolting) killer-counterparts, and accordingly isn't discussed either. Also, partly because of space constraints, few prehistoric animals are addressed; I've generally maintained focus on the creatures of our current epoch. Similarly, Godzilla notwithstanding, I generally avoid more generalized "monsters" that possess animal characteristics, although again I feel that what follows will be useful for thinking about them too. Despite its boundaries, I hope that the reader will be satisfied with the bestiary compiled herein, and find fascination in considering the emotional effect of our toothy brethren of fur and fin and their (at least alleged) delight in dining on people. It's not strictly necessary to have seen the films mentioned here before reading about them—but I'd encourage it. I can't say that this is a "spoiler free" book, but I do avoid divulging the details of films unless doing so is necessary for serious discussion (and sometimes it is). As to the structure of the book: we'll begin with cinematic animal horror's first grand success, *King Kong* (1933), but I'd prefer not to perform extended introductions here. Instead, I'd ask that, as you proceed, you allow these daunting beasts to clamber or crawl or swim or slither up to you more naturally, with your eyes peeled but your mind open.[80]

1

Going Ape

King Kong

*K*ING *K*ONG TOWERS IN CINEMATIC and cultural influence, an inspiration for numerous films in which self-determining and often semi-sympathetic nonhumans smash through a metropolis, from *Godzilla* to *Rise of the Planet of the Apes* (2011). Although we perhaps tend to think of *Kong* as a work of unprecedented originality, the fearsome monarch of Skull Island had plenty of forerunners, albeit few with the same seismic impact. The jungle quest was a popular genre in the era of Kong,[1] and directors Schoedsack and Cooper's opus was preceded by the now-lost films *Man Hunt* (1926), as well as *Ingagi* (1930), the latter a faux-documentary in which gorillas lay claim to local women. In the crime melodrama *The Unholy Three* (1925, remade in 1930), a crook who runs a pet store uses a gorilla as a weapon against his traitorous accomplice. Further back, French sculptor Emmanuel Frémiet's *Gorille enlevant une femme* (Fig. 1.1 on page 22), had won its creator the 1887 Medal of Honor at the Salon, the official art exhibition of the Académie des Beaux-Arts in Paris. In Frémiet's vivid carving, a cantankerously open-mouthed ape clutches a struggling bare-breasted beauty with ease under one arm. The poet Charles Baudelaire declared the work's sexual subtext in his contemporary review: "this is not about eating," he wrote, "but rape!"[2]

Perhaps the first Western narrative tale of ape-terror (as well as the first modern detective story), Edgar Allan Poe's "The Murders in the Rue Morgue" (1841), reveals its killer to be an escaped "Ourang-Outang"

Figure 1.1. *Gorille enlevant une femme* by Emmanuel Frémiet (Musée des Beaux Arts de Nantes).

(orangutan). From a tuft of hair in evidence, detective Dupin guesses the assailant to be no man, despite the attack initially suggesting the sophistication of a human attacker. The tale was very loosely adapted for the screen by Robert Florey in 1932, with the ape's sexual appetite amplified. Ted Gott and Kathryn Weir credit Poe's tale with fostering the link between gorillas and crime, also evident in *The Gorilla* (1930, remade in 1939); a series of brutal murders during the late-1920s were referred to in the press as the work of "Gorilla Men,"[3] presumably influenced by Poe's evocative imagery. More directly influential on *Kong* was Edgar Rice Burroughs's adventure sensation *Tarzan of the Apes* (1912), the eponymous hero of which clashes with a number of cranky primates. As a teen, Tarzan battles gorilla Bolgani, bests his long-term ape enemy Tublat, and deposes ornery tribe-leader Kerchak. After the tyrannical ape Terkoz abducts marooned Englishwoman Jane Porter (prefiguring the abduction at the center of *King Kong*), the jungle hero slays his rival, paving the way for his and Jane's famous romance. As in Frémiet's figure, the abduction suggests the brute's violation of sexual boundaries between species: "Then [Jane] was dragged toward those awful fangs which yawned at her throat. But ere they touched that fair skin another mood claimed the anthropoid."[4]

The sexual threat again emerged in Cecil B. DeMille's precode epic *The Sign of the Cross* (1932), in which prisoners are flung into the Colosseum arena with all manner of creatures to be mauled and mangled for the perverse excitement of Ancient Roman onlookers. At one point, a gorilla darkly appraises a naked and trussed-up blonde beauty (Fig. 1.2), although whatever happens next is thankfully outside our view. Our biggest concern in these moments is the virtuous Christian girl Mercia (Elissa Landi), who waits in a dungeon for her turn to die. The subjection of the girl ahead of her to this bestial terror is sadistically erotic: what awaits poor Mercia is not merely death but also horrifying sexual degradation.

After the stomping success of *King Kong*, of course, the killer gorilla theme hardly abated: a poorly received sequel, *Son of Kong* (1933), was rushed out the same year; later, *The Ape* (1940) featured Bela Lugosi and a savage primate pet; and a gorilla guards a white woman in the jungle

Figure 1.2. A gorilla ominously approaches a bound beauty in *The Sign of the Cross* (Cecil B. DeMille, Paramount, 1932). Digital frame enlargement.

in *Nabonga* (1944), the poster of which repeated the Frémiet motif of a damsel clutched under a powerful primate arm. In general, erotic themes have been especially well represented. After a plantation manager murders his boss for love in *Bride of the Gorilla* (1951), he's cursed by a local witch to transform into a gorilla, the beast that apparently exemplifies his wild desire. In the exploitation film *Kong Island* (1968), the villain threatens to lock his two female prisoners in a cage with two hyper-aggressive gorillas who are, he sadistically chuckles, "getting excited." The possibility of interspecies arousal is even used to poke fun at male narcissism in the zoo-centered comedy *Fierce Creatures* (1997): arrogant investment heir Vince McCain (Kevin Kline) knows his crush (Jamie Lee Curtis) is smitten with another, and mistakes her devotion to a gorilla as evidence that this must be the man, launching immediately into a mocking derogation of his "rival." "But let me ask you," Vince raves competitively, "how much does he earn—how much does Mr. Gorilla take home at the end of the week?"

Consistently in cinema the ape presents an ambiguous human analogue: a creature comparable in appearance and perhaps interiority, including (especially in horror) a human-oriented sexuality that challenges the border between human and animal. Kong is of course king among these representations, the angry ape virtually unrivaled among cinema icons more broadly, suggestive of his enduring archetypal resonance. Yet what of our sympathy for Kong? What of Kong the protector, who shields his would-be mate from Skull Island's meat-eating megafauna?—the Kong whom even contemporary audiences couldn't help but pity? As John C. Wright puts it, Kong "roars a challenge to tormentors to do their worst," and when they do "pour machine-gun fire, efficiently and mercilessly, into the great ape's breast" and he finally falls, "The audience does not cheer."[5] There's obviously something in this strange creature that stymies our pleasure in his defeat; this chapter explores the four central versions of the epic tale of the angry ape (from 1933, 1976, 2005, and 2017) as powerful evocations of the shared evolutionary impulses of human and animal.

Beauty and the Beast: *King Kong* (1933)

Few movie plots are as famous, but we'll summarize the events of *Kong* for the forgetful or uninitiated. An audacious movie director Carl Denham (Robert Armstrong) spots blonde waif Ann Darrow (Fay Wray) on the streets of Depression-era Manhattan and offers her a part in his next film, before he and his crew embark on a voyage to Skull Island in search of the fabled "Kong." They disturb a scene of sacrifice by the indigenous islanders, dedicated to the mysterious monster, in which a local girl is to become the "bride of Kong." The natives offer to trade Ann for several native women (picking the white girl as a rarer specimen for sacrifice) and after their offer is unsurprisingly declined, they abduct Ann from the boat anyway. After the supersized gorilla (the ingenious stop-motion work of Willis O'Brien) strides through the jungle to retrieve the offering, by which he is immediately enthralled, the crew mounts a rescue mission, which Kong jealously attempts to thwart. Thankfully, he also defends his unwilling bride against Skull Island's other hair-raising residents, including a Tyrannosaurus and a giant serpent. To the rescue is Jack Driscoll (Bruce Cabot), Ann's hardboiled human admirer, who snatches her away but with Kong in hot pursuit. Under the instruction of the enterprising Denham, a trap has been laid: Kong is gas-bombed into submission and transported to New York for exhibition (Fig. 1.3). Degradingly chained up for the awe of New York theater-goers, Kong flexes his muscles and snaps his manacles before laying a path of destruction through Gotham to regain his bride. With Ann in his hairy hand, Kong scales to the

Figure 1.3. The captured king: the mighty Kong manacled for public amusement in *King Kong* (Merian C. Cooper & Ernest B. Schoedsack, RKO, 1933). Digital frame enlargement.

top of the newly erected Empire State Building (1931). Yet the jungle monarch is no match for humans' high technology of violence, and he's gradually picked off by a swarm of biplanes, plummeting from his iconic pedestal to his death. The director Carl Denham tells us, standing by Kong's body below, that "It was Beauty killed the Beast," repeating the epigraph with which the film began (a so-called "Arabian proverb" actually fabricated for the film).

The ambitious ape isn't successful, but the movie was. Accordingly, *King Kong* has generated a wealth of scholarship. The giant gorilla has been seen as a fearsome representative of a barbarous racial Other, in line with his remote home and dark-skinned worshippers,[6] but as Noël Carroll points out, we've also heard about "Kong as Commodity, Kong as rapist, Kong enraptured by L'amour fou, Kong as Third World, Kong as dream, Kong as myth, Kong according to Freud, according to Jung, and even according to Lacan."[7] Carroll's own essay "Ape and Essence" works to highlight a "survival of the fittest" theme that reflects a strain of Social Darwinism embedded in laissez-faire economic attitudes during the period. Carroll first points out a series of symmetries between Kong's jungle home and his new urban environment: for example, Kong battles a serpent on the island, and later smashes a serpentine monorail in New York. Such echoes equate the city with the jungle in a "literalization of a banal but persuasive American belief about the nature of society."[8] The jungle world of Kong, Carroll contends, echoes the brutal world of capitalism specifically: "the Darwinian jungle," he writes, "was a readily accepted figure for the market in the culture in which Kong was made," and this Darwinist metanarrative reflects an American economy depressed at the time of the film's production. Degrading though Kong's exploitation may be, that his captor Carl Denham receives no moral reprimand within the film suggests a culture open to "celebrating unselfconscious opportunism."[9] Yet for Carroll, Kong nevertheless attracts our sympathy as a naïve victim of this system "because he is exploited as a commodity, displaced for the sake of business, befuddled, and smashed to a pulp in the modern jungle. . . . Kong is not only the biggest country bumpkin ever to be crushed by the city; he is also a metaphor for the Depression Everyman, lowered in the course of Denham's promotional bid for the showbiz pot of gold."[10]

This is a persuasive reading. However, Carroll's perspective can be valuably complemented through reference to Darwinism as more than a symbol or stand-in for the machinations of capitalism, allowing further interpretation of ape (and human) "essence" as the film presents them. As indicated in this book's introduction, while still relatively little-noticed by the humanities and social sciences, many researchers in the cognitive sciences have busily applied the implications of Darwinian theory to human personal and social behavior. This research has given rise to fields variously titled sociobiology, evolutionary psychology, human behavioral ecology, and Darwinian psychology.[11] Supported by voluminous experimental and anthropological data that show innate and cross-cultural aspects of humanity,[12] evolutionary psychology demonstrates that personality, behavior, and social organization cannot be explained solely in terms of arbitrary "social constructs."[13] Consequently, it's becoming increasingly appreciated that any thoroughgoing explanation of human motivations and behavior simply cannot exclude evolutionary thinking, thereby beginning, as Jerome Barkow puts it, "the mighty labor of shifting humankind from our privileged position in the land of the non-animals to the natural world."[14] A film like *King Kong*, which centralizes archaic animal forms and primal desires, can be usefully considered with reference to the aims of those desires, and the way they evoke the animal in the human and, necessarily, the human in the animal.

At the center of evolutionary psychology is the encoded "selfish" goal of advantageous gene replication,[15] the premise that organisms tend to seek for themselves situations that maximize opportunities for successful reproduction. It's an appreciation that Darwinian goals are not only the business of the past: human behavior is still dependent on brains that, like those of other animals, prioritize gene replication, and brains that evolved to their current form by responding to the pressures of ancestral environments. This means that the "jungle" of Depression-era New York City in *King Kong* isn't just an economic metaphor; those who live there are still in the "jungle" psychologically as well. This is not to simply equate capitalism and Darwinism, or suggest that capitalism is the "desirable" product of evolved human nature; it is to say that capitalist New York is inevitably a domain of behavior for human creatures molded and motivated by evolutionary imperatives.[16] When director Carl Denham finds his soon-to-be star homeless, thieving an apple from a cart, he immediately references her value in the most brutal biological terms. While there may be many homeless women around, he tells her, there's "not many who look like you." Crude as his observation may be, what he means is that Ann is possessed of a primitive sexual currency that ought to preclude her homelessness—she's a genetically "valuable" female. The status-obsessed Denham isn't actually interested in Ann sexually, but he's very clear that his motives are not altruistic: "I'm not bothering with you out of kindness," he says, before pitching her the part in his film. Denham only wants a woman in his film to appease female viewers, and sees Ann as a pathway to a greater return on his investment and social status. In the world of Cooper and Schoedsack's film, nothing is truly free, but part of an evolutionary logic of self-advantage. The suggestion of a primal nature just below the thinnest social veneer is again evoked once Ann is aboard the ship bound for Skull Island. She quickly runs into unsentimental sailor Jack Driscoll, who's standoffish toward her, although he makes clear that his apprehension is because of the trouble he thinks she'll cause through the promotion of sexual rivalry between the ship's men. "Women can't help but be a bother," he tells her, "Just made that way I guess" (Fig. 1.4). On this male-only ship, mating opportunities are normally deferred until their next stop at port; Driscoll is foreshadowing a disruption of efficient comradery through intrasexual competition.

Despite his standoffish, tough-guy persona, Driscoll quickly enough falls for Ann. It's at this point that Denham first mentions his "beauty and the beast" thesis, warning Driscoll of the dangers of getting distracted by women: "It's the idea of my picture. The Beast was a tough guy too. He could lick the world. But when he saw Beauty, she got him. He went soft. He forgot his wisdom and the little fellas licked him. Think it over, Jack." The remark clearly links Kong's nature and desire with Jack's, but on the surface Denham's idea is a little confusing. As Noël Carroll notes, his hypothesis "holds the unlikely idea that sex is unmanly and unmanning."[17] Yet his words make enough sense for the hyper-competitive character

Figure 1.4. While acknowledging her beauty, Jack Driscoll (Bruce Cabot) is nevertheless initially unfriendly toward his lovely female shipmate, Ann (Fay Wray) in *King Kong* (Merian C. Cooper and Ernest B. Schoedsack, RKO, 1933), wary that she'll generate intrasexual male rivalry. It won't be on the ship, but Jack will find a rival, all right. Digital frame enlargement.

who utters them: Denham's obsession with status means that actual sex seems perpetually deferred. When he says, "The little fellas licked him," what we might say he evokes is the rampant competition between men, in which any number of "lesser" competitors await the smallest sign of mediocrity or inattention.

On the island, primal logics are of course in powerful motion, as the crew spies and disturbs the sacrificial offering to the beast. As with any such sacrifice, the tribe offers up to the terrible unknown something of value in the hope that the future will manifest itself in their favor. The sacrifice is not arbitrary: a beautiful young girl, a potential mate, adorned with flowers in accentuation of her beauty and fertility. They explicitly designate her the "bride of Kong." Ann is of course soon captured by the island natives and offered in tribute to their god instead. While Kong clearly can't have sex with Ann, he explores her through the "erotics of touch,"[18] removing items of clothing, and smelling the fingers that have touched her, the film obviously signaling the young woman as a valued object of sexual possession.

Yet the relationship is not entirely one-way—at least not for the viewer. The powerful Kong actually performs as a highly desirable and enthusiastic mate in several key ways. Commenting on the conditions that influenced our psychology and mate-preferences, David M. Buss encourages us to

> imagine living as our ancestors did long ago—struggling to keep warm by the fire; hunting meat for our kin; gathering nuts, berries, and herbs; and avoiding dangerous animals and hostile humans. If we were to select a mate who failed to deliver the resources promised . . . our reproduction would be at risk. In contrast, a mate who provided abundant resources, who protected us and our children, and who devoted time, energy and effort to our family would be a great asset.[19]

Just as other animals have evolved mate preferences in response to the adaptive problems of their environment, human's mate selection has been affected by problems significant in our natural history. Given humans' unusually long period of gestation and period of dependency in infancy (the longest of any mammal), pregnancy requires a tremendous biological investment for the female relative to the male, interfering with her own resource acquisition (and further mating opportunities). Accordingly, evolutionary psychology hypothesized an evolved female preference for stability of resources and capacity to acquire them, which has been repeatedly confirmed,[20] and replicated even across periods of profound cultural change.[21] Relative to men, women across all studied cultures also tend to prefer mates higher in social status.[22] This follows logically, given that social hierarchies are universal among human groups, and higher male status is linked with greater access to resources.[23] "King" Kong's persona is wrapped up in his status at the very top of Skull Island's social dominance hierarchy: in that world, he's quite a catch. Athletic ability is also a significant trend in preferred male mates, obviously as an indicator of genetic health beneficial for reproductive success, but also for the physical protection that would have been crucial in the unpredictability of the ancestral environment: "A man's size, strength, physical prowess, and athletic ability," explains Buss, "are cues that signal solutions to the problem of physical protection,"[24] which again would have become a high priority during pregnancy and child-rearing.[25] Skull Island provides a thrilling vision of nature "red in tooth and claw," as Tennyson put it, a landscape prowled by dinosaurs, sea monsters, and serpents. And in this physically volatile environment, who is as physically capable, and in that sense desirable, as Kong?

Virtually as soon as Ann is situated in his realm, Kong begins fending off threats to her survival, persistently demonstrating his capability as a protector against the perils of this revived ancestral landscape. Kong is hierarchically unrivaled in his domain—he is, after all, King Kong, the one whom the puny human natives beseech for benevolence. It's during these sequences of stunning protection that our identification with and admiration for Kong builds. Kong cares—with impressive force. After he defeats the Tyrannosaur and the serpent, he proudly pounds his chest before his desired mate, displaying his credentials.

Our sympathy for Kong, and the tragedy of his demise, is enhanced by the film's relative lack of interest in Jack Driscoll. Driscoll is of course Ann's "proper" lover, the one implicitly endorsed in attractiveness, social standing, and species. But the great gorilla is unmatched by his human rival in the mate qualities he powerfully displays. Unlike Tarzan, who challenges and supersedes his ape rivals' skills in ever-increasing challenges, Jack never faces Kong on the island but rather stealthily snatches his bride out from under him. Later in the film, Kong even knocks Driscoll unconscious with absurd ease while reaching for his "bride" through a hotel window. Neither does Jack directly participate in Kong's death, arriving on the scene only after he has toppled from the building. Jack fulfills the role of the romantic partner while offering only paltry investment compared with his huge and hard-working counterpart.

Anthropomorphic though Kong may be, and as much as we may be able to understand his desires, Ann is not a gigantic gorilla; she's a petite modern girl from a modern world. While she too may have mate preferences inherited from deep history, Kong is in competition with men not only more successful in the civilized environment to which Ann is (to her relief) repatriated, but also rather more handsome than Kong is. Kong may be wide-eyed for Ann, but he presents no corresponding "beauty" for her. At least in Tarzan, Jane Porter is smitten with her muscular and athletic jungle hero; Ann is not attracted to Kong, and she never will be. As Kong wiggles his eyebrows at Ann upon first examining her, flashing a toothy grin as she famously screams her lungs out, the point is the profound mismatch between how each one sees the other. Despite the big brute's devoted and energetic displays of protection, he never had a chance. This allows our sympathy for Kong much of its tragic tenor: our recognition of how conscientiously he fulfills his desired role, while never qualifying at all.[26] As Wright puts it, "For better or worse (but probably for the better), we are not so callous toward the masculine weakness for the weaker sex."[27] And when Kong falls, so far and so hard, we see a guy not merely defeated but also rejected (Fig. 1.5).

It's in this light that we can consider the final words of the film—"It wasn't the airplanes; it was Beauty killed the Beast." But it wasn't beauty, was it? And it was the airplanes. . . . Perhaps literally, yes. But let's imagine that Kong hadn't been killed: Ann, of course, would be no more compliant—would no more return his flirtation or interest. The

Figure 1.5. The weary Kong, riddled with bullets, seconds before falling from his great height in a fate that also symbolizes his romantic rejection, in *King Kong* (Merian C. Cooper & Ernest B. Schoedsack, RKO, 1933). Digital frame enlargement.

proverb's application is more coherent if we think that attempts to secure female attention open one up to rejection, and the grander the attempt, the more crushing the collapse. "Beauty" itself is not simply "in the eye of the beholder" (as virtually all of us wish it was). While influenced by cultural context to some extent, physical attractiveness is far from a merely arbitrary cultural construction; it's made up of preferences for particular bodily and facial shapes and symmetries (clues to genetic benefits) that turn out to be remarkably consistent across cultures.[28] While Ann may be the fragile emblem of "civilization," Denham's proverb hints that beauty itself is a "primal" and powerful force. The ugly and cantankerous Kong may well be spurred to action by female beauty, but not everything is in his control. It's Ann who gets to choose, and Kong doesn't make the cut. In the game of sexual selection, the sex whose biological investment in reproduction is more expensive is going to turn out to be the choosier about whom she mates with.[29] As feminist evolutionary anthropologist Sarah Blaffer Hrdy writes, "to an extraordinary degree, the predilections of the investing sex—females—potentially determine the direction in which the species will evolve. For it is the female who is the ultimate arbiter of when she mates and how often and with whom."[30] The power of what Darwin called "female selection" is foreshadowed earlier in the film through Ann's human admirer: Driscoll had admitted his love for Ann not without fearfulness—"I guess I kind of love you. I'm kind of scared of you too." Even a tough guy like Driscoll knows that confessing interest to Ann opens him up to rejection—highlights her power over him. That is how Beauty may slay a Beast. But this fate is reserved for tragic Kong, as Denham's moral reaffirms that it is the female who is ultimately in control.

Emphasis on naked evolutionary objectives of survival, status, and mate selection is entirely characteristic of the work of directors Cooper and Schoedsack. In *The Four Feathers* (1929), also starring Fay Wray, a man declines his soldiering duties because they'll get in the way of his wedding. The fiancée, far from being pleased by her lover's devotion, is appalled and calls the whole thing off. The rejection is directly linked to his refusal of a protective role: only after demonstrating his heroism and fighting prowess is he restored in her esteem and the union proceeds. Filmed at the same time as *King Kong* (and using some of the same sets), *The Most Dangerous Game* (1932) drags its characters again into the animal world, recognizing their continuity with nonhuman creatures when an eccentric big-game hunter, Count Zaroff (Leslie Banks), takes to hunting humans on his jungle island because "man is the most dangerous game." The hero (Joel McCrea) must fend off the human predator and protect his female companion (Fay Wray again) in a fight-or-flight scenario evocative of prehistoric struggles. Embedded in Cooper and Schoedsack's filmmaking is a fascination with the "animal" in the human that prefigures the man/ape hybridity of Kong's character, and the primal "jungle romance" in which Ann Darrow is embroiled.

Every Ape-Man for Himself

Kong is more than an aspiring lover; he is, with ferocious pride, an individual, and this holds tremendous dramatic and affective appeal, and can also be elucidated through evolutionary perspectives. The shift from Skull Island to Manhattan, initiated by Kong's capture, undoubtedly amplifies our sympathy for the ape. In the theater, Kong's arms are chained akimbo as if he were on a crucifix: the "god" of the island exposed to earthly capture and torment. His exhibition also resembles a pillory, with the individual specifically displayed for humiliating social exclusion. The mysterious Kong was the beneficiary of sacrifice earlier; now it is he faced with powerful unknown forces—however, not submitting to his tormentors, Kong refuses to sacrifice anything. As mentioned above, Noël Carroll sees our sympathy for Kong as part of an economic subtext of an everyman smashed up by the "jungle" of capitalism.[31] I disagree here, since King Kong is not really an "everyman." After capturing the monarch, Denham announces, "He was a king and god in the world he knew, but we'll teach him fear, boys." But they never do. As Charles Derry writes, "even on a simplistic level it is obvious that King Kong represents an aspect of man that man has managed to suppress,"[32] and below that surface level what we see in Kong is a tragic allegory of the self-determining individual besieged by the demands of the group.

Humans are social animals, having spent our natural history in small tribal groups, yet we're also genetically predisposed to prioritize our individual interests: a process of negotiation and (at least) inner conflict that can never be permanently settled. As David Barash writes, "As difficult as it must be for any creature to balance its various competing demands . . . such choices are probably most confusing in the social domain."[33] He suggests that the theme of individuality versus the social—"self versus group, selfishness versus altruism, callow youth versus responsible adulthood, individual needs versus society's expectation"—has been central to literary history because "it is a conflict that may reside, literally, in our genes."[34] Kong has immense status and power, but he hasn't learned any form of sociability that requires concessions to a group. Kong is the exemplary empowered individual. He belongs to no coalition—he's the only one of his kind. His only interactions are with the animals he fights or the nervous humans from whom he receives offerings. Philosopher René Girard has written that "no culture exists within which everyone does not feel 'different' from others. . . . There exists in every individual a tendency to think of himself not only as different from others but as extremely different"[35]—part of what social psychologists refer to as "false uniqueness bias." Still human enough to garner our sympathy, the ape titan is a fitting metaphor of the "otherness" of selfhood, and his rampage and demise a potent expression of the primal tension between the drive to fulfil individual desires and the necessity of social compromise.

Kong's representation of an empowered, presocial state of existence is enhanced by the brute's intermittent childishness throughout the film. Back on the island, when Driscoll lances Kong's finger with a knife (just a pinprick for the giant ape), Kong pulls back his hand and looks at it with confusion, as an infant would. Carroll also observes that the giant's relationship to Darrow makes her appear as a toy in his possession.[36] Kong the big kid evokes a time before compromise, sacrifice, and impression-management become accepted features of our social existence. He's the monarch of the self, to some extent recognizable to all of us, but finally ousted and trammeled by social coercion. It is worth noting that while modern viewers may pick the Empire State Building that Kong scales as a triumphant apex of industrial progress and civilization, Martin Rubin points out that, really, in the early 1930s "it was widely considered a folly—a relic of the pre-Crash real-estate boom" that at the time of the film's production consisted of largely unleased space.[37] Outwardly spectacular, the heights of civilization are dissatisfyingly hollow. Kong's extreme difference ensures a tragic view of individual compromise. Kong can never be integrated or accepted to his own advantage; he has nothing to gain from the society of others—he's too animal to be assimilated. But more fundamentally, he's also recognizably too human. In this beast's individuality, character and autonomy, we recognize much of what we specifically admire in humans, and attributes that Kong staunchly refuses to curb.

As Rubin points out, *King Kong* combines the elements of numerous genres and traditions.[38] Consequently the film offers multiple pleasures and sustains many interpretive approaches. Nevertheless, clear, potent, and primal in Cooper and Schoedsack's film are themes of status, mate selection, animality, and promethean resistance befitting the Darwinist setting from which its manlike monster is imported. As Denham advertises, it's a tale of "Beauty" and a "Beast," and one that, like the fairytale, implies the human hidden in the animal, but also the animal hidden in the human.

Crude Motives in *King Kong* (1976)

Primal desires are also at play in the film's 1976 remake, produced by Dino De Laurentiis and directed by adventure specialist John Guillermin. In this version, Kong comes to life through a combination of ape suits and animatronics rather than stop-motion, and he's discovered on an obscure Indonesian island by a petroleum vessel searching for oil. The leader of the expedition is Fred Wilson (Charles Grodin), eager representative of Petrox petroleum, although also on board is Jack Prescott (Jeff Bridges), a stowaway academic convinced that the massive carbon dioxide emissions from the island indicate an enormous organism rather than an oil deposit. Unlike in the original, the expedition isn't out to make a movie, yet on the way the all-male crew encounter a lifeboat containing beautiful ingénue actress Dwan (Jessica Lange), the only survivor of a shipwreck, who quickly takes a shine to Jack upon awakening.

The film's focus on prehistoric time, with talk of ancient oil reserves maturing over millions of years, subtly hints that we're also entering the zone of prehistoric psychological phenomena. The original film's Great Depression setting is replaced by a climate of energy uncertainty (the first oil crisis occurred in 1973), in which discovering a jackpot of black gold will send Wilson's prestige through the roof—if he's successful. Used to the sheltered office life, the company man has staked his entire reputation on this expensive quest. He's convinced the bounty will be discovered either way, and makes several references to corporate competitors who would steal away his profit and glory. Wilson is a modern version of the tribal hunter in pursuit of big kill to impress the village and bolster his worth and status. It turns out the oil on the island is geologically undercooked and useless for human purposes, but once they discover Kong, Wilson's contingency plan brings him further into line with the ancestral archetype: he will conquer and bring back the beast. There's of course no desire to actually eat this impressive animal, as in the prehistoric paradigm, but instead they'll subject him as an exhibit to capitalist "consumption," allowing the oilman another avenue for the lucrative adulation he desires.

The girl is again at the center of conflict between Kong and his human foes, and the strength of her sexual currency is inflated for this new era. Jessica Lange's performance as Dwan is stylized glamour and coquetry in every hair-fiddling, lip-biting gesture. Immediately upon being brought aboard, unconscious, this sleeping beauty is subject to near-feverish male interest. When a crew member prepares to administer first aid and asks the crowd of onlookers to leave the room, another guy suspiciously queries, "I suppose you'll have to undress her," clearly concerned that a rival might gain some unearned sexual access. Contemplating her loss at sea, Wilson murmurs, "Sure have to be a careless yachtsman to lose this one overboard." One would have to be pretty careless to lose anyone, but we know what he means: to these men, Dwan is a female of very high value. After she awakens, she reveals a smiling, playful and utterly unguarded personality. This is when we learn her name, which she's modified from "Dawn" to make her seem "more memorable"—a goofy stylization that plays into her openness and naiveté. And once she is up and about the ship, the men all virtually trip over themselves to be of assistance (Fig. 1.6).

Kong's motivations in Guillermin's version are more explicitly erotic than they are in the original film. After Dwan's abduction, we see Kong awaken in the foreground of the frame, before rising to reveal Dwan, lying parallel in the background, as if they've been lying in a gigantic bed together (as Dwan's tanned garments seen at a distance provide the momentary optical illusion of post-coital nudity). As Kong slides off Dwan's heavy ceremonial necklaces and tries to stroke her top down over her breasts, he becomes more explicitly an ogling and unwanted male admirer: "Damn chauvinist pig ape!" Dwan snaps. Yet the captive's time on the island begins the process of humanizing Kong, with Dwan (more than her 1930s counterpart) coming to appreciate her admirer's personality and protection. While the original leaves the viewer to infer Kong's virtues, Dwan actively espouses them to the male crew after she is rescued. This allows the film to develop an anti-capitalist subtext:

Figure 1.6. The beautiful and flirtatious Dwan (Jessica Lange, center) quickly becomes the center of attention upon awakening in *King Kong* (John Guillermin, Paramount, 1976). Digital frame enlargement.

more explicit empathy for Kong renders more despicable his circus-like abuse later in the film. Moreover, in this film the greedy entrepreneur is juxtaposed with the countercultural young professor Prescott, who wants to conserve rather than cash in on this natural wonder.

While it's the woman who initially advocates Kong's noble nature, the film's treatment of Dwan seems ultimately unfavorable. Once Wilson rigs up Kong in a gaudy Petrox-sponsored circus, the fame-hungry Dwan can't help but accept a starring role (despite Prescott's objections). And when the big guy breaks loose, the professor is naturally reinforced as the voice of reason. Dwan and Prescott are informally a couple, yet as this chaos unfolds, Prescott questions their compatibility in light of Dwan's intense aspirations of social ascent. The two share a drink in an abandoned bar, where she flirts with him but gets only skepticism back: "You know how much an associate professor earns?" he asks, while complimenting her furs. He might have some small measure of status, but Prescott knows he can't compete with the kind of men who will pursue this glamorous beauty. Again, in the mating game we see primal anxieties roiling just below the surface (Fig. 1.7).

With Kong dead at the end of the film, Dwan stands and stares tearfully, separated from Jack as a throng of reporters close in with their promise of fame. Jack doesn't rush to reach his would-be lover. Perhaps he takes her loss as inevitable; perhaps he sees her as too much implicated in Kong's demise, since she took the glamorous gig in Wilson's grotesque

Figure 1.7. "You know how much an associate professor earns?" Despite the romantic setting, Jack (Jeff Bridges) begins to count himself out as a competitive mate for the high-maintenance starlet Dwan (Jessica Lange) in *King Kong* (John Guillermin, Paramount, 1976). Digital frame enlargement.

cavalcade of exploitation. Whatever the case, Dwan achieves her longed-for fame, but at the ironic cost of deterring her lover, the only sensible guy in the film. Consequently, the conclusion of Guillermin's version seems to align Prescott and Kong. They're both earnest but underresourced male suitors left behind, and the tragedy of Kong's destruction seems to emotionally overlap with the destruction of romance generally.

Beauty of the Beast: *King Kong* (2005)

Peter Jackson's lavish 2005 remake film pays loving homage to the original, restoring several characters (with some modernization) and reproducing key plot points and dialogue, while re-suppressing the erotic subtext. It also produces the most sympathetic incarnation of Kong to date, while casting further disdain on his human captors' greed. With Kong's savagery and sexual desire diminished, so too is much of the story's Darwinist undertone; Jackson's film reinvests in *Kong* as a tale of far-flung exploration whose sublime mysteries become tragic prey for exploitation. By now Kong is played by actor Andy Serkis in collaboration with sophisticated motion capture and digital animation technology. He's also modeled explicitly after a western lowland gorilla, complete with silvered back. Cooper and Schoedsack's original film was released in the era when gorillas were still targets for traveling big-game hunters, and dead ones were displayed in museums.[39] For the modern viewer, however, Kong is now a wonder to be protected and an animal against which violence is culturally abhorrent.

Immediately after Ann (Naomi Watts) is abducted, we see the human side of Kong. She attempts to communicate with her captor through a pantomime-filled "conversation" in which the furry giant roars and huffs a range of emotions familiar to human viewers. As Ann dances in an attempt to amuse him, Kong is bored by her more sophisticated routines but shows a childish delight in slapstick humor, his playful responses underscoring his pre-civilized "innocence." When Ann scolds her captor, he responds with a tantrum that she, quite like a firm mother, refuses to indulge. Kong retains his violent temper, but in this version he's violent only within clearly decipherable (even condoned) human frames of logic (primarily self-defense or in defense of Ann). In other words, he's the soft-hearted tough-guy—and, of course, he's still a hell of a protector (Fig. 1.8).

Ann stands apart from the exploitative paradigm of conquest and profit trumpeted by the film's men, and it is here that the film expands her role beyond the sexism of her 1970s predecessor. Unlike the ditzy Dwan of Guillermin's film, Ann rehearses scenes on the boat that suggest within her a deep melancholy, foreshadowing the film's tragedy but also prioritizing her sensitivity. A struggling Depression-era actress, the

Figure 1.8. Kong faces off against a Tyrannosaurus in Ann's (Naomi Watts's) defense, in Peter Jackson's *King Kong* (Universal, 2005). Digital frame enlargement.

principled Darrow nevertheless longs for emotionally meaningful productions. She's also reluctant to leave her gigantic admirer when rescued, and later (unlike her earlier counterparts) declines to participate in the theater showcase, opting out of this despicable and destructive parade of male dominance.

Our amplified sympathy for Kong is also wrapped up in the film's reinterpretation of the "beauty and the beast" theme. In this film the motif is first mentioned by Ann herself as she sits with Kong and they both gaze out at Skull Island's magnificent sunset (Fig. 1.9). "Beauty," she utters, naming their shared sense of the sublime. This moment not only deeply humanizes Kong, since appreciation of beauty strikes us as

Figure 1.9. Tough guy, soft heart: Ann (Naomi Watts) approaches Kong, gazing contemplatively over Skull Island at sunset, in *King Kong* (Peter Jackson, Universal, 2005). Digital frame enlargement.

a particularly human trait, but also paints the noble and contemplative Kong himself as a thing of beauty—part of this wondrous natural scene. In Jackson's film, "beauty" swerves away from the sexual, becoming something more ineffable but also elegiac. The gorilla's threatened status plays into the composition, the sunset emblematic of something slipping away. When Denham (Jack Black), standing by Kong's body at film's end, gives us that same line, "Beauty killed the beast," this time the summary seems different somehow. Now it seems to hint at the beauty of the beast himself, and the vulnerability of the sublime to exploitation.

Gorilla Warfare: *Kong: Skull Island*

The next major Kong feature, *Kong: Skull Island* (2017), was not a reiteration of the established narrative, but a reboot linked to the studio's previous *Godzilla* revival (2014) and intended to be woven into a broader "Monsterverse" franchise. To suggest a shared world between the two titans, Kong has been made substantially larger and thereby more consistent with his Japanese kaijū counterpart. The bulk of the film's action takes place in 1973: a secret government bureau receives approval to scour the island for cryptids under the guise of a geological survey. Using choppers provided by their military escort, they rain seismic charges down onto the verdant island landscape, sending animals scurrying in fear. The jungle spectacularly strikes back with Kong, who batters and swats and smashes the choppers like bugs, and leaves the survivors scattered and lost below. The humans encounter an aging American pilot, the comical Hank Marlow (John C. Reilly), who fills the intruders in on what they've seen. Kong, he explains, is the island's cranky caretaker who prevents it being overrun by a skull-faced reptilian race living below ground. The Americans' seismic blasts stupidly stir up these "skull-crawlers," against whom both human and ape are eventually drawn into spectacular combat.

In accordance with its new influences and franchise aspirations, *Skull Island*'s style is more overtly pulp than that of its forerunners. The structuring romance is excised: the film has none of the drama of mate rivalry, and it's without the ultimate tone of loner tragedy that hit its peak in Peter Jackson's version. Yet lingering from previous incarnations is the use of the Skull Island setting and its ape-man inhabitant to again underscore themes of status and dominance—a primitive landscape for primitive (yet persistent) human desires. The leader among the military escort is the embittered Colonel Packard (Samuel L. Jackson). America has just announced withdrawal from Vietnam, and as we first meet Packard he runs his hand over his bald pate in subtle tribute to Marlon Brando's Colonel Kurtz. He woefully examines his medals, secured in the service of a failed and ignominious war. "All this, for what?" he murmurs to himself. But later, as men scream and his gunships fall blazing from Kong's wrath, Packard does not run: he stubbornly stares, now obsessed with his new enemy.

From that point, Kong becomes the white whale to his Ahab, but more importantly the new "rival tribe," defense against which is unfinished business: guerillas become a gorilla, consolidated in Packard's mind into this massive jungle monster. Kong is thus a target through which Packard seeks to restore his badly wounded prestige. He seeks, through hunting Kong, to perform an unprecedented act of hunting and protection: "We're soldiers, we do the dirty work so that families back home don't suffer!" he shouts, touting his bravery as he plots the downfall of his new nemesis.

When explaining the island ecology, Hank articulates a clear dominance hierarchy in which Kong keeps the skull-crawlers in check. Packard wants to surmount this, and uses species difference to justify his enmity: "It's time to show Kong that Man is King." Yet Packard's brutally status-minded motives conceptually align him with the skull-crawlers, and we cheer for Kong to escape and avenge his hateful wrath—that is, we recognize Kong as more admirably "human" than his maniacal hunter.

While the links between Kong and human characters and motives are diluted in this newest film (especially given the absence of the central romance), we still get a glimpse of overlapping primitive intentions, evoking shared human/animal goals. More generally, we can see in the Kong films exemplary instances of nonhuman primates as fascinating boundary blurrers, creatures suggestively human enough to share our interests—or garner our sympathy—yet not always human enough to get what they want. I've focused on the *Kong* films here because horror is my subject, and the *Kong* films carry the mutant gene of the monster movie, although these themes stretch further. In action-adventure *Congo* (1995), a gorilla strapped with a device that vocalizes her sign language struggles with her position between worlds. Thus able to "speak" rudimentary English, she is human enough to communicate and defend her human friends against a tribe of killer gray gorillas, but not human enough to feel as though she truly belongs among people. And the recent *Planet of the Apes* films (2011–2017), more extensively than their 1960s and 1970s forerunners, ask us to contemplate where we draw the line between "us" and "them": a pressing question when they decide they've had enough of us, and attained the ability to say so. Whatever the fate of these primates, in their rage, heroism, horror, struggle, or sadness, they hold up for us an uncanny mirror, providing glimpses into an ancient and animal world of which we are still very much a part.

2

Out of Our Depth

Surviving Marine Monsters

Several of the creatures in this book, such as bears or giant snakes, provoke desperate evasive action: the human characters they stalk need to be somewhere else, and to put a lot of effort into getting there Yet the terrors of marine environments, most notably sharks, are pretty easily avoided. The difference between the water and land is obviously profound for these animals in terms of mobility. For us, simply choosing to remain on land, the environment to which we are after all adapted, places us safely out of reach. Yet such creatures also live on the other side of an ecological fringe of which many of us, as it happens, are especially fond. The beach is a significant domain of human enjoyment, family life, socialization, and trade, and thus consequently also a provocative zone of skirmish.

We might like the ocean's leisure opportunities, but we're not at our most capable there. The shark is an optimal ocean-borne source of anxiety, seeming to answer with dark and silent confidence many of our physical incapacities: whereas water renders us sluggishly limited in speed and movement, sharks are astonishingly speedy and whippily maneuverable. Olympic-level freestyle swimmers can sustain around five miles per hour in short events; shark species will reach over forty.[1] Unlike the arboreal or dry-land environments of our primate ancestors, the ocean offers no hiding places, footholds, or obstacles to put in a predator's path. Indeed, standard for the shark film (especially post-*Jaws*) are shots of humans from below as they bob on the ocean surface, unaware of what lurks beneath them, kicking feebly without traction and bereft of sudden evasive options. "The fear of being eaten is ingrained in people," says marine biologist Mike Heithaus, "if we feel like we have some control or [a] fighting chance, a situation isn't as scary [but] with sharks there are no trees to climb, and you can't outswim a shark."[2] Australian shark thriller *The Reef* (2010) further emphasizes our ocean-going ineptitude through the threat of dehydration: its characters, like Coleridge's ill-fated Ancient Mariner, have water everywhere "nor any drop to drink."[3] In contrast, sharks don't need to drink, absorbing and purifying water through their gill tissues. In a domain where our senses are severely impaired, the shark is the master detective: its underwater vision is far superior to our own thanks to a specialized tissue of light-reflecting crystals behind the retina,[4] and it's able to sniff blood diluted in seawater to as little as one part per million,[5] perfect for tracking us like a submarine Terminator. And what could be more symbolic—even mocking—of our aquatic incompetence than the familiar pop-cultural image of the shark circling around its human prey, dorsal fin ominously protruding from the water's surface?

An investigative tour through shark films shows that aquatic assailants regularly toy with the limits of our abilities. But they also demonstrate how much we attribute to some scenic locations, which run on their own ecological programs and may not be nearly as tantalizing as they seem. Fearsome fish are my main focus here, but I'll also detour to discuss water-borne reptilian hazards—crocodiles and alligators—another set of apex predators presiding for millions of years over their respective ecosystems, and which may similarly snap up human intruders. We'll see that these onscreen animals powerfully challenge the confidence of our control over our surroundings and sense of importance within them. Additionally, though, in several films marine monsters are used to dramatize more personal fears that lurk below comfort and contemplation. They play on our bodily clumsiness, but the challenge is also psychological. Characters are confronted with their evolved physical inadequacies but also with opportunities for beneficial psychological adaptation.

The Bite Perimeter of *Jaws*

Sharks are premier predators in animal horror, the frequency of their appearance indicative of their ability to elicit a level of fear rarely matched by other animals. We can easily see that the shark's jaws, razor-lined and in multiple rows, are capable not only of inflicting fatal damage to our soft human bodies but also of consuming them. "How the world loves to gaze at this maw," Antonia Quirke suggests, considering the motif's popularity in animal photography. The image, she suggests, is the clearest signifier of death there is. We can be bitten by a spider. Stung by a jellyfish. Mauled by a bear. Gored by a bull. Constricted by a python. Trampled by an elephant. Eaten by a shark. Only through the shark's jaws is the other side visible—the actual place where the victim will be moving to. It is a topological description of the after-life. You can be swallowed by a whale and still live. But the shark's jaws are the physical gates to the next world. A portal at which you stare and stare trying to discern the other side of life.[6]

While not the first film with such an aquatic attacker, *Jaws* certainly looms large as the most influential shark movie. Spielberg's film places extraordinary emphasis on a clash between human and animal "territory," in which we war for a location to which we are poorly adapted and our dominance is downgraded. *Jaws* commences by immediately contrasting human and animal worlds as a prelude to conflict. As the opening credits appear, our gaze is that of the lone and roving predator, steering coldly through its underwater world and scanning over the bleak weeds of the ocean floor. The cut that marks the end of the credit sequence juxtaposes the creature's perspective with the warmth and conviviality of a teenage party on the beach—noise, conversation, kissing by firelight. What will emerge to snatch Chrissie (Susan Backlinie) in a few minutes, we already know, is a thing from a fundamentally oppositional realm.

At the party, a gathering of holiday spot Amity Island's local and visiting youth, Chrissie sits alone on the sand. She and a boy (Jonathan Filley) make eyes at each other over the fire before he strolls over to meet this mystery girl. But it's not going to be that easy: from the seemingly shy girl comes a burst of delighted sexual autonomy as she dashes off over the dunes, urging the boy to give chase. She wants to see what this guy's made of first, to test his interest, investment, sense of humor—he's going to have work a little for this "catch." She begins stripping off as she runs and dives into the ocean, leaving him to follow after. Away from the (perhaps morally judgmental) group, Chrissie seems freed to inhabit her environment instinctively. In her spontaneity, casting her clothes any which way and diving nude into the ocean, she surely seeks to embrace a kind of utopian "animal" or "natural" state of being. She demonstrates her playfulness by raising one foot in a dainty gymnastic maneuver above the water's surface as she waits for the boy to undress at the lapping early-morning shoreline.

Chrissie's attempt to embrace a natural state is aggressively cancelled when she ends up devoured by that which is brutally instinctive. Quirke points out that as the shark approaches, we see Chrissie's silver hoop earrings: "They surprise you, remind you that she is human. Not a siren come from a coral cave to bewitch a sailor. Not a mermaid who belongs in the sea."[7] Immediately after her gymnastic display, from below comes the shark's perspective, reassigning to Chrissie a position of profound vulnerability—she is not, despite her confidence, in control at all. And indeed, when the shark strikes, it doesn't simply pull her under, as we might expect: she's tugged below only briefly before being propelled from side to side, her torso remaining above the surface. A moment ago Chrissie was playfully "toying" with the young man; now the shark is horrifyingly toying with her (Fig. 2.1).

The shark's first attack seems sexually prohibitive: animal attack as a punishment for autonomous female sexuality. But this interpretation isn't sustained by later attacks in the film: the next victim is a child (the asexual subject par excellence), followed by an attempt on a bumbling if ambitious fisherman. The horror of the encounter is more usefully considered through its insult to human autonomy and control. As well as viciously underscoring human helplessness in water, the attack implies a broader conflict of territorial zones of "belonging"—specifically, conflict between "civilized" (and leisure-ready) human space, and "wild" animal territory. The playful Chrissie might have wanted to be a wild child, but she was fatally out of her depth.

Given Amity Island's status as a holiday destination, the opening attack is an explosive prelude to a broader crisis around the meaning projected onto untamed natural space. The decision to close the beach is of course broached to businessmen who display serious consternation. And once panic has seized the town, the vandalism of a billboard (a shark-fin spray-

Figure. 2.1. Mistaking the ocean for a domain of spirited leisure, Chrissie (Susan Backlinie) becomes herself the plaything of the predator in Steven Spielberg's *Jaws* (Universal, 1975). Digital frame enlargement.

painted behind a bikini-clad boogie-boarder) reinterprets its promotional text, "Amity Island Welcomes You!" as grimly sarcastic. The graffiti addition makes clear the "vandalism" the shark has wrought on this holiday idyll. The environment of Amity has been recoded, with human-centric recreation, commerce—even survivability—now brutally contested and ridiculed.

Police chief Martin Brody (Roy Scheider) takes the lead. The recently relocated city cop must now investigate and intercept a far wilder type of criminal. The film's interest in spaces of perceived and proper belonging is again centralized through Brody's own outsider status. Amity's locals regard him with a suspicion of city-slicker ignorance or insensitivity, as a cop probably uncalibrated to policing a small seaside town. His foreignness is signaled early as his wife Ellen (Lorraine Gray) coaches him on the proper Amity dialect; and yet Ellen is exposed to the true extent of the town's nativism after she herself is told by a local that she'll never truly be "an islander," which requires one to be born on Amity. While the islanders' right to ownership, enjoyment, and commercialization of seaside space is contested by the shark, Chief Brody's right to act as their representative is implicitly suspect. The mayor, for whom the beach is a major attraction, is particularly intent on keeping his head in the sand (as it were) and ignoring the police chief's concerns. It's only once preteen bather Alex Kintner (Jeffrey Voorhees) has been dragged to his death in a geyser of blood, before a gasping crowd of onlookers, that Brody's warnings sink in. This hazard of nature will not fall in with the charming and profitable image of Amity that the mayor desperately desires to maintain; it will compromise the whole thing. As Quirke points out, the horror of *Jaws* is not merely the horror of its single aggressor, but a kind of contamination that permeates and destabilizes beyond its physical reach, "the inflection of a whole landscape with fear."[8]

The shark's aggressive "re-wilding" of civilized human space is compounded by its being staged around the beach as a location of family fun. Thought of as a recreational outpost of the domestic sphere, the beach is ideally a utopian world in which children are secure; but it's also at the very threshold of our ability to maintain that ideal. Accordingly, the crisis also becomes one of paternal protection, and Brody's challenge an extension of his fatherly identity. After the death of young Alex (similar in age to Brody's own son), the boy's mother (Lee Fierro) punishingly blames the police chief for his failure to have the beach closed earlier. Later, having abandoned his obsessive shark-focused study, Brody relaxes with his wife—only to be again plunged into anxiety as he spots his son playing in a sailboat tied to the jetty. The rhythm of this scene—its anxious cycling from relaxation to agitation—implies that there is no psychological safety from the enemy. The aggressor must be confronted, for it has invaded zones of control and relaxation both literally and psychologically. Interestingly, Brody himself already hates the sea. On the one hand, this flourish suits his character as the representative soldier of a dry-land species (playing up the collision of conflicting realms), but it also establishes the shark as a more personal psychological obstacle to be overcome.

He won't face this terror alone. The man hired to coordinate the shark hunt is fisherman Quint (Robert Shaw), an outsider who scrapes a living from a working-class trade unlike the middle-class tourism operators around him, and who'll bring to the conflict the revival of an age-old masculine adventurism. Importantly, Quint operates on the margins: he's at home in the wilderness and has a touch of the animal—of the wild—crucial to the task. During the town meeting he drags his clawed hand across a blackboard behind him to command attention, and before speaking he shoves a chunk of biscuit into his mouth and begins slowly masticating, like the chalk drawing on the blackboard of a shark masticating a man. As Nigel Morris points out, "Quint's $10,000 demand immediately establishes his greed,"[9] also suggestive of his animal nature. Yet for this grim and surly character (much influenced by Melville's Ahab) to actually succeed in killing the shark would imply a triumph of the aggression and nihilism he represents. Brody, on the other hand, is an identifiably "normal" man of restraint, of communal and familial decency—a man better suited to represent the stable world the shark threatens. Quint is possessed of valuable pugnacity, but he's also eventually possessed by it—losing himself in his unreasoning aggression. Too much a part of the wild world out there, the crazed shark hunter will be finally devoured, screaming all the way down (Fig. 2.2). As Morris puts it, "Quint's nemesis incorporates him when he slides into the shark's

Figure 2.2. Already psychologically consumed by his own animal aggression, Quint (Robert Shaw) is now literally consumed by the animal in *Jaws* (Steven Spielberg, Universal, 1975). Digital frame enlargement.

gaping maw."[10] Accordingly, the shark hunter's death works to clarify the line between the civilized and the wild: one may engage "wildness" to battle nature on its own terms, but one cannot give oneself over to its ravening bloodlust.

As a force of terror, the shark has been interpreted as a manifestation of various political or cultural concerns: as a metaphor for oppressive male power;[11] as terrifying female power;[12] as imbued with the tensions of Watergate, or Vietnam;[13] or the possibility of nuclear war, with some interpretations more plausible than others.[14] As he studies up on the animals before the expedition out to sea, Brody tells his wife, "People don't even know how old sharks are: they don't know if they live two, three thousand years—they don't know." It's as if this beast might be immortal, mythological, a dragon—an archetypal opponent ready to symbolize any number of fears. Yet, as Morris notes, the embodiment of the threat as such a natural one means cultural concerns are subordinated;[15] whatever else we might imagine the shark to "represent," it remains more immediately a man-eating shark—that's quite threatening enough. But as a shark, its menace is also tied up with profound contestation of geographic space: the intrusion of the amoral violence of nature into a zone of human leisure, and the accompanying challenge to restore order.

Second, Third, and Fourth Courses

With the offending shark blasted into fish food at the end of *Jaws*, it's a new toothy transgressor creating havoc for Amity's humans in *Jaws 2* (1978), directed this time by Jeannot Szwarc. First a shark chews up a party of divers poking around the sunken wreck of Quint's boat from the original film; later, a female water-skier and her driver are devoured. An orca is found washed up on the beach, unusual prey for a shark: we're dealing with a fiendish violator of natural order, the vanquishing of which thus becomes a moral necessity. Brody must again answer this challenge (with the site of the first attack suggesting that it's personal), but he's again hindered by the tide of community disbelief. Much of the sequel's threat focuses around the town's teenage population, especially as they seek to evade parental scrutiny and naïvely see the water as a site of fun, freedom, and potential sexuality (as did Chrissie). Since disobeying adult instruction may be fatal, the film appears to surpass its predecessor in sexual moralism. But rescuing these wayward teens allows Brody the chance to reinforce his paternal care, while reasserting his role as trusted guardian of the coast against the malevolent realm that laps at the doorstep of dry land.

The next installment, *Jaws 3-D* (1983), with direction by Joe Alves, brought (or strove to bring) the marine mayhem closer through looming graphic inserts designed to pop out at a theater audience wearing polarized glasses. More importantly, the aquatic action was relocated from Amity Island to SeaWorld Orlando, where a man-made lagoon connected to the ocean becomes the theater of mayhem. This faux ocean theme park is a curated space of human enjoyment, but again the human attempt to regulate the watery wilderness is doomed. The lagoon is meant to grant humans privileged access to nature's pleasures, yet this pleasant simulation is really more suited to the shark (which in its behavior will simulate nothing). If you build it, they will come: first the creature snatches a burly mechanic repairing a faulty gate to the ocean outside. Later it drags down two poachers stealing coral from the lagoon floor. After the attack, their inflatable raft sits on the still water in the moonlight before that too is pulled under. It's unlikely that the shark would clean up its own crime scene, but when the killer leaves only calm water behind, the film suggests its deep connection to and collaboration with its natural environment—we might have claimed this bit of sea, but the shark is its true native. When the beast finally appears for all to see, it does so as a perverse and unwanted park exhibit, its dorsal fin speeding alongside stunt water-skiers, before it terrorizes the public frolicking in the custom-made cove (Fig. 2.3).

At one point, the SeaWorld staff attempts to snag the shark for a park attraction, to corral it into a kind of domesticity. They have some initial success, relocating it to a pool. But after it awakens from its tranquilizer, it suddenly dies as tourists look on. It turns out this was

Figure 2.3. A fatal attraction: the shark sails in to cause tourist terror in the SeaWorld lagoon in *Jaws 3-D* (Joe Alves, Universal, 1983). Digital frame enlargement.

merely the juvenile offspring of the bigger beast, which will now wreak its revenge. Despite this, the film never courts an animal rights interpretation, choosing to preserve the shark's demonic character. In one scene, the SeaWorld dolphins ram the shark, attempting to deter it from human targets. As these dolphins come to our defense, the film implicitly reinforces a distinction between what are seen as humanized, domestic, cooperative, and generally "good" animals, and the sharks, who are still the pernicious people-eaters of the earlier films. Rather, this captivity critique seems grounded in opposing categories of "wild"/"domestic" and the general stupidity of attempting to treat one as if it were the other.[16]

As the title of *Jaws: The Revenge* (1987) suggests, the cinematic shark's vindictive character is reconfirmed in the franchise's final film, in which it targets one of Chief Brody's sons, Sean (Mitchell Anderson), then the other one, Michael (Lance Guest), now a marine researcher working in the Bahamas, promptly transforming that tropical paradise into a forbidding wilderness. Since the sharks of every previous *Jaws* film have been spectacularly slaughtered in the denouement, this is again by logical necessity a different animal. Yet these vengeful attacks on the Brody clan construct the shark as a singularized force of negativity, personalized to the family and ready to symbolize whatever unaddressed thing still haunts them. Chief Brody himself has passed away, and his widow implies that his fear was what took him to an early grave. This touch means the shark is recharged as a violator of paternal power to be confronted by the sons—if they're brave enough. The *Jaws* sequels' proposition that a new shark keeps emerging to assume the diabolical, Brody-hating mantle of the original is admittedly absurd. But their utility as horror opponents against which characters can struggle for self-realization has remained high because the ocean depths remain outside our zone of comfort, belonging, or easy surveillance, and can always replenish their danger.

Turn Yourself In(ward): *Orca*

Taking inspiration from *Jaws*, Michael Anderson's *Orca: The Killer Whale* (1977) upped the ante by focusing on another apex predator. Unlike *Jaws*, the film embraces an animal rights subtext, albeit around the orca specifically, based on its unusual intelligence and suggested emotional similarity to humans. In the film's opening scene, we see an orca pod frolicking in sublime sunset-dappled waters, yet fisherman Captain Nolan (Richard Harris) busts up the family bliss when he kills a mother orca, leaving him subject to the wrath of the male mate left behind. Nolan knows that he's done wrong and steers clear of the harbor, but the orca won't be so easily put off: it begins sabotaging the catches of fellow

Figure 2.4. Facing judgment: Captain Nolan (Richard Harris) sails out to confront his nonhuman nemesis in Michael Anderson's *Orca* (Paramount, 1977). Digital frame enlargement.

fishermen, then targeting Nolan's crew members one by one, until the captain is drawn into confrontation (Fig. 2.4).

With his transgression twisting him up internally, Nolan asks a priest whether one can really sin against an animal. "You can commit a sin against a blade of grass," the priest tells him, for "sins are really against oneself." Accordingly, the orca begins to assume a more anthropocentric role of manifesting Nolan's neglected conscience. The captain's crime is further personalized when we learn that his wife and child were killed by a drunk driver many years earlier; this symbolically intertwines the two beings but also underscores that Nolan of all people should have known better. In its fateful deadlock of human and animal, *Orca*, like *Jaws*, echoes *Moby-Dick*. Yet in both Melville's novel and Spielberg's film the fisherman is propelled by his own electrifying and unstoppable hatred; in *Orca*, the confrontation becomes instead the grim moral duty of admitting one's spiritual crimes and facing justice, and Nolan's aquatic foe is foremost a punitive animation of his own sin-soiled psyche.

Holidays from Hell: *Open Water* and *The Reef*

Following *Jaws*, later shark films have continued to appall any assumption that the ocean's role is to enhance the meaning of human lives. Among the most despairing is the independent film *Open Water* (2004). In documentary style, the film follows affluent professionals Daniel and Susan (Daniel Thomas and Blanchard Ryan), who escape to the Caribbean to defuse the stress of their hyper-productive work lives and revive their flagging romance.

Upon arrival, Susan stretches out on a deck chair as Daniel jumps into the shallow water; later they take a romantic stroll along the sand, the location dutifully serving its purpose—so far. The holiday is not without hiccups: the air conditioning in their bungalow is broken, the mood dries up during a sexual exchange, and a bug bothers them in the middle of the night. They're minor, but these creeping agitations indicate a location that isn't the cure-all it seems. What isn't minor is the couple taking a diving tour, where they marvel at a sublime undersea world, before resurfacing to find themselves abandoned. A tour operator has performed a negligent headcount and left Daniel and Susan bobbing alone in the Atlantic. And just like that, the zone of leisure becomes one of danger and distress.

The couple's agoraphobic immobility in this environment is apparent. The space can't even be intelligibly mapped: Daniel had mentally marked the boat's original position (probably the best place to wait for rescue) via some underwater feature, but the tide quickly carries the couple away. When they become a target for sharks, the creatures attack with terrifying anonymity and stealth, snapping at their legs and seen only (if at all) in the flick of a fin. In an environment that places humans at such a bleak disadvantage, the threat may approach without being sighted, much less evaded. Like any of us, the couple can play and luxuriate in such an environment under only the most carefully contrived and monitored conditions. Take those away, and the environment will gradually pick them apart.

The holiday was intended to rejuvenate Susan and Daniel's strained relationship and serve as a distraction from daily stress, but here are the sharks: nature at its most stress-inducing. The couple bicker under the pressure, digging up past resentment, yet by the film's conclusion, with little hope of survival, they reassert their love for each other—perhaps ironically, given the disastrous nature of this romantic tryst. Romantic love is affirmed against the threat of nature's deathly meaninglessness. Held afloat by his wife, Daniel dies of blood loss from his bite wounds, and Susan releases him to be subsumed by the ocean (Fig. 2.5 on page 54). A few moments later she too loses consciousness and slips below. We hear ritual tribal singing over the soundtrack, a choice that, in its evocation of traditional cultures, seems to ritualize the otherwise bleak scene, perhaps erecting some paltry meaning against the abyss of death—or perhaps suggesting the futility of trying.

Australian writer-director Andrew Traucki's *The Reef*, based on true events, also hinges on the natural environment's indifference to the characteristics that humans project onto it. Luke (Damian Walshe-Howling) has the enviable job of sailing boat purchases to their new owners, and invites his former flame, Kate (Zoe Naylor), her brother Matt (Gyton Grantley), and his fiancée Suzie (Adrienne Pickering) aboard a stylish yacht

Figure 2.5. Susan (Blanchard Ryan) sorrowfully releases her dead lover, Daniel (Daniel Thomas), shortly before she too slips permanently under in *Open Water* (Chris Kentis, Plunge Pictures, 2004). Digital frame enlargement.

for a brief holiday off the tropical Australian coast before he delivers the vessel to Indonesia. Kate's brother and his fiancée immerse themselves in all the romance that befits a sun-kissed getaway, swimming hand in hand as they marvel at the beauty below the water's surface; but this brings into relief the awkward ambiguity of Kate's relationship to her ex-boyfriend Luke. The boat stops by a secluded beach, and the two kiss on the shore, yet Luke interrupts the encounter, unsure of his would-be lover's intentions (romantic or purely sexual?), and the mood grinds to a halt in the hesitation. The two decide to trust each other despite their doubts. But when the underside of their boat is dashed open on some coral, so are any hopes that the tropical scenery will make a propitious setting for their renewed romance.

The vessel is capsized, and the crew huddles on the exposed hull before deciding to use boogie-boards (paddling is now not so leisurely) to find a nearby island—to remain is to risk death by exposure and dehydration. Only Warren (Kieran Darcy-Smith), a fisherman assisting Luke on the journey, refuses to leave: he knows the kind of creatures that patrol these seas. The water might look luxurious, but it's home to the world's largest marine carnivore, the Great White. As the trio moves along the surface, with the look of seals but none of the speed, they are forced to understand themselves as potential prey in an ecosystem outside the tranquil holiday ideal they'd signed up for. Early into the journey they discover the rotting remains of a sea turtle, likely a victim of one of the predators against which Warren warned. As the three of them struggle through ambiguous ocean, we see shots that place the lens half in the water, dividing the frame, suggesting the fundamental instability of their surroundings. Genre-typical, low-angle shots from beneath the water capture human legs kicking awkwardly, visually disconnected from their owners' torsos—human swimmers are so clumsy they can't even see what their own bodies are doing. Warren's worries are well founded: Matt falls prey to a shark and bleeds out, and the survivors have no choice but to leave him—Suzie's fiancé is now tragically the same kind of biological trash as the sea turtle. Then she too is dragged below, vanishing in a liquid cloud of her own blood, leaving only Luke and Kate remaining.

As in *Open Water*, the previously divided couple reaffirm their love: for all their previous bickering and uncertainty, the crisis has demonstrated to them the importance of their connection. The shark itself remains purely Other, beyond the realm of identification or sympathy, a force that through its contrast underscores human warmth and connection. But warm feelings aren't of much use out here: Luke is yanked below, leaving only the thoroughly traumatized Kate to be rescued. A textual overlay informs us that despite an extensive search, no traces of Warren or the capsized yacht were ever found. For all its tantalizing tropical glory, the marine environment becomes haunting in its capacity to erase us altogether.

Fin-clement Weather: *Bait 3D* and *Sharknado*

Australian-Singaporean production *Bait 3D* (2012) gave the well-worn battle-at-sea formula of *Jaws* and *Orca* a novel touch by bringing the predator inland. During a tsunami on Australia's Gold Coast a twelve-foot shark is flushed into a flooded supermarket, the creature's untamable anarchism a provocative addition to an otherwise banal suburban space. Sealed off by rubble from the outside world, a motley crew of characters is trapped inside as the shark swims between the main shopping area and the carpark below (Fig. 2.6 on page 56). The survivors must band together to devise a plan to defeat their common enemy and re-civilize their territory from this frontier intruder. The absurdity of this situation provides many opportunities for comic relief: surrounded by water but dry on the inside of their BMW in the carpark, an affluent teen couple stupidly bicker as the shark swims around them. Heather (Cariba Heine) refuses to let her boyfriend Kyle (Lincoln Lewis) use the heel of the $300 Guccis he bought her to crack the window, only to be informed that they're not real Guccis anyway. Forget the shark—for Heather,

Figure 2.6. Deli section: tidal wave survivors take refuge on the tops of shelves and refrigerators as a great white shark patrols the flooded supermarket in Kimble Rendall's *Bait 3D* (Darclight Films, 2012). Digital frame enlargement.

this is the true horror. For the story's major players, however, the shark is symbolic as well as literal, with each of them held prisoner by their regrets. Trapped are an ambivalent armed robber (Julian McMahon), hankering after money to pay off his brother's drug debt; a teen girl (Phoebe Tonkin) who abandoned her dying mother because she couldn't handle the stress; as well as her father (Martin Sacks), with whom she is at odds. Most centrally is Josh (Xavier Samuel), who blames himself for his friend's death by a shark attack a year earlier, driving his separation from his former fiancée (Sharni Vinson), who's also trapped below and mournful of their breakup. The subtext ascends to the surface when the sympathetic armed robber remarks, "Today Mother Nature saw us all as sinners down here."

Sealed off from the world by rubble, the bizarre environment becomes a suspended, purgatorial realm in which past mistakes can be corrected. Accordingly, the oceanic aggressor is deployed as a morally malign opponent against which the human spirit must demonstrate superiority, not despair. And not likeness, either: also trapped below is a vile drug dealer, Kirby (Dan Wyllie), who regards the situation with nihilistic inhumanity and only doubles down on his villainy by attempting to use a fellow captor as bait to distract the shark—naturally, he'll be eaten himself. Kirby's death is obviously wrapped up in his refusal of the film's moral program, but if we peel away this layer we can see a working demonstration of the age-old relationship between animal predators and social cohesion. As H. Clark Barrett informs us, predation by animals "is thought to be a major factor in selection for sociality in primates. . . . Reduction in predation risk could have provided benefits that outweighed the various costs of social life."[17] The characters of *Bait 3D* are marked not just by past sins but also by their disconnection or even antagonism to each other. When primal threats of predation are reactivated, refusing cooperation means you don't last in the long run. It isn't surprising that Kirby is a drug dealer specifically, a figure commonly seen to actively undermine community.[18] This crook not only tries to go it alone, but also preys on the group itself—which might work for him normally, but in this primal scenario he is quickly selected out.

Made-for-TV sensation *Sharknado* (2013) continued the shark as a symbol of chaos whose defeat promises human redemption, albeit mainly in a horror-comedy vein that subtracts some of *Bait 3D*'s moral angst. Again, the weather (a potential passage between land and sea) is amusingly exploited to provide a city setting with an unlikely sea creature contamination. The location is a sunny beach idyll in Southern California: people play volleyball; surfers slip up and down the waves; and bikini-clad beauties stride along the sand. But soon a hurricane pummels the coast and deposits a few snapping sharks onto land, even sending one shark flying through the window of a seaside bar, before a female bartender, Nova (Cassie Scerbo)—with a vendetta against sharks, as we'll discover—harpoons its head with a billiard cue. As the storm worsens, the bar's owner, Fin (Ian Ziering), Nova, and a few customers and friends flee inland to rescue Fin's estranged wife, his son, and his daughter—all this as a hail of sharks dramatically transforms the landscape of Beverley Hills.

Even more than in *Bait*, the shark in *Sharknado* is the essence of the anarchic and uncontrollable—more so, because there are more of them, crashing into and gnawing on anything in range. *Sharknado* was first film of a series, each installment striving to up the absurdist ante. These fiends are not even slightly cowed by their airborne predicament, ravaging everything in reach like angry animal missiles. A bird's-eye-view shot of the city shows several sharks "beached" atop skyscrapers, waggling furiously like stranded automatons. The novel ways these incorrigible creatures attack is part of the film's fun, cultivating delight in decontextualized silliness over the slower-burning spatial horror of *Jaws*. We see sharks swimming down city streets and chowing down on pedestrians; a flying shark knocks out a news reporter; another collides with a billboard

Figure 2.7. A shark is lobbed through a California billboard in Anthony C. Ferrante's cult hit *Sharknado* (The Asylum, 2013). Digital frame enlargement.

(Fig 2.7); another slams into an electrical tower and (once sufficiently charged up) explodes. Pedestrians are flattened as sharks belly-flop from the sky, and sharks begin raining into the pool of a retirement community as anxious seniors hurry out. And of course, as the film's title promises, we see a great swirling tornado flinging sharks around its perimeter.

While there's perverse pleasure implied in all this havoc, the shark threat again offers characters the chance to conquer personal challenges. For Nova, sharks have been an enemy since they ate her grandfather and left her with a score of teeth marks on her leg. For Fin, battling the sharks is a chance to repair his fractured family, with his courage impressing his daughter and estranged wife. At one point he abseils down a bridge to rescue children marooned in a school bus, and also rescues his ex (Tara Reid) as her new boyfriend is eaten after failing to take the threat seriously. Indeed, this character's name "Fin," suggests that the sharks are obstacles tailored to his character.

Produced amid rising public and political concern over climate change, *Sharknado* nevertheless engages with the topic only peripherally. Early in the film, a televised news report blames global warming for the hurricane, and the first victims of the sharks are fin poachers putting profit before ecological concern, which might suggest a moral reckoning. Yet the crisis is tackled and solved by characters with no environmental penance to complete—indeed the primary shark hater, Nova, is an environmentalist. A conservationist subtext is additionally buried by the enjoyment the film promotes by showing these mindless eating machines flung (often fatally) every which way across urban California. It may be that the film's brief acknowledgment of climate change allays the guilt of ecological degradation by showing a consequence that can be received by an audience only as disposably silly.[19] In any case, it's really the sharks' lack of more nuanced symbolism that allows them to serve as obstacles through which various personal issues may be resolved.

Detour: Beasts from the Backwater

If we steer momentarily toward more out-of-the-way locations, we find some evolutionarily distinct, yet hardly less intimidating, aquatic antagonists that have managed to make a bloody splash of their own in horror—albeit through many of the same conventions of the shark film.[20] Snap-happy reptiles feature in a number of better- and lesser-known films, among them *Eaten Alive* (1977), *Alligator* (1980), *Dark Age* (1987), *Killer Crocodile* (1989), *Crocodile* (2000), *Lake Placid* (1999), *Rogue* (2007), *Croc* (2007), *Primeval* (2007), and *Black Water* (2007). Given that they sport the nasty, gnarled look of a dinosaur, a snout replete with overhanging teeth, and have little problem snatching human prey, the presence of these creatures in horror movies is hardly any surprise. Not typically encountered on popular beaches, crocodiles haven't been a cinematic threat of the same magnitude as sharks, but crocodile and alligator enemies also bring into relief the human body's poor marine mobility and haunt the borders of putatively "human" spaces.

Given the regional and secluded locations that reptiles of the order Crocodilia often call home, horror films typically find them there as hazards for holiday misadventurers and others who dare trek beyond the boundaries of civilized city life. Befitting its reputation for rapacious beasts, Australia is a favorite location. The country has averaged at least one fatal crocodile attack per year since 1971[21]—not a high number relative to other causes of death, but dramatically newsworthy, pricking our deep fears of predation. The size and power of the Australian saltwater crocodile, the world's largest reptile and the usual culprit in fatal incidents, makes it a formidable ready-made horror monster. Philosopher Val Plumwood's oft-cited account of being attacked in Australia's Northern Territory in 1985 positions the attack as violating expected divisions between human and animal. She writes that it integrated her into an ecosystem in which she became materially "food" to another creature, this realization undermining humans' supposed mastery of a "malleable" nature.[22] An "ethical order" valued by humans (and through which we understand ourselves), Plumwood writes, does not map directly onto the "ecological order" around us.[23] Plenty of movie characters learn this too: in *Crocodile Dundee* (1986), Big Apple journalist Sue Charlton (Linda Kozlowski) bends down to refill her canteen by a peaceful stream scattered with lily pads before a croc launches out at her (Fig. 2.8). She's saved in the nick of time by the film's roguish human hero, Mick Dundee (Paul Hogan), but the attack stuns us with the volatility of obscure aquatic territory. It hits us with how uncertain the edge of land and water can be for a human species otherwise superlative in its capability, sophistication, and technological advance.

Perhaps partially inspired by *Crocodile Dundee*'s success, the thriller *Dark Age* (1987), a British-Australian co-production also set in the Northern Territory, provided further crocodile commotion. When a particularly big brute starts snacking on humans, wildlife ranger and conservationist Steve Harris (John Jarratt) is charged with bringing it to heel. With a sensible respect for the local wildlife, Steve wants to stop the croc while preventing a crew of mad hunters (eager for any excuse to indulge their bloodlust) from taking to the creeks and killing everything they can. In a nod to *Jaws*, the local bigwig (Ray Meagher) is concerned about tourism: Japanese investors set to build up the town mustn't be scared off. *Dark Age* depicts an outback culture whose powerful players are in hot pursuit of modernization and money, yet whose wildlife presents a challenge to those commercial plans, an inexorable and ancient ecological force that will never submit to human designs. Aboriginal elders,

Figure 2.8. Her surroundings seem tranquil, but journalist Sue Charlton (Linda Kozlowski) is poised to be prey for a saltwater croc as she refills her canteen from a pond in *Crocodile Dundee* (Peter Faiman, Rimfire Films, 1986). Digital frame enlargement.

the land's ancient custodians, warn the ranger of this creature's special significance. In addition to its size, this croc is "proper old" and "wise," they say. The animal is a figure in their Dreaming mythology, and they refuse to participate in killing him: with their long view of the land's history, they maintain a respect for the predator and his domain. Given that the film's initial attack is against racist night-time poachers, the film fuses this water-wariness with an anticolonial subtext, evoking a land stolen and its ecology foolishly ignored.

Given the regional environments they inhabit, crocodilians are sometimes linked cinematically with humans from the same obscure areas. In Tobe Hooper's *Eaten Alive*, a deranged motel owner in remote Southern Florida, Judd (Neville Brand), feeds guests to a pet crocodile lurking in a pond by his porch. Alligators are native to the area, but Judd boasts of the special size and ferocity of his imported African pet. As crazed as its master, the croc overlaps and magnifies the predatory nature of the humans who (the film would have us imagine) might thrive in this isolated area, an association consistent with Hooper's earlier portrayal of Southern lunatics in *The Texas Chainsaw Massacre* (1974). The director's later film, *Crocodile* (2000), also set in the southern United States, features the same rapacious breed, this one glutting itself on teen spring-breakers (Fig. 2.9). And, as in *Eaten Alive*, the ill-mannered

Figure 2.9. Having gobbled a few of them by now, a giant African crocodile eyes off another appetizing teenage morsel (Caitlin Martin) in Tobe Hooper's *Crocodile* (Trimark, 2000). Digital frame enlargement.

animal is fed and fostered by a local hillbilly grotesque. *Crocodile* draws extensively on the familiar theme of contested territory. The teens hire a houseboat and prepare for a holiday of hedonism, but at the location they're forewarned against any recklessness by the cops, for whom this is the busy season and no holiday: in other words, the film develops tension between competing human claims before the animal stomps in with a terrifying title of its own.

In *Lake Placid*, a secluded expanse of water in rural Aroostook County, Maine, provides a fitting-enough home for the human-eating habits of a supersized prehistoric croc. The film begins with soaring aerial shots of the waterway and its splendid forest surroundings, before switching to a view below the murky water from which the reclusive beast will emerge. As we now know, visually inviting environments aren't always what they seem. A conservationist diver is the first victim, propelled along the water's surface by some unseen attacker much like Chrissie in the opening scene of *Jaws*. The local sheriff, Hank (Brendan Gleeson), watches on from a dinghy in alarm. He catches the screaming man's arms and tries to haul him onboard but, gorily, only the diver's top half cooperates. An exploration party is soon on the case, a squabbling team who, as in *Bait 3D*, must operate cooperatively to survive in the domain of the primeval predator. We later learn that the beast is being fed entire cows by an eccentric senior, Mrs. Bickerman (Betty White): Hank spots the old woman leading a blindfolded bovine out to the water's edge while the croc waits incongruously like a cheerful dog. An amusing twist on the theme of a conspiring local, Bickerman's feeding of this dreadful "pet" also blurs the boundaries between the domestic and the wild, rewarding this animal's deadly intrusions.

Crocodiles return to stir up dread Down Under again in *Black Water* and *Rogue* (both from 2007). In *Black Water*, three Aussie adults, Grace, Lee, and Adam (Diana Glenn, Maeve Dermody, and Andy Rodoreda), seek a break from the grind of working life (much like the hapless protagonists of *Open Water*) and settle on a cruise up a Northern Territory waterway. Their small boat is swiftly overturned and their guide (Ben Oxenbould) gobbled up, leaving them stranded in the mangroves at the water's swampy edge, petrified by what patrols just below. What was initially a scenic holiday locale and escape from suburban routine is reoriented as a site of age-old and lethal peril. Stranded in trees for the majority of the film, these human characters take the place of their arboreal primate ancestors, fearfully enmeshed in the local ecology. The connotations are compounded when one of the group tries to entertain the others by singing a childhood rhyme: "Three cheeky monkeys sitting in a tree, teasing Mr. Alligator, 'can't catch me.'" Apparently, he thought this would be funny, but it cuts too close to the bone for that.

Greg McLean's big-croc thriller *Rogue* also treats us to enticing aerial scans of the landscape (the setting again Australia's Northern Territory) before shots at ground level subvert the scenic overview. A water buffalo approaches the water to drink, but out of nowhere a croc snaps onto it like a metric-ton mousetrap in a shocking display of the animal's ability to stalk and strike at the boundary of land and water. Shortly after, American magazine writer and city slicker Pete (Michael Vartan), incongruously suit-clad in this dusty outback locale, steps off a bus in a remote Territory town. He walks into a dingy milk bar and orders a coffee from the eccentric attendant (Barry Otto), mentioning that his bags were lost at the airport. Despite this inconvenience, Pete embarks on his writing assignment, boarding a boat for a crocodile-watching river cruise with a handful of other tourists (Fig. 2.10), some Australian, some English, American, and Irish, and headed by young local guide Kate (Radha Mitchell). Toward the end of the tour, the group spot a flare further up river and, as Captain Kate explains, maritime law obliges them to respond. But she accepts the duty to investigate reluctantly: they're now coasting through sacred Indigenous land, and a rock painting of a crocodile looms ominously on a cliff above as they drift by. Similar to *Dark Age*, *Rogue* implies the native inhabitants' knowledge of and fearful reverence for the primal predator—a wisdom we negate at our deep peril.

They find the wreck of a boat just as their own is viciously rammed from below, and Kate hastily powers the vessel, gushing water from a rupture in its side, to a tiny island in the middle of the river. Here the

Figure 2.10. A boat full of tourists cruises down a scenic waterway in the Kakadu region of Australia's Northern Territory in Greg McLean's *Rogue* (Village Roadshow / Emu Creek, 2007), before the wildlife makes the excursion a lot less agreeable. Digital frame enlargement.

passengers will remain marooned and anxious as a croc stalks the water around them. The crocodile's superb striking ability at the border of land and water, demonstrated initially through the buffalo, is soon repeated on a human, as the brute snatches a tourist from the shoreline without anyone else even seeing. Waiting around for rescue isn't an option, we learn, as this island disappears with the tide. This is a high-stakes and high-stress situation, and the tour is made up of disparate and squabbling individuals, each with different ideas of what to do (and what they're willing to do). Accordingly, McLean's film places particular emphasis on the animal attacker as a pressure toward sociality: selfish impulses must be put aside because cooperation is crucial.

As Fuchs points out, McLean's film participates heavily in an initial idealization of the Australian outback: "The landscape is both repeatedly turned into a visual spectacle and idealized on a verbal level, such as when the Australian guide Kate wonders, 'Why would I leave this?,' as the tourist boat is making its way through a magnificent canyon."[24] As in the shark films discussed above, the animal will violently invalidate human projections onto its domain. One tourist (*Dark Age* star John Jarratt) is there to solemnly scatter his wife's ashes, perhaps imagining the area as a sublime distraction from the trauma of death, but instead it will mercilessly deal out more of it. For a mother (Heather Mitchell) who's terminally ill, the holiday is intended as a treasured excursion with her daughter and husband before her death; one half of an American couple (Robert Taylor) remarks how horny the sultry environment makes him, annoying his wife (Caroline Brazier) with his aphrodisiac interpretation of their surroundings. Most central is the reluctant travel-writer Pete, who during the crisis snaps at Kate that, despite its adventurous image, his job is actually prissily bourgeois. "I write stupid articles about hotels and restaurants and resorts," he tells her, "and I fucking hate animals—especially ones that can kill you." Struggling to control his agitation, Pete is not the steely male wanderer she might have expected in a crisis. Yet the catastrophe is also a chance for him to prove himself and push past his urban fragility and apprehension.

A hardy young local, Neil (Sam Worthington), comes to the group's aid but is unexpectedly devoured: the reluctant foreign hero must face his fear and assume a leading role in resistance against the reptile. And when Kate is mauled and carried away to the croc's burrow for a later meal, Pete braces himself for the rescue, venturing deep into the dragon's lair to rescue the imperiled maiden—now proving his resourcefulness and credentials as a protector. As the film closes, we see that Pete has made the local paper: his photo is among the newspaper clippings stuck to the milk bar wall (the display a sort of grim "greatest hits" of local crocodile attacks). He overcame his self-doubt, but the film's final images are hardly triumphal. In a spot we might expect photographs of the region's leisure activities and attractions, the display is instead evocative of crime-scene photographs, a testament to the water as a domain of giddy terror and deterrent to human intrusion.

Beach Therapy in *The Shallows*

After some time out to sea, the shark film surged back in 2016 with Jaume Collet-Serra's *The Shallows*. Medical student Nancy (Blake Lively) escapes her high-pressure life to an obscure Mexican beach, the same one that her late mother traveled to surf when pregnant with Nancy. After a shark tears at her leg, she becomes stranded on a rock, and recreation is replaced by a desperate struggle to outwit and escape the continuously patrolling predator. *The Shallows* dramatizes a powerful refutation of humans' symbolic colonization of the beach, but it also expands the shark's role as an emissary of unaddressed psychological conflict, thereby crystallizing the thematic tendencies of earlier shark films.

Almost immediately in the film, the meanings assigned to natural environments are subject to contestation, a process soon to be urgently amplified by the shark. While he will show her there, Nancy's Mexican guide (Óscar Jaenada) won't tell her the name of the beach, presumably to protect it against tourist takeover. This difference in perspective persists: as they arrive at the glorious and unspoiled spot, Nancy points to a mountain off the coast whose hills, she says, are the shape of a pregnant woman lying down. The guide doesn't see it. "Oh well: it is for me," she says (Fig. 2.11).

Upon hitting the waves, she demonstrates her surfing prowess, reveling in the location as a zone of escapist leisure and one imbued with

Figure 2.11. "This is the island of the pregnant woman, no?" Nancy (Blake Lively) gestures to the formations beyond the water, in which she sees her mother symbolized, in *The Shallows* (Jaume Collet-Serra, Columbia, 2016). Digital frame enlargement.

personal significance. Taking a break, she calls her father and sister back home, and we learn that her escape is from the stress of her medical studies, but also triggered by the recent death of her mother from cancer. Her father disapproves of her withdrawal from everyday life—he knows this is really all about her mother's passing—and urges his daughter to persist in her studies: her mother was a fighter, he reminds her. "She fought too hard, and for what? It all ended the same," Nancy glumly responds.

But the natural environment is not some "time-out" from the world, a utopia beyond the stresses that have torn apart Nancy's otherwise comfortable life, and it soon reveals its savage side. Before the attack, the weather darkens as evening approaches: the tide relaxes and sharp rocks breach the surface; crabs crawl up onto the beach; flocks of birds turn in, and the rhythm of the waves becomes noisier—the location shedding its leisure status. Nancy is startled by some unexpected undersea thing, but it turns out to be a pod of dolphins—a moment of fright transformed into inspiring invitation. Yet as she paddles toward the playful animals, she suddenly encounters the corpse of a dead whale swarmed by ravenous seagulls, the romantic moment immediately overturned. This landscape is fundamentally unstable, with cruelty concealed beneath the sublime. Then comes the shark: lured into the bay by the rotting whale, it barges her off her board and sinks its jaws into her thigh. Badly bleeding, Nancy makes it to a rock sticking out of the sea with the surface area of a car roof, where she'll be stranded, with the beach absent of human help.

The shark, stealthy and swift and pitiless, is again the icon of nature's ruthless amorality and nihilism. Injured and under siege by the creature (to which her trickling blood is as tantalizing as the smell of the dead whale), Nancy is forced to recognize herself as part of the natural landscape, and not merely a tourist. Marooned on the rock with her, and indicative of her integration into the wilderness, is a seagull with an injured wing, the bird unable to fly away or (for the same reason as Nancy) enter the water (Fig. 2.12). The scenario is bleak, certainly not the escape from death this student of medicine wanted, but it is a chance to reckon with it, and to decide that survival is worth fighting for. A surfer shows up, but the shark makes short work of him; he does however leave his helmet behind, mounted with a small digital camera. Nancy uses the device to record a message to her father and sister in case she doesn't survive, affirming her willingness to fight: dystopian nature becomes a zone in which she can confront her internal emptiness and despair.

As in *Jaws*, grasping the potential cruelty of nature and accepting the challenge it presents is not the same as descending to its level. The positioning of the seagull as a "character" in the film (Nancy talks to it during her isolation) is not so much a degradation of humanity as an opportunity for interspecies sympathy, given their shared situation. Using

Figure 2.12. Trapped on a small rock after a shark attacks her, Nancy (Blake Lively) inspects her wound as a similarly stricken seagull looks on, in *The Shallows* (Jaume Collet-Serra, Columbia, 2016). Digital frame enlargement.

her medical knowledge to reposition its dislocated wing, Nancy chooses to help the gull despite its not holding any benefit to her. In her current position, she must accept the savagery of nature, but she doesn't need to internalize it—compassion is worth hanging onto.

In her commitment to resistance, Nancy will take her mother as inspiration; she'll fight, she tells her father in her recorded message, "like she taught us." She cannot simply escape into a fantasized world of communion with her mother, but she can take her mother's example (and her father's guidance), fighting despite the odds. This time the fighting isn't for nothing: Nancy makes it, and gasps for life on the shore as rescuers are alerted. As she recovers, she glances once again at the formation shaped like a pregnant woman, now parallel with her own horizontal form (Fig. 2.13). A vision of her mother appears over her. In place of

Figure 2.13. Washed up on the shore and lucky to be alive, Nancy (Blake Lively) in *The Shallows* (Jaume Collet-Serra, Columbia, 2016) again looks to the mountains that remind her of her mother, having embraced her fighting example. Digital frame enlargement.

Nancy's presumptuous perspective when she arrived is now a link to the landscape that she's earned, and earned through deep identification with her mother's (fighting) spirit.

In an epilogue we see Nancy with her younger sister, ready to surf at a beach in their hometown of Galveston, with city buildings within view. A large scar from her ordeal is stamped into her leg. Despite this, she hasn't been deterred from the water altogether: she's instructing her sibling—further sustaining her surfing mother's spirit. As Nancy rides the waves, casting off spume, pop artist Sia's song "Bird Set Free" plays over the soundtrack: the track underscores Nancy's freedom from danger and from the melancholia of her mother's death, but it also reminds us of her affinity with her animal companion (whom she herself freed). The ocean's danger isn't disavowed in this conclusion: the girls have just a selected a more predictable spot, a beach closer to home.

Despite our tremendous impact on and dominance over our environment, this planet's surface is mostly ocean, which makes water a potent domain for our power to be contested. I've focused here primarily on sharks and crocs as the most prolific aquatic threats, yet the conventions and concerns of such films can be seen in those featuring other types of marine menace, from the ravenous fishes of Joe Dante's *Piranha* (1978) to various lesser-known pictures featuring human-hunting barracudas or eels. Even in Jules Verne's *Twenty Thousand Leagues Under the Sea* (1870, filmed in 1954 by Richard Fleischer), submariner Captain Nemo's ultra-romantic view of his aquatic home is challenged by the sudden slippery attack of a giant squid. Nemo (James Mason) thrums with disdain for what he sees as human civilization's corrupted character, although despite charming appearances the underwater world, as in numerous shark movies, houses viciousness of its own. However, as its persistent reappearance in horror films implies, the shark seems to present the ideal avatar of humans' marine helplessness: a creature familiar in that it occasionally encroaches on our real-life seaside endeavors, but never close enough to be comfortable. Difficult for characters to even clearly see, the shark may well be the cinematic animal aggressor that operates most intimately within (and as an extension of) its wild environment, an environment into which we fit quite well as food. Through films as tonally diverse as *Jaws*, *Sharknado*, and *Bait 3D*, sharks may also be positioned as agents of something submerged in our personalities, not only demons of deep water but also demons of our deeper selves.

3

Man versus Wild

Bears, Wolves, and the Men Who Fight Them

WE DON'T NEED AN INVOLVED demographic survey to tell us that the majority of the film-going public doesn't live in forests. As the antithesis of civilization (at least to Western culture), the deep wilderness, when it appears in horror movies, is not a site of ease or belonging. As environments unmarked by human institutions or enterprise, not crafted or organized to meet human needs, wilderness locations easily confound human navigation and survival. We see this process dramatized in numerous films in which lost characters quite plausibly discover themselves to have been moving only in pointless circles as their well-being worsens. Of course, they're also geographies in which a range of animals alarming in domestic or suburban settings, like bears, wolves, or big cats, are right at home, in terms of both their survival capacity and their lethality. The wilderness is an ideal cinematic location for horrific confrontation between human and animal, a domain in which our adeptness at navigating our own sophisticated social landscapes (our practiced "civility") counts for troublingly little. We've previously explored the terror and sometimes triumph of humans battling wild aquatic foes; now we turn to humans in drier (yet no less dire) trouble within various untamed earthbound environments. The wilderness might not be accommodating, but it's also often viewed as a domain of masculine self-sufficiency, a tough terrain in which a man can enact a suite of physical skills prioritized by popular versions of manhood. In wilderness-based survival thrillers and horror films we see characters forced to test their resourcefulness without the crutch of civilization.

This process resembles the ordeal faced by the female protagonist of *The Shallows* in an aquatic setting, although that film remains something of an outlier in gender and geography. When it comes to surviving the perils of the wilderness, it's mainly men whom cinema puts to the test. As the largest of forest carnivores, bears are often implicated, appearing in numerous films, including *Grizzly* (1976), *Day of the Animals* (1977), *The Edge* (1997), *Grizzly Rage* (2007), and *Into the Grizzly Maze* (2015). In Alejandro G. Iñárritu's conspicuously male-focused *The Revenant* (2015), Hugh Glass (Leonardo DiCaprio) is acting as a guide for fur-trappers in the frigid American wilderness in 1823 when he's mangled at shocking length by a grizzly. Marginally alive, and with a wincingly obscene set of injuries, Glass will then be abandoned to the wild by an ingrate companion: the narrative will focus primarily on the agonizing test of endurance the harsh environment presents.

The writing of Val Plumwood postulates a suite of interlocking dualisms that undergird Western culture, "a fault-line which runs through its entire conceptual system" including the "nature/culture" binary.[1] For her, these oppositional terms define each other through contrast, but they're also hierarchical and ultimately oppressive. She writes that "the dualisms of male/female, mental/manual (mind/body), civilized/primitive, human/nature correspond directly to and naturalize gender, class, race and nature oppressions respectively."[2] For her, categorizing concepts as oppositional to each other means one inevitably assumes superior status—male is conceived as superior to female, reason is superior to nature, and so on. Moreover, these terms (superior or inferior) are "interlocked" in a system of shared meanings—male is understood to be aligned with "reason," while the female with "nature" and "animality."[3] Various dualisms are mobilized in horror cinema, especially known/unknown, alive/dead, and good/evil. Conceptual oppositions like these emphasize differences between familiar and unfamiliar, and thereby enable dramatic conflict between a force with which an audience can identify and something they can't. And as we know already, the dualism of nature/culture is of particular importance to animal horror. The wild is a fundamentally "different" place, and not just geographically: the norms of the wild aren't the same as those of the civilized world either. But is our "entire conceptual system" dominated by a grid of corresponding dualities? I hardly think so. In survival thrillers at least, neither "nature" nor its associated animal attackers are aligned with "the feminine"—in fact, quite the contrary. The feminine (or more simply women) are typically taken as the wilderness's threatened opposite, that which must be kept safely at a distance. In what follows, I explore some of the more significant wilderness-set horror-thrillers over the past fifty years, including *Grizzly* (1976), *Day of the Animals* (1977), *The Edge* (1997), and *The Grey* (2011). And as we'll see, this subgenre has a habit of intertwining masculinity—in its potential for violence, aggression, and territoriality—with the wild animals that populate it.

Beasts of Men: *Grizzly* and *Day of the Animals*

William Girdler's *Grizzly* and *Day of the Animals*, both penned and produced by Edward L. Montoro, show an increasing interest in blurring the distinctions between out-of-control animals and the men who fight back against them. Both films launch their narratives from loose environmental premises, yet the stories that follow instead fixate on the potential "wildness" of masculinity. In *Grizzly*, camping season has begun at an American national park, and head ranger, Michael Kelly (Christopher George), briefs his crew on keeping the tourists safe and the environment unspoiled. They've got a challenge ahead: a couple of young female campers are soon slashed to bits by some unseen colossus. It falls to Kelly to sort out this massive menace with the help of his fellow rangers, as well as the park's chopper pilot (Andrew Prine), and a naturalist (Richard Jaeckel), who attributes the attack to a fifteen-foot living prehistoric grizzly bear (Fig. 3.1).

As Dan Whitehead points out, a combination of elements both stylistic and narrative, including concerns over tourism, point-of-view shots, and the assistance of an intrepid scientific expert, demonstrate the

Figure 3.1. Both jaws and claws: the colossal carnivore of *Grizzly* (William Girdler, Columbia / Film Ventures 1976) closes in on its prey. Digital frame enlargement.

profound influence of *Jaws* on *Grizzly*.[4] Yet far more than in Spielberg's film the animal aggressor is attributed a kind of rabid masculinity. The medical examiner's initial suspicion that the attacks might be the work of a female bear protecting her cubs is specifically dismissed, and when a crew of hunters, assuming a female culprit, use a lost bear cub as a lure, the brute discovers the infant and swiftly kills it. This monster has none of the care-giving impulses with which it is initially credited, and the naturalist explains that only male bears will commit such an act. The event has no lasting purpose, but it's an opportunity for the film to underscore the animal's gender and attribute to it a kind of obscene masculine excess.

The bear's violence is also framed in terms of predatory (human) male sexuality: virtually all of the grizzly's victims are female, with these attacks afforded the most screen time. But dialogue is also used to link the predator to sex. After the first attack, Kelly tells his superior that "one of our bears got lonesome, came out for a little action." Later, as he scans the forest from a helicopter, Kelly tells the pilot beside him that the bear "likes women, and he keeps moving." "Sort of like me," jokes the pilot, before he shifts the subject to Kelly's sex life: "What about that filly you've been ridin'?" However, Kelly's disapproving glare brings the rascally sex talk to an end. "Oh, I didn't know it was that way now," his buddy smirks. These men are usually "animal like" in their appetites and vocabulary, and Kelly is only recently domesticated by his latest love.

The staging of the bear's next attack doubles down on the sexual connotations. In a take reminiscent of the opening of *Jaws*, we see a group of campers gathered around a series of evening campfires. Away from the hubbub of children playing, a married couple nestle and kiss before the wife smilingly departs for the tent behind her, leaving her husband to finish his drink and follow after. In the tent, she applies some perfume, undresses, and readies herself for her man, but it's not the kind of action she expects when the grizzly suddenly tears through the tent wall. Later on, a lone female ranger (Victoria Johnson) is appraised from the bear's point of view as she swims in a stream while her lover checks the surroundings. The brute waits for her to strip to her underwear before making its move, panting heavily with this barely clothed beauty in its sights—again the creature's attack framed as a sexual assault.

As mentioned above, ranger-in-charge Kelly declines to participate in sex talk that would align him with the animals he oversees—refuses to talk about his new "filly." The girl who has tamed this wild man is a photographer, Allison (Joan McCall). Yet early in the film, when assigning his underlings, Kelly bars a young female ranger from teaming up with her handsome male colleague, thereby placing a subtle sanction on a rival male. Allison tells Kelly, "Every face tells a story," and when he asks what story his face tells, she refers to him as "a dissembler: you hide everything behind that tight jaw; one day it's gonna break." He laughs off her cheeky assessment, but it zeroes in on his repression, and later he mentions to her a brief marriage he couldn't handle. The implication of Kelly's stifled sexual appetite, while the bear indulges a sexualized literal appetite, hints at the grizzly as an overblown projection of the ranger's own desire, which he must confront and vanquish. Through this link, Girdler's film engages the wild/civilized binary to suggest a tension within heterosexual masculinity in which "wild" sexuality lies just beyond, and may encroach threateningly upon, the desire for domesticated relationships.

Girdler's later film *Day of the Animals* performs an even more feverish connection between "wildness" and what it sees as a precivilized male sexual appetite. Christopher George stars again, this time as tour guide Steve Buckner, an affable outdoorsy type who, along with Native American colleague Daniel Santee (Michael Ansara), leads a diverse group of hikers through scenic mountain terrain. An opening textual insert informs us that aerosol sprays have been found to damage the ozone layer and the events that follow speculate the possibilities of this depletion, attributing to excess solar radiation both the heat of which the characters will complain and the numerous animal attacks to follow. The tour group includes a glamorous TV journalist, a middle-aged man battling cancer, and a few squabbling pairs (a couple trying to revive their marriage; a single mother and the son from whom she feels alienated). Traveling alone is brash advertising executive, Jenson (Leslie Nielsen prior to comedy fame), around whom the film will eventually reach its climax of macho hysteria.

Day of the Animals is filled with enticing overhead shots of the American landscape, yet a hawk that oversees the travelers as they depart indicates the area's hidden menace, and the first attack comes from a raptor's swift and vicious swoop. The two guides, Buckner and Santee, are baffled, although the Native American Santee shares an intuition that something in nature is amiss. They plan to guide the group toward a supply station, although another tourist is targeted—a young woman savaged by a wolf in her tent. As the incursions continue, and as befits his macho arrogance, Jenson challenges Buckner for control of the party. The obnoxious ad-man derides their defenselessness against the threats around them, touting his superior leadership. In essence, he forwards himself as the legitimate alpha of the group, eventually asserting his power by socking Buckner in the face, splitting the group and taking several travelers with him. We've deduced that only nonhuman animals are affected by the solar radiation, yet the implication is that Jenson, too, has been somehow mysteriously energized, suggesting his latent and brutal animality.

Leading his new group, the shirtless Jenson slashes a path through the foliage, his face sweaty and dirt-smeared as thunder rumbles ominously in the distance. His aggression grows, and he clobbers the divorcee and threatens her son (Fig. 3.2). Several people challenge him, but he fends off their attacks. A strong leader initially seemed beneficial, but now Jenson is a predator himself. He points to a young woman: "I'm in charge of this trip and I take what I want—and right now I want you! Come on baby, you're going to have a real man now!" Her husband comes to the rescue, but the deranged Jenson impales him on a branch and resumes his reign of terror: "I own you!" he roars, struggling with the woman on the muddy ground as the rain thrashes down around them. This demented primal display reaches its zenith as a grizzly roars onto the scene, staggering forward on its hind legs. Jenson's fellow hikers scream and flee, but the bare-chested and power-drunk Jenson charges his new challenger, testing his animalistic dominance against the forest animal alpha. Of course, the madman has bitten off more than he can chew this time, and is conquered by this literal incarnation of the primal, pre-ethical power he has embraced and inflicted on others.

The broader crisis is resolved with a deus ex machina: the radiation level corrects itself, and the rogue animals suddenly die. Yet it's a human who has formed the most striking and memorable antagonist, stoking our fear of what might lie beneath civilized facades. When deriding the guides, Jenson sarcastically refers to Buckner as "hot shot" in the

Figure 3.2. Jenson (Leslie Nielsen), left, grows increasingly bestial as he intimidates a young camper, Bob (Andrew Stevens), in *Day of the Animals* (William Girdler, Multicom / Film Ventures, 1977). Digital frame enlargement.

language of big-city male rivalry, and he irritates Santee with a parody Native American accent, his vain masculinity tied to an insensitive colonialist arrogance. The animals affected by the radiation, we note, are all predators (big cats, wolves, birds of prey); and for the predatory Jenson what once was sublimated is now supercharged. *Day of the Animals*, like *Grizzly*, is narratively clumsy—even whimsical—yet both of Girdler's films manage to imply a connection between wild animal attackers and a volatile masculinity similarly lurking at the edge of civility.

Like a Bridge over Feline Slaughter: Rising to the Big Cat Challenge in *The Ghost and the Darkness*

In *The Ghost and the Darkness* (1996) it's 1898 and John Patterson (Val Kilmer), an Irish-born English soldier and engineer, has been charged with constructing a bridge in troubled Tsavo (now Kenya) in British East Africa (Fig. 3.3). But once he arrives there, his valued assignment is undermined by a wave of carnage. Two man-eating lions crash upon the camp, leaving workers mauled and dismembered and striking fear and unrest into those who remain. Based on the historical Patterson's 1907 memoir *The Man-Eaters of Tsavo*, the film tracks the beleaguered engineer's attempts to end the animals' reign of terror. The task will elevate him from boyish naivety to heroism, preparing him first for leadership and, finally, for fatherhood.

Figure 3.3. Eager to impress, the clean-cut engineer John Patterson (Val Kilmer) has little sense of the chaos that awaits in Africa in Stephen Hopkins's *The Ghost and the Darkness* (Paramount, 1996). Digital frame enlargement.

In the tradition of the archetypal hero, Patterson does not depart without some reluctance: his young wife Helena (Emily Mortimer) is pregnant with their first child, and he'd promised to be present for the birth. The comfort of home is tempting, yet Helena selflessly urges her husband to pursue his dream of visiting the continent and the opportunity to climb up the career ladder. Upon arrival, Patterson is drawn into sublime awe of the landscape around him: having read voraciously of Africa's wildlife, he virtually switches roles with his guide Angus (Brian McCardie) on the train ride toward the camp, pointing out the animals (hippopotamuses, hyenas, elephants) around them. There's something distinctly boyish about the polite young engineer as he thrills at this land of adventure and wonder: "I've been longing for this all my life," he says. The situation in Tsavo, crammed with workers hauling iron and leveling dirt, is less idealistic. The bank picked for construction, Patterson realizes, will test his engineering skill, and a nearby hospital is full of patients running fever. Moreover, the labor force is on the constant verge of collapse. When Patterson meets the Kenyan foreman, Samuel (John Kani, who also narrates the film), the local indicates a landscape without order: "Nothing works here; Tsavo is the worst place in the world." The local Africans don't like their Indian coworkers, and the Hindu Indians barely tolerate their Muslim countrymen. Bringing the diverse team together is now Patterson's problem, an immediate challenge to his idealistic wish of "bringing worlds together" through the bridge. But things will get much worse before they get better.

A rare social equilibrium is shattered when a man is carried into the hospital with his leg dangling bloodily beneath him from a man-eater attack. Patterson shoots a lion dead that night, earning him instant praise from his terrified crew. But as we sense, it won't be that easy: the attacks continue, the work of a ferocious feline double-team willing to drag men screaming from their tents or leap down from rooftops. Patterson puts plans in motion, but the cunning beasts outmaneuver his every attempt. As the death toll mounts, Tsavo lives up to its name—"slaughter" in Kamba language—and Patterson's loftier ambitions are thoroughly degraded in this zone of social fragmentation and bloody chaos.

In its focus on friction between civilization and wilderness, Hopkins's film also takes on the characteristics of the western: the hero must render the frontier safe against (in this case) animal outlaws so that community can thrive. But the film also conjures around its felines an aura of mythic evil: regarding the first victim, we hear that a lion "licked his skin off so he could drink his blood"—and then devoured the man feet first. Such monstrosity redraws the culture/nature dichotomy in Manichean terms of good and evil, but also depicts the African frontier as a haunted landscape requiring exorcism, an image enhanced by the natives' supernatural view of their two predators, whom they name "the ghost" and "the darkness" (Fig. 3.4).

On the one hand, we might say that these demonic lions shrouded in native superstition and terror are positioned for conquest by sober and heroic European reason; yet on the other, the film puts its real emphasis on Patterson's own haunting by these specters of untamed exotic nature. His wife Helena, back in England, is the film's only woman, so she is portrayed as a paragon of fragile English femininity that underscores the incompatibility of the two worlds, although she expresses her wish to visit after their child is born. In perhaps the film's most gripping scene, Helena has arrived in dusty, sun-burnt Tsavo, dressed in a pristine Victorian dress. She carries her bonneted baby boy across the railway platform toward his father for the first time, and he makes his way toward wife and child—but not fast enough: from the long grass, a lion dashes up to the platform and collides with Patterson's dainty wife like a 400-pound linebacker. Patterson watches helplessly at a distance as (thankfully out of frame) the big cat begins crunching mother and baby in its ferocious maw—but then he wakes up, drenched in sweat. It was just a dream, though one that appallingly dramatizes the "wild" threat to civilization. The vision reinforces his need to render the landscape tenable for human—especially domestic, female—habitation, and to rise to the challenge of protection, here linked explicitly to his pending fatherhood.

But the genteel Patterson (despite some hunting experience) is no frontier tamer—or not yet. Enter Charles Remington (Michael Douglas),

Figure 3.4. "They are not lions—they are the ghost and the darkness": The twin man-eating terrors of the East African village of Tsavo in *The Ghost and the Darkness* (Stephen Hopkins, Paramount, 1996). Digital frame enlargement.

a traveling American big-game hunter hired for the kill by Patterson's anxious boss back in England. In contrast to the clean-shaven and well-groomed Patterson, Remington is unkempt and unshaven and clad in a dirty leather vest—the ever-wandering gunfighter of any number of westerns (some of whom were played by Douglas's father). Like Quint of *Jaws*, Remington arrives as a mentor of aggressive masculinity; volatile and adept at confrontation, he has the streak of wildness that this situation requires. The hunter participates in a native Masaai ritual in which, by the flickering firelight, he drinks the blood of a sacrificial bull (Fig. 3.5). The ritual aligns him with the carnivores he hunts, especially with the lion, which, it was said, "drank the blood" of its victim. In order for a man to combat or protect against a predator, he must acknowledge, as though it were the Jungian shadow, his own predatory capacity. By introducing Remington, the film does not maintain strict culture/nature, human/animal binaries, but rather suggests a necessary measure of cross-pollination. The two men are marked by differences from each other, yet the film situates Remington as Patterson's darker double, enabling this transfer of knowledge or spirit to occur. The American expert indicates that on a previous hunt he too had tried one of Patterson's failed capture methods (and he defends the failure of his device in identical phrasing). It's through his friendship with the aggressive hunting veteran Remington that Patterson will be able to acknowledge and awaken the "animal" within himself.

Remington may lead Patterson to acknowledge an element of nihilistic animality within himself, but he cannot truly be a role model

Figure 3.5. The wild touch: Charles Remington (Michael Douglas) drinks the blood of a bull during a Masaai tribal ritual in *The Ghost and the Darkness* (Stephen Hopkins, Paramount, 1996). Digital frame enlargement.

for the younger man. Early on, he indicates that hunting does not bring him satisfaction in life; it's something he pursues, he says, "Because I've got a gift." When Patterson asks him whether he's ever failed, he flatly responds, "Only at life," and later voices his regrets over never having started a family. Like the eponymous hero (Alan Ladd) of *Shane* (1953) or Ethan Edwards (John Wayne) of *The Searchers* (1956), Remington is a wanderer whose violence may assist civilization, but who can't find a stable place for himself within it. Remington is eventually killed—dragged out of his tent and torn apart during the night. This allows the confrontation with the beasts to escalate and paves the way for Patterson to demonstrate his own newfound "animal" edge. But Remington's brutal killing also suggests that, like Quint before him, the hunter has finally succumbed to the aggressive animal world that he too closely embraced.

Having finished off the feline threat with anger ignited by Remington's death, Patterson repairs the social chaos of the terrified workers. Through his ordeal, he leaves behind his boyishly sublime view of the world around him, after which point his parenthood can proceed. The intrepid engineer has successfully created a zone of protection for his family and, accordingly, the film concludes with his wife and son safely visiting. As he rushes to the railway platform, we notice his costuming has altered from his earlier tidy white ensembles to an outfit matching the brown hues of the landscape around him, and complementing his sun-browned skin, indicating his belonging. He shares some words in an African dialect with local Samuel and a gesture of friendship with a previously rebellious Indian foreman—there exists now a social unity to prefigure the literal unity of bridge building. Patterson embraces his wife and child, the latter seen for the first time. He glances to the long grass, but knows the threat is dispelled—the landscape now cured of malice and chaos.

Bearing a Resemblance in *The Edge*

In Lee Tamahori's *The Edge* (1997), penned by David Mamet, surviving the wilderness, especially a cantankerous Kodiak bear, is also crucial to the protagonist's sense of self. But in this case that sense of self is jeopardized by primal threats that persist within civilized life. English billionaire Charles Morse (Anthony Hopkins) is accompanying his noticeably younger model wife, Mickey (Elle Macpherson), to a lodge deep in the Alaskan wilderness for a photoshoot. The elderly Charles's status as a legitimate match for this prized beauty is under serial scrutiny, with male attention piqued by the possibility that this woman is feigning her marital satisfaction and thus still discreetly "available." Charles is acutely aware of his May-December romance as a social curiosity. A handsome young mechanic marvels at the billionaire's private plane on the tarmac, and Charles mistakenly (but understandably) thinks this young buck's erotic attention is attuned to the woman stepping out of it. They arrive at the secluded lodge by smaller seaplane, and the proprietor (L. Q. Jones) grinningly asks the billionaire, "Who's that beautiful lady?—your wife?" Charles confirms, but asks the reason for the question. It also happens to be Charles's birthday, and thus an unwelcome reminder of his age. Charles can read the signs: he'd better watch out. And he'd better watch out especially for cynical, cigarillo-smoking fashion photographer Bob (Alec Baldwin). Charles sits privately outside reading an old survival manual gifted to him by an employee, as Mickey, gussied up in a Native American costume, pouts and poses for Bob and his clicking camera. Her buckskin bra at one point slides south, and the two giggle as she corrects it, with none of this flirtation overlooked by the troubled Charles.

After a night at the lodge, Charles, Bob, and another photographer, Stephen (Harold Pirreneau) have the seaplane pilot whisk them upriver in search of a local Native hunter to pose for a snap. On the ride, having totaled up his suspicions (which the viewer by now certainly shares), Charles makes himself explicit: "So, how are you planning to kill me?" he calmly asks his rival (Fig. 3.6). Despite the matter-of-fact phrasing, Charles's question acknowledges intentions that breach the men's otherwise "civilized" milieu. Bob seems stunned, and simply looks at the older man,

Figure 3.6. "So, how are you planning to kill me?": aging billionaire Charles Morse (Anthony Hopkins) calls Bob Green's (Alec Baldwin's) jealousy likes he sees it, moments before their plane crashes, plunging them into the wilderness, in *The Edge* (Lee Tamahori, 20th Century Fox, 1997). Digital frame enlargement.

unable to form a response. Nor does he have time to: a flock of gulls slam into the seaplane's engines (an early act of animal unpredictability), and the plane falls to the forested earth below, leaving Stephen, Charles, and Bob alive. Alive but lost, and in dangerously primal terrain—inserted back into a brutal ecology just as civility was breaking down.

But hope is not lost: Charles's well-read mind is a storehouse of survival trivia. In his new and savage environment, he takes the lead, showing exemplary ingenuity, demonstrating a suite of skills that he earlier admitted was "purely theoretical." The towering Kodiak who stalks the trio (animal actor Bart the Bear) is the men's primary test, the culmination of this landscape's lethal volatility. The beast snatches Stephen, leaving Bob and Charles the only survivors. While Bob despairs, the tenacious Charles devises a plan to kill the beast and, after wearing it down with a booby trap, the two lance at it with spears like stone-age hunters, with Charles striking the fatal blow. Having re-achieved mastery over the animal predator, the two men confirm their triumphal reenactment of an ancient past by fashioning crude garments of bearskin to wear against the harsh conditions. The victory is Charles's especially. Earlier at the lodge, the proprietor had challenged him to guess the Cree motif on the other side of an old canoe paddle, a mountain lion painted on one side. Charles correctly predicted its prey, a rabbit, yet one smoking a pipe symbolic of its ability to outwit its stronger predator—a brains-over-brawn motif he has now put into practice. And, of course, having otherwise failed to secure food, the men roast chunks of the animal's flesh. After conquering their foe, they finalize their dominance by reversing the feared order of consumption: they will eat him.

The bear embodies the threat of the wilderness more broadly; once the animal is defeated, no further threats arise. Through Charles's leadership and intelligence, toppling the apex predator signifies the men's recovered ability to survive and dominate the landscape. Facing down a bear is of course an uncommon activity for modern Western men, but it taps into narratives of masculine mythmaking. Robert Bieder suggests that for white settlers, bear hunting also "served as a ritual entry for manhood, as in the stories and legends associated with early nineteenth-century American frontier hero, Davy Crockett."[5] Yet the film also associates bear hunting with Indigenous culture: the Native American man sought for Bob's photoshoot is seen in a photograph at the lodge clutching a rifle after a bear hunt, and Charles's plan is partly inspired by the illustration of a bear-battling Native on his matchbook cover. More pointedly, as he attempts to motivate his flagging companion, Charles tells him, "Did you know Indian boys used to run up to the bear, slap him—count coup on him as a test of manhood?" This reinforces the masculine status value of their achievement, while success generally implies their competence in a landscape beyond the comforts of Western civilization.

The animal threat in *The Edge* must also be seen in more specific connection to an age-old threat still present in domestic life: that of having a valued mate poached by a rival. On the crew's first night in the cabin, Charles walks downstairs to make his wife a sandwich, where he notices the front door ajar and a ham foolishly left uncovered—a virtual invitation to scavengers. To the aging man's alarm, the beast roars and rears up behind him on hind legs, right there in the cabin. But—"surprise!" a chorus of voices announce—it's just a birthday prank: the animal is Bob draped in a bearskin, head and all.

The lights come up; the startled Charles takes a moment to let relief sink in before receiving his gifts. Bob is again linked with the animal predator after the actual bear's defeat, and Charles's suspicions about his wife and Bob are finally confirmed. The two men reach relative safety when they find an old cabin. Looking in his jacket for some paper to light a fire, Charles finds a warranty slip containing the order request for the engraved watch his wife gave him for his birthday. There's another order written on it, for a watch engraved to Bob: "For all the nights." There it is, plain as day. Bob no longer needs Charles for his smarts, and the older man now watches as his co-traveler loads a rifle he's found inside the cabin, preparing to kill him. Bob mutters to his rich rival while drinking his courage: "You had no business with that broad anyway," he tells him. "You know you don't, Charles." Bob takes Charles outside, but before he can do the deed, he stumbles backward into a pit, impaling his leg—he has fallen prey to a deadfall bear trap. While the bear is the film's immediate antagonist, its overlapping with Bob indicates that similarly primal threats still stalk the civilized world.

After the plane crash, the pressures of the new environment mean that competition will be familiarly suppressed between these two so that the benefits of group cooperation can manifest: they might be at odds, but they need each other's help to survive. As soon as the outside threat disappears, though, Bob seeks to wipe out his rival. But it turns out that Bob needed a little more help than he thought. Despite everything, the benevolent Charles still renders assistance to Bob after he falls in the pit, but Bob's injuries are too severe and he won't survive long enough to be rescued. Since we're never told how Charles actually made his fortune, the film leaves open the question of whether he truly deserves it: what cut of a man is he, really? Stripped of the spoils of wealth, Charles will demonstrate his skill and industry, thereby re-earning his status against the humiliation of his cuckoldry by the younger man, who would murder him, marry his wife, and reap his fortune.[6]

At the film's conclusion, Charles, the only survivor, embraces his wife, but reservedly, placing the telltale watch in her hand before walking toward the crowd of reporters who have gathered to hear his story. Ironically, having outlasted his rival in a mating arena reduced to its most savagely competitive, Charles will let go of Mickey. The struggle may have re-empowered the aging man, but he rejects the amoral competitiveness that characterized his mate-rival, who would have killed him for the woman. Despite Charles's deep immersion in all things wild, he will choose to hang onto some human dignity. What's more, he preserves the dignity of his opponent. When asked by the crowd how his friends died, Charles considers not Bob's murderous treachery, but instead the journey's broader contribution to his own revived sense of self: "My friends, they died saving my life."

Fighting for Meaning: *The Grey*

Joe Carnahan's *The Grey* (2011), also set in Alaska but in a region ruled by wolves, pushes the man-versus-wild theme into the existential. Again, lost men must demonstrate their resourceful resistance against nature, but in *The Grey* this project comes to symbolize living more generally as a kind of resistance. John Ottway (Liam Neeson) is at the end of the world physically and the end of his rope emotionally. A sharpshooter for a petroleum company, he keeps rogue wolves from preying on workers at a remote site. The camp culture is intensely and stereotypically masculine; having finished his shift (where he stopped one creature's swift and soundless dash toward its human prey) Ottway enters the on-site bar, a pandemonium of brawling and rock 'n' roll. Yet the isolated Ottway's thoughts are with a woman who's left him, imagined alongside him in a bed. His voiceover narrates a letter he's written to her, not yet delivered. Back outside, with his despair having reached its terminus, he kneels in the snow and places the end of his rifle into his mouth. But his attention is diverted by the sound of unseen wolves baying far up in the mountains. Later, he boards a plane with his rowdy workmates, all headed back to their home lives, but they crash in the blizzard conditions, leaving Ottway and a handful of survivors stranded in the hostile wilderness (Fig. 3.7 on page 84). The survivors soon find themselves prey to wolves, and spend the remainder of the film in attempts to evade their fierce territorial foes. Ottway takes the lead: he has the more developed survival skills, if little personal will to live. However, after his companions gradually fall prey to the wilderness, the exhausted Ottway is the only one left alive to contend with the dark and ominous alpha wolf at the film's conclusion.

Figure 3.7. John Ottway (Liam Neeson) tries to formulate a plan to escape certain death after a drilling crew's plane crashes in the Alaskan wilderness in Joe Carnahan's *The Grey* (Open Road, 2011). Digital frame enlargement.

The division between "wild" and "civilized" territory is starkly invoked in Carnahan's film: the group find themselves displaced and disempowered in a blizzard-blown terrain with which they have no familiarity. After the first victim is snatched up, Ottway observes that the wolves are stalking survivors not as much for food as because the men "don't belong." As Gregersdotter and Hållán suggest, "The urban human's penetration into nature not only makes him or her prey for predatory animals," but a border crosser also becomes "the target of violence precisely because he or she violates the border between worlds."[7] After the crash, the men must flee, and remain in flight, hoping that within forested terrain they won't be as vulnerable as in the snowy tracts that hinder their visibility and protection. Yet despite this pressure there are moments of retaliation and conquest. After the men manage to kill one wolf with a sharpened stick attached to a shotgun shell (all working firearms have been destroyed in the crash), they cook the creature on a spit. As in *The Edge*, the men's consumption of their predator announces that they still have the ability to dominate the ecosystem: "You're not the animals—we're the animals!" one man gloats triumphantly to the remaining wolves, skulking somewhere in the darkness beyond.

Alternating her discussion between the film and the novella on which it was based, Dawn Keetley suggests that *The Grey* blurs the lines between species, depicting a "process of dissolving into an animal substratum."[8] The human/animal similarities are made overt in the wolves' protection of their territory just as Ottway had monitored human space earlier. Moreover, gathered round the campfire, the men overhear the ominous alpha wolf suppress a challenge from a rival; a moment later, Ottway, the group's informal leader, similarly puts down a challenge from a mouthy driller, Diaz (Frank Grillo). Keetley summarizes: "What the film and novel depict . . . is the possibility that, in some way, the men have always been wolves, something the wolves have recognized from the beginning," and that *The Grey* consequently "unsettles the usually fixed ontological border between human and animal."[9]

For Keetley, these themes motivate a "posthumanist" interpretation in which "the human" as a distinct conceptual category is subsumed. This process is initially evident (the film develops it explicitly), but it doesn't go the distance of the film. For one thing, the wolves themselves are not strictly literal animals: they're especially large and heavily built, and their eyes glow demonically in the darkness. These are not creatures rendered with realism as a first priority, suggestive of a more metaphorical resonance (for the humans they hunt). It is the anti-human symbolism of death that they carry; obviously the wolves bring literal death, but they also symbolize it. Ottway's memories throughout the film, and the note he has written addressed to his wife, convey the despair of a man unable to reconcile himself to a separation or divorce. Yet as he prepares to face the alpha at the film's conclusion, the flashbacks of her go further—we see an intravenous drip by her bedside. His wife is dead, we now realize; they'll never be reconciled, and the letter he has composed will never be delivered. He begins the film in despair, his narration describing his feeling "damned." He and the other men have sought to evade death this entire time, but the death of which Ottway is most afraid has already occurred. Accordingly, this flashback injects crucial thematic significance into what we see as Ottway faces the massive black alpha wolf alone. The creature becomes symbolic of death as not just something that ends life but also a challenge to the meaning of any of it (Fig. 3.8).

Figure 3.8. Man versus Wild: the alpha wolf, black as the death it brings, scatters its subordinates to face John Ottway (Liam Neeson) alone in *The Grey* (Joe Carnahan, Open Road, 2011). Digital frame enlargement.

In the final confrontation, *The Grey* reaffirms the need for human narratives of meaning, and seems to elevate something exceptionally "human" out of the nihilism of animality. Ottway will fight back: he smashes single-serve alcohol bottles taken from the plane and tapes the broken glass to one fist as the alpha approaches, and straps a bowie knife in the other hand. Earlier in the film, Ottway had spoken of his hardy Irish father, and an untitled poem he'd written. He recalls the verses again now: "Once more into the fray, The last good fight I'll ever know / Live and die on this day, Live and die on this day." Formerly fixated on what is lost, Ottway will take his father's instruction to "live and die on this day"—to boldly engage life until the end. Keetley sees the knife and jagged glass taped to Ottway's hands as improvised wolf claws,[10] but they're also tokens of the father whom Ottway earlier mentioned was "a drinker, a brawler." As Ottway prepares himself, a flashback shows him as a young boy, seated on his father's knee: the little boy faces the same direction as his father, toward the lens—now sharing his defiant view (Fig. 3.9).

Ottway faces the alpha in a battle of "brute" aggression, but as he does so the lines between human and animal are redrawn and *The Grey* becomes a powerfully humanist film. The framing of the confrontation as an emblematic western-style "showdown" (complete with light/dark color coding) underscores the two creatures' differences. Ottway's moving recollections of his father attribute to him something above the nihilism of nature—identity, inspiration, philosophy—distinguishing him from the dark and pitiless predator approaching him. In its focus on parental

Figure 3.9. John Ottway of *The Grey* (Joe Carnahan, Open Road, 2011) remembers himself as a child (Jonathan Bitonti), his perspective now aligned with that of his defiant father (James Bitonti): "Once more into the fray." Digital frame enlargement.

inspiration as a source of strength in a world of emptiness and death, *The Grey* is almost a male companion-piece to *The Shallows*. The film concludes just as man and beast collide, refusing us the comfort of knowing whether Ottway survived or not. Yet after the credits, a brief, tight shot lets us at least glimpse the aftermath: the wolf lies on the snowy ground, breathing slowly and heavily, perhaps dying, but presumably injured. Ottway lies slumped against his opponent, alive or dead we cannot tell. We don't get to know the outcome, but we can tell that the wolf didn't have it easy. Ultimately, the fight may end up being for nothing, but in both *The Shallows* and *The Grey*, protagonists are moved to embrace an identity that allows them to at least face the void unflinching.

As in *Jaws* and *The Ghost and the Darkness*, in *The Grey* characters need enough "animal" in them to face the cruelty of the world; but they also need something more than that. We see this play out in the death of Diaz earlier in the film. Doubtful of rescue and too emotionally exhausted to continue, Diaz collapses. He's had enough—he'll die here, he tells the others. Like Ottway, Diaz has no one waiting at home. As the group had shared stories of their loved ones by the campfire, in testament to their desire to live, the most Diaz could think to say was, "I just want to fuck one more time." In other words, he is the most "animal" of the group, indeed the one who had boasted to the wilderness around them: "You're not the animals—we're the animals!" The two remaining men reluctantly accept his wishes and press on without him. Walking away, the only other survivor comments to Ottway that he'd seen a man with Diaz's defeated look only once before: Ottway himself, the night he left the bar, intending (we know) to commit suicide. Diaz has plenty of animal aggression, but without anything of deeper "human" value, why not resign the whole game? In this sense, Diaz is a cautionary mirror of Ottway—and as they say goodbye to each other, they learn that they share the same first name.

In each of the markedly male-centered films discussed above, nature is a zone of merciless volatility in opposition to the comfort of civilized life. In *The Edge*, it provides a proving-ground for male resourcefulness and intellect against a mate-rival: a latent primal conflict placed into a properly primal domain. *The Ghost and the Darkness*, set on the uncertain borderlands of civilization, depicts a wild terrain that must be cleansed of menace in preparation for fatherhood. As we see through several characters, when struggling against nature one cannot become too wild, taking life as a brutal and ultimately empty struggle for gratification or dominance. But as we also see, a bit of the brute is still necessary to survive in this wild world.

4

Creepy Crawlies

Intelligent Ants, Sickening Spiders, and Other Ill-intentioned Invertebrates

Despite their diminutive size, arthropods—especially insects and arachnids—cast a large shadow in horror film, sometimes literally. The individual tininess of these creatures obscures their ecological significance, but also their sheer numbers: in terms of biomass, the planet's insects vastly exceed humans (or any other animal), and once bacteria are exempted, insects comprise approximately 80 percent of the world's species.[1] In the domain of the insect we see a parallel world to entrance and alarm us: of armies, invasions, courtship, cannibalism, a world of alien singlemindedness and intensity. Belgian playwright Maurice Maeterlinck wrote that there is "an instinctive and profound inquietude inspired by these creatures so incomparably better armed, better equipped than ourselves, these compressions of energy and activity which are our most mysterious enemies, our rivals in these latter hours, and perhaps our successors."[2] At the more extreme end of inquietude is the pathological fear of insects, entomophobia. If we breach taxonomy briefly to corral spiders into this category, the United States is estimated to contain almost nineteen million entomophobes.[3] In light of such a number, and the captivating aggression of the insect world more generally, it's unsurprising that fantastic cinema might consider ways to more intimately enmesh the human world with the one that carries on at our feet.

Bugs are called upon as objects of horror in numerous films. In *Indiana Jones and the Temple of Doom* (1984), the adventurers find the floor beneath them a thick and writhing carpet of roaches, beetles, centipedes, worms, whip scorpions, and other anomalous arthropods. Sheltered nightclub singer and germophobe Willie Scott (Kate Capshaw) is particularly terrorized as all manner of creepy crawlies scale over her (Fig. 4.1). Moments later, she must pull a hidden lever to save the life of her co-travelers by first pushing her bare hand past a gauntlet of twitching micromonsters.

According to producer Frank Marshall, while there were snakes on set, they were fairly easy to deal with; in fact, "people were much more scared of the insects." Capshaw confirms: "The bugs were really gross, really bad. I think I took a Valium."[4] Ants writhe beneath the sheets of criminal profiler (Sigourney Weaver) in *Copycat* (1995), a disgusting sign that her most private living space has been invaded by the sadistic killer she traces. In *Hostel: Part III* (2011), a young woman is tortured by having cockroaches encouraged to invade her esophagus—implausible as a mode of death but repugnant enough that credibility doesn't seem to matter.

On the bigger side, in *The X-Files* episode "Folie à Deux" (1998), a disturbed telemarketer takes his officemates hostage at gunpoint, convinced they have been zombified by their boss, whom he claims is really a gigantic parasitic insect in disguise (and it turns out he's right). In *Mimic* (1997), massive roaches lurk in the underground railway tunnels of Manhattan, mutated to human size through an accident of genetic engineering. As we'll soon see, 1950s horror cinema contains plenty of giant pests, oversized incarnations that have lasted into later decades through films like

Figure 4.1. Dainty nightclub singer Willie Scott (Kate Capshaw) squeals in disgust under a virtual ecosystem of insects in *Indiana Jones and the Temple of Doom* (Steven Spielberg, Lucasfilm, 1984). Digital frame enlargement.

sci-fi actioner *Starship Troopers* (1997) and *Arachnid* (2001).[5] Naturally, many buggy characteristics have been hybridized in the concoction of new monsters: the hyper-predatory Xenomorph from the *Alien* franchise has the eusocial organization of insects (focused around a central queen with numerous drones) but also the endoparasitic reproduction of some wasps, who implant their eggs within a host organism.

In his book *The Infested Mind* (2013), entomologist Jeffrey Lockwood suggests that the widespread apprehension toward insects is linked with disgust through age-old fears of contamination. Pathogens are a constant threat for most organisms, leading in many animals to the development of immune systems to combat infections. However, mounting immune responses is costly in terms of an organism's energy: it's advantageous to develop strategies that mitigate the risk of contamination before it occurs.[6] Disgust helps us out here, and this is thought to be its primarily adaptive purpose.[7] Consequently, disgust centers prominently on cues to disease hazards, such as feces, mucus, maggots, or putrefying food. Disgust motivates us to avoid potential threats, creating concern around oral contamination; it provokes nausea and acquired taste aversions based on links between food and previous illness.[8] The majority of insect species with which humans come into contact are harmless, and may even be beneficial;[9] however, bugs like cockroaches, beetles, and flies have indeed presented potential disease hazards throughout our natural history, and continue to do so today. Several species may bite or sting in medically significant ways, and the others may be avoided through precautionary bias. Insects or invertebrates can also display characteristics, like the mucus of worms or slugs, that trigger our disease-aversion impulses whether a real threat exists or not.[10]

Dark lord among diminutive terrors is of course the spider. And there are a lot of them. In early 2017, several news outlets posted with mischievous glee the news, deduced from an article in *The Science of Nature*, that the world population of spiders would be sufficient to consume all humanity within a year. Spiders eat between 400 and 800 million tons of prey per annum,[11] which while comprised of over 90 percent insects and other hexapods, is at least as much as the combined weight of the world population of humans.[12] Fortunately, spiders don't appear interested in any such conspiracy, and generally busy themselves with far smaller prey—but that doesn't stop our imagining. Despite their unimposing size, spiders regularly rank among the most feared animals. In a U.K. study, 32 percent of women and 18 percent of men indicated that spiders caused them to feel anxious, nervous, or fearful,[13] and evidence suggests that men underreport their phobias in line with cultural expectations of masculinity.[14] There are numerous recorded accounts of individuals inadvertently burning down their own homes while attempting to exterminate spiders with improvised aerosol-can flamethrowers—such is the fear these tiny creatures inspire in some people. And we also recognize spiders' distinctive morphology as the template for many a made-up monster, from the mythological Arachne to the scuttling face-huggers of *Alien* (1979).

The exact reason for the anxiety that the arachnids generate has been subject to considerable discussion. Fear of spiders is typically explained in terms of biological preparedness stemming from spiders as an evolutionary hazard.[15] Since some spiders have presented a threat to hominins throughout our natural history, spider fear is likely an evolved response. The evolutionary hypothesis is supported by research into attentional bias, focusing on hardwired mechanisms for the speedy detection of specific types of threats. New and German point out that experimental evidence demonstrates that spider shapes are exceptionally likely to draw our alert focus, an effect observed even among those who consider themselves unafraid of spiders.[16] In the introduction to this book, I mentioned that for snakes we have an evolved perceptual mechanism designed for snake detection, and it turns out that the same is likely true for spiders. As New and German write, "Dedicated perceptual templates may make very few forms, such as the human face and body, snakes, and spiders uniquely capable of capturing attention."[17] We're always alert to spiders; and if something appears in the telltale spider shape, we'll notice that too—just in case. Evidence for the evolutionary origin of spider fear has been recently reinforced by research at the Max Planck Institute, which demonstrated that babies as young as six months will demonstrate stress responses to images of spiders and snakes relative to other stimuli, well before such responses could have been learned or socialized.[18]

The puzzling part is that the fear of spiders is grossly disproportionate to the actual danger they present, since the vast majority of them are harmless to humans. As Katarzyna and Sergiusz Michalski point out, while the U.K. study cited above found pronounced spider fear among men and women, the country is deficient in spiders of serious medical concern.[19] Injuries thought to be spider bites are routinely misdiagnosed by their victims, and many spider species have been incriminated on unreliable evidence.[20] As noted earlier, adaptations are driven by cost–benefit calculations, and it may be that on the basis of a few dangerous spiders it was beneficial for humans to develop heightened apprehension toward the whole lot. The idea here is that errors are costly, and even if a spider turns out to be harmless, there's no upside to engaging with it. Such asymmetry in cost–benefit means it was probably better for our evolving psychology to err on the side of anxiety (referred to as "error-management theory")[21]—after all, it's better to be safe than sorry.

Intriguingly, a long-running observation of researchers into spider fear has been that the arachnids elicit not only fear but also responses consistent with disgust, owing to perceptions of spiders as somehow dirty.[22] But spiders aren't especially dirty, and are less likely to carry diseases than (for instance) beetles, which may invade and contaminate human food products (yet to which we have fewer phobic responses). Whatever the case, cinematic spiders certainly appear to suggest this feared dirtiness regularly. *Spiders* (2000) provides a particularly vivid example: in this film the already intimidating funnel-web spider is spliced with alien DNA, leading to a parasitic species that inserts eggs into a host when it bites. The faces of the spider's infected victims swell and bulge, straining with pulsating cysts, their skin clammy and oozing in clear signifiers of contagion. The first monstrous birth emerges from its host's mouth, suggesting oral contamination (Fig. 4. 2). And as we venture further into the spider's cinematic den, the consistency of this theme will become apparent.

While the following exploration touches on only some significant and intriguing features in the landscape of arthropod horror, I hope it will outline and elaborate key themes with utility for a broader range of films. In addition to how "disgusting" some onscreen arthropods may be, we'll see that filmic focus on creatures who live in their multitudes all around us calls into question the idea of unique, stable, and specifically "human" space. Bugs violate the distinction between human and

Figure 4.2. Disease-threat: a spider emerges from the mouth of its infected host in *Spiders* (Gary Jones, Trimark, 2000). Digital frame enlargement.

nonhuman territories; they provoke recognition of the ever-communal reality of our living spaces, placing us within a broader—and often more brutal—spectrum of creaturely life.

The Big Bad Ants and Outsized Arachnids in *Them!*, *Tarantula*, and *The Black Scorpion*

The reader may be relieved to know that giant bugs are impossible. Numerous features of insects and arachnids mean they can't biologically afford to get too big, perhaps most fundamentally that exoskeletons won't support significant weight.[23] Horror movies, of course, aren't usually held back by technical quibbles. The first film to sensationally inflate insects was Gordon Douglas's *Them!* (1954). When a little girl is found by State Police wandering in the desert of New Mexico, she's so shook up that she's only able to murmur "them" when asked who exterminated her kin. Investigators find a series of wrecked homes and the local store partially demolished, but authorities cannot explain the cause. The federal government eventually sends father and daughter scientist duo, Drs. Harold and Pat Medford (Edmund Gwenn and Joan Weldon), from the Department of Agriculture, who figure out from the evidence that the culprits can only be carnivorous ants, but ones upsized through exposure to atomic energy (Fig. 4.3).

Figure 4.3. An oversized flesh-eating ant makes a sensational first appearance in *Them!* (Gordon Douglas, Warner Bros., 1954). Digital frame enlargement.

Ants seem like unlikely horror villains, with the insect world containing far scarier little fiends. However, in a study asking people to rank bugs in terms of the anxiety they provoke, ants came in third. When participants of another study were asked to indicate their affinity for arthropods, only scorpions did worse than ants.[24] It seems there's plenty of ambivalence out there toward the humble ant, and its appearance in horror isn't as idiosyncratic as we might assume. In Douglas's film, after the revelation of "them" we receive a video lecture on the complexity of ant life that impresses on us their skill in engineering and organization, but also in the perpetration of violence. "As you see," Harold Medford commentates, "ants are savage, ruthless, and courageous fighters." The video suddenly reveals a kind of extraterrestrial intelligence on Earth, a connotation compounded when a fighter pilot mistakes a migrating queen ant for an alien craft. Eventually these migrating queens take up residence in the storm drain system of the Los Angeles River basin, a space created by but unlivable for humans. The infrastructure's concrete grooves and tunnels, so similar to the ant's native environment, imply that spaces we create are not necessarily our spaces. The film insinuates that even now we share our spaces with typically unseen insect others, urging us to look anew at the world around (and below) us.

Spiders are scarier than ants; accordingly, if big ants were successful onscreen, then big spiders could only do better. In Jack Arnold's *Tarantula* (1955), a surly biologist experiments with a nutrient serum on a variety of varmints, producing oversized mice, guinea pigs, and a tarantula that escapes during a laboratory fire to continue its accelerated growth. When we first see the spider, it's twenty-two days old and roughly man-sized. Yet after it escapes and roams the desert, it feeds on cattle and the odd human until it achieves terrifyingly titanic scale.

As in *Them!*, we receive a video lesson on the predacity and tenacity of the tarantula, ensuring we know all about its thoroughly nasty nature. "We must accept them as we do the rest of God's creation," the instructor concludes. "Each has a function in its own world." Yet as the doctor-protagonist (John Agar) explains, this spider has grown beyond its ecological niche, and is now "something that's fiercer, more cruel and deadly than anything that walked the earth." The creature's starkly black appearance, more and more prominent as it grows, suggests not only its moral evil but also the "dirtiness" associated with spiders, and we sense that this obscene creeper must be decisively cleansed back into obscurity (Fig. 4.4 on page 96).

Hot on the invertebrate heels of *Them!* was Edward Ludwig's *The Black Scorpion* (1957), with another suitably bad type of bug. A series of volcanic blasts in Mexico let loose from their subterranean prison a

Figure 4.4. The chemically enhanced arachnid lumbers downtown in Jack Arnold's *Tarantula* (Universal, 1955). Digital frame enlargement.

horde of cranky house-sized scorpions, a prehistoric species back to vie for dominance. Ludwig's film centralizes nature's inherent volatility; the prologue depicts a volcanic fury threatening to incinerate anything in its path, indifferent to the prayers of endangered villagers. The beasts themselves, animated by stop-motion master Willis O'Brien, are naturally without the sympathy of anthropomorphic giants like King Kong (also O'Brien's creation). As fearsome bugs go, the scorpion is an apt choice: dark, shielded by a heavy exoskeleton, conspicuously armed, and thoroughly carnivorous (indeed often cannibalistic).

The critters are gassed in their den by the geologist heroes, but several escape and lope toward Mexico City. On the way, they fiendishly snatch an express train from its track, before turning on each other—these bugs are too nasty to even collude. Eventually an alpha emerges, striking dead its smaller rivals and lumbering into town to assert itself as the monster to worry about. In the final showdown, the scorpion supervillain is bombarded in a stadium by the best of human military might, and finally subdued. But it doesn't go down easily: it snatches one circling gunship from the sky, then another, slam-dunking them to the ground and ramming its stinger home like a harpoon.

Again, the bugs are like an alien species on earth: a mysterious pulsating accompanies their attacks, linking them to an extraterrestrial sense of the unknown. When the heroes venture into the volcanic chamber from which the pests arose, they wear protective jumpsuits and visors suggestive of space explorers as they navigate this rocky, quasi-lunar terrain. While the threat is of course finally defeated, the creatures' emergence also insults our sense of control over our environment, beginning with the volcanic blasts, which prayers fail to abate. Indeed, in both *The Black Scorpion* and *Tarantula* there's a struggle to consider such creatures consistent with a benevolent god, troubling us with the savage aspects of life on Earth that aren't easily reconciled with our more romantic sensibilities.

Picking on Someone their Own Size in *The Incredible Shrinking Man* and *Honey, I Shrunk the Kids*

The Incredible Shrinking Man (1957), also directed by *Tarantula*'s Jack Arnold, had the distinction of physically demoting the man rather than upscaling the arachnid. Arnold's film is almost totally confined to domestic settings, its unlucky protagonist not transported beyond his comfort zone but rather transformed within it, providing an engrossing exploration of the overlapping living space of bug and man. Months after Robert Scott Carey (Grant Williams) is exposed to a mysterious mist while on vacation, he notices his clothes no longer fit, and his suspicions of some strange happening are confirmed when his doctor's measurements indicate that he's gradually diminishing in size. He eventually shrinks to the scale of a thimble, becoming lost and presumed dead within his own home. While Carey isn't dead, his condition plunges him into a strange new world in which death is a perpetual possibility, and one lorded over by an intimidating arachnid menace.

The first half of Arnold's film offers a powerful subtext of acquired and incurable disability. Carey's shrinkage triggers his panic and surly introversion; he loses his job, fears that his wife will reject him, and questions his validity, particularly in gender terms: "I felt puny and absurd," he narrates. Gwendolyn Audrey Foster suggests that Carey's shrinking highlights the conditional nature of his social power—losing size triggers the whole thing to come apart.[25] Positioning this shrinking man within banal domestic space also provides the film with an effective means of visually indexing his regression, as well as reconfiguring his everyday surroundings into something more foreign. As Carey, by now the size of a small child, sits or moves about his living room, the ordinarily familiar environment is uncannily transformed (Fig. 4.5).

This is a stepping-stone to the greater uncanniness faced by a far more miniaturized man. When Carey, not much bigger than a rice grain, finds himself in the basement, the immense landscape around him becomes comprehensively recoded, a new wilderness ahead—the floor, he narrates, "stretch[es] before [him] like some vast primeval plain." As befits this description, his new environment is also fundamentally unstable, and what is secure one day is not so the next. The matchbox shelter he discovers is subject to a siege by the spider, and later this ad hoc home is soaked through from a leak in the water heater. The ordinarily dull environment becomes one in which dramatic feats must be performed, and there's genuine tension as Carey attempts to cross a ravine that is, in reality, not more than the space between two old boxes. In desperate need of nourishment, the shrunken man discovers a mousetrap the size of a car, baited with cheese, and struggles dangerously to disarm the contraption to secure a precious meal. The moment powerfully reminds us of humankind's attempts to regulate the boundaries of its space, brutally imposing "pest" status on anything that crosses over (even in a virtually unused location like this basement). In doing so, the scene surely elicits our sympathy for the rodent (never shown) trying to meet its basic needs, whose interests and hazards this human being now shares.

Figure 4.5. Poor Carey (Grant Williams), dwarfed by the domestic in Jack Arnold's *The Incredible Shrinking Man* (Universal, 1957). Digital frame enlargement.

The showdown with the spider, the apex predator of this hostile country, provides the film's dramatic climax. Dark, hairy, and fang-faced, the brute seems to grope massively around its domain, as if sinisterly tasting the environment, moving with the confidence of one invulnerable to attack. Yet it can also emerge from crevices in which its darkness is disguised with all the familiar spidery stealth, albeit now on a massive scale. Carey takes on the monster with a pin yanked from a pincushion and brandished as a sword; he bends another pin into a hook and attaches a cotton-thread rope to make a grapnel—putting all his human ingenuity into combat against a much stronger foe (Fig. 4.6). The spider as a source of disgust is powerfully evoked as, struggling beneath it in combat, Carey gazes up at the black and salivary maw looming down on him.

Carey triumphs, dominating his new world, reasserting human supremacy by rising above the top predator. Yet, remarkably, the conquest does not trigger feelings of gratification, nor lead to any narrative re-promotion to the world of bigger beings. Instead, as he continues to shrink, Carey has an epiphany in which he feels new acceptance and integration into "the vast majesty of creation." While his previous worldview had been "in terms of man's own limited dimension," he now recognizes all life—large and small—as both unified and infinite under nature: "The unbelievably small and the unbelievably vast eventually meet—like the closing of a gigantic circle." This conclusion is so holistic, the film can only terminate, since philosophically unifying all life means dramatic conflict

Figure 4.6. Carey (Grant Williams) battles the spider in *The Incredible Shrinking Man* (Jack Arnold, Universal, 1957). Digital frame enlargement.

disappears. In its final decentering of its hero, the film encourages us to think beyond our anthropocentric view of the world around us. The spider, now defeated, is reframed not as an obstacle to human superiority, but as a catalyst for deeper awareness of the diversity of existence: the reality of human "smallness" in the grand scheme.

While hardly a horror film by any stretch of the imagination, family adventure *Honey, I Shrunk the Kids* (1989) nevertheless draws substantially on the big-bug vocabulary of animal horror cinema in its depiction of towering arthropods. Inventor Wayne Szalinski (Rick Moranis) slaves over an innovative shrink ray only to be disappointed by its results, battering the device apart. Little does he realize that the contraption not only works but that it has miniaturized his two children, as well as two kids from the family next door. Having swept up the spilled parts of his broken machine into the garbage and placed the bag by the back gate for collection, Wayne has also swept up his tiny kids, forcing them to begin the long journey back to the house to get their parents' attention. The size of pinheads, the children are confronted with massive fronds of their family's overgrown grass, casting a canopy above. The lawn is no longer a homogenized, benign, and domestic space, but a landscape teeming with action and danger. Early on in the children's quest, a butterfly squeals by, its wings sounding like a chopper to their tiny ears; later, one of the children is accidentally carried off by a bee after falling into a flower. Having realized their error, the parents scour the yard using stilts and slings to keep them aloft, and with magnifying instruments peer deeply into the ordinarily unacknowledged landscape beneath their feet, now hyper-aware of the teeming world they usually crush underfoot.

The children's first sustained encounter with a (now) supersized arthropod is with a juvenile ant, roughly the size of a car. The male children tackle the beast, seen as part of a frontier wilderness to be tamed as they ride it into passivity like a bucking horse. Newly named "Anty," the insect becomes their day's transport; and once they decide to let the ant go, it emits a "purring" indicative of its desire to stay, having been successfully domesticated and now appreciative of its human masters. However, this complementary and anthropocentric encounter with the insect is juxtaposed with the encounter with a much larger scorpion, which rams its fat claw toward one kid as he sleeps, thoroughly reviving the danger of this backyard wilderness. Now we know that the jungle of miniature life will not offer a mere vacation (like that which one of the families were set to embark on before their kids were zapped and lost). In contrast to *The Incredible Shrinking Man*, the film is pointedly anthropocentric, with Anty sacrificing himself for his domesticators in battle with the scorpion, dividing these bugs into broadly Manichean roles. Yet the film still offers a compelling vision of a microworld bursting with drama and violence at odds with the benign human domestic space that geographically contains it.

Life on Earth: *Phase IV*

Unlike the immense insects of *Them!*, Saul Bass's *Phase IV* (1974) focuses on ants of more humble size, but granted additional intelligence through a cryptic series of cosmological adjustments. In the U.S. desert, ants are observed extending their power across the local ecology, and a duo of scientists, entrenched in a high-tech base of their own design, begin various experiments to solve the riddle of this mysterious escalation of ant conquest. The desert research team consists of Lesko (Michael Murphy), an expert in animal communication, and the older Hubbs (Nigel Davenport), a mathematician who provokes the ants by exploding the enigmatic obelisk-like mounds they've constructed. While Lesko focuses on the possibilities of communication, Hubbs is increasingly fanatical and warlike in his approach, at one point turning on sprinklers of yellow poison to annihilate everything around them. The fatal brew showers an elderly couple running for shelter, leaving only their granddaughter Kendra (Lynne Frederick) alive. The scientists bring her into their base, but Hubbs refuses to call the police, unwilling to have his experiments disrupted. He's obsessed with furthering war against their insect rivals, intent on teaching the creatures through conflict, and striving to reimpose human superiority.

The ants have gained their new intelligence through strange planetary movements, but the causal process of this remains utterly ambiguous. The premise strongly recalls Stanley Kubrick's *2001: A Space Odyssey* (1968), in which arcane extraterrestrial intelligence directs human evolutionary advance. This allows *Phase IV* to capitalize on ants' alien appearance, but also to complement and further mystify our view of their cognition and behavior. The film is perhaps most remarkable for its macrocinematographic sequences tracing the ants' motion, travel, and routines. Under the deeply investigative documentary gaze of the camera, ant burrows become corridors and caverns, with all the reality and function of human spaces. Much of the film's action really takes place outside human awareness, and collectively these images and techniques coalesce to challenge our centrality as a species. While animal horror typically does not depict the animal antagonists communicating with each other, we see ants engaged in cryptic communication through the kind of countershots used for human conversation. After an attack by the men, we even see the ants arranging their dead ceremonially (Fig. 4.7), a display that demonstrates the gravity of the humans' attacks in moral terms, but also contrasts with the insensitive Hubbs, who carelessly causes human deaths and carries on the confrontation with the ants as if it were a mere game.

As in *The Incredible Shrinking Man*, territorial overlap is of key significance to Bass's film. In one moment, an ant crawls along coils of complex machinery within the base and begins gnawing its wires, only to be ambushed and mauled from above by a praying mantis. Here human-contrived equipment becomes the setting of a specifically insect conflict, part of the décor of their world, of which we are now fascinated spectators. The spatial conflict with humans is emphasized more directly when Hubbs tears apart the same control room in search of a single ant. As this occurs, we see close-ups of the insect scurrying for cover, negotiating the nuances of the room in a way no human ever could—the environment becoming as much theirs as ours.

Toward the end of the film, with Hubbs dead and Kendra missing, Lesko feels the ants have won and an armistice will never be achieved. Outside, he ventures into a massive burrow, the film spatially fusing human and ant worlds. Within a tunnel Lesko discovers Kendra and embraces her as his voiceover explains that the ants desired a sexual union of the two to make them "part of their world," initiating some existential change in the couple. They will, it seems, become the Adam and Eve

Figure 4.7. An ant has arranged its dead in Saul Bass's *Phase IV* (Paramount, 1974). Digital frame enlargement.

in a union of ant and human intelligence, although the film concludes without explaining what this means. Nevertheless, like the conclusion of *The Incredible Shrinking Man*, the ending of *Phase IV* implies a union of perspectives and experiences. Rather than restoring human dominance, the film speculates a more transcendent—if ambiguous—interspecies worldview.

Frozen in Fear (and Time) by *Arachnophobia*

Arachnophobia (1990), as its title suggests, is perhaps the definitive spider-fear film, not only swamped with adventurous and angry arachnids, but also centering a character pathologically petrified of them. Dr. Ross Jennings (Jeff Daniels), his stockbroker wife Molly (Harley Jane Kosak), and their children move to the country for Ross to assume the practice of an aging local doctor. But also immigrating to this rural idyll is an especially malign spider species from an obscure Amazonian cavern. The insidious import mates with a local arachnid in the Jennings's barn, producing a litter of lethal offspring that branches out to terrorize the small town. Ross is haunted by the memory of a spider strolling across his naked body as a young child, and the crisis will culminate with his showdown against his darkest, hairiest horror.

As with many animal antagonists, the spiders erode the boundaries around civilized domestic life. The threat is exotic: transported inadvertently by an entomological expedition in South America—a concoction of the deepest wilderness.[26] By contrast, the Jennings family are typical middle-class city-slickers. Their barn, where the spiders will mate, is an emblematic rural feature for which they have no use, suggestive of their displacement in this "wilder" country environment. Inside is dark, dingy, and festooned with cobwebs—a point of wildness within the domestic sphere. Moreover, since the lethal brood are the hybrid offspring of common and exotic varieties, the film further muddies any categorical clarity, investing otherwise familiar intruders with fresh menace.

The breakdown of the family home as a human-exclusive area begins quite literally. Performing DIY work, Ross discovers his floor is partially termite-eaten—the house not only inhabited by other creatures, but also literally undermined by them. We're soon drawn into appreciation of the ease with which spiders can also sneak stealthily around. When a teenage girl reaches behind her to adjust the shower nozzle, she plunges her wet hand into a spiderweb, benign domestic space having been repurposed by an arachnid engineer. The girl's concerned father calls in Delbert (John Goodman), a muttering and eccentric exterminator, to investigate a possible infestation. Delbert runs a gloved hand around the back of the toilet bowl, just as one of the creatures scuttles just beyond reach. He confidently gives the wrong diagnosis: "There's no spider here." They might be our houses, but they provide space for any number of tiny squatters, whose presence is difficult to detect, let alone control. The shower incident also develops anxiety around the automation of our physical movements. We expect our homes to be highly predictable environments; we don't have to waste energy considering what we might encounter. These stealthy spiders make us aware that we constantly expose our skin to attack, and that we can't very well be looking everywhere we touch.

The ease (even superiority) with which arachnids can navigate human environments is only amplified as the film progresses. When the family lock themselves in an upstairs bedroom, the spiders simply dance under the door and through the lock—literally any aperture renders human space distressingly pregnable (Fig. 4.8). To stop these leggy hordes permanently, Ross must locate and destroy the egg sac before it emits its unstoppable multitude. The slimy pulsating structure in the barn is symbolic of a dark inversion of domesticity; it promises to establish for the spiders a "family" of their own—the Jennings home to be totally colonized by the arachnid Other.

Not only can these spiders crawl from any unlikely crevice, challenging our control over the spaces in which we live, but they can do so with unnerving speed—spiders' capacity for unpredictable movement is a commonly identified element of spider fear.[27] As I earlier mentioned,

Figure 4.8. No room of one's own: with the door closed against them, the spiders begin trickling under it in *Arachnophobia* (Frank Marshall, Hollywood / Amblin, 1990). Digital frame enlargement.

humans seem to be evolutionarily preset to detect spiders. Our attention arranges concerns hierarchically, and spiders and snakes always rise to top priority—they won't be ignored. *Arachnophobia* makes great play with this visual bias, toying with our compulsion by making sure we have our spider-spotting work cut out for us. Toward the film's conclusion, the Jennings house is veritably besieged by the tiny terrors, with spiders crawling up walls and abseiling from the ceiling. In this scene the spiders are obviously disturbing "safe" domestic space, but with new threats popping out seemingly everywhere, they're also creating cognitive panic: our hierarchy of attention is being repeatedly hijacked to keep track of all these little terrors.

Arachnophobia also dramatizes responses of disgust and contamination associated with spiders. The spiders' initial home, the dark and disused barn, is a hygienically unmaintained area, and the massive web lurks amid dust and debris as if a concatenation of its invasive potential. More importantly, scares in the film are frequently staged around fears of contamination. When a spider leaps on the teen girl in the shower, we see a close-up of the dark creature sliding over her clean, fair, soap-covered skin, evoking not simply the threat of its bite, but also a malevolent dirtiness (Fig. 4.9).

Fears of oral contamination emerge several times. As Ross, the coroner (James Handy), and the sheriff (Stuart Pankin) inspect the house of a victim, the sheriff peers with infinite care inside a row of mugs

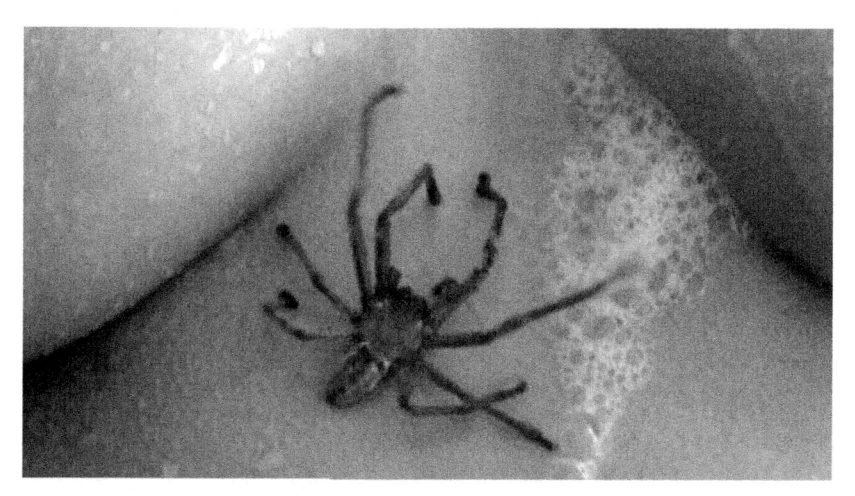

Figure 4.9. A spider slides down the soapy clean skin of teenage girl after it leaps on her in the shower in Frank Marshall's *Arachnophobia* (Hollywood / Amblin, 1990). Digital frame enlargement.

hanging in the kitchen, fearful that the suspect may be nestled inside. It isn't—phew. Having relaxed, however, he helps himself to fistfuls of cereal from a nearby box, unwittingly pulling out the culprit. Thankfully, the spider is dead, but the horror here arises not simply from the spider's unanticipated appearance but from how close the sheriff came to eating it. Later, the town's medical examiner and his girlfriend are bitten, a spider struggling up from within their bowl of popcorn, poised to be ingested. When their bodies are discovered and inspected in situ by the dim light of the television, the offender suddenly gropes its way out of the male victim's nostril. Again, it's not just the bite that is threatening here; it's the suggestion of bodily contamination.

As we know, it's Ross, the shrinking urban arachnophobe, whom the film centralizes and who must overcome his deep-rooted apprehension. Early in the film he describes the experience of the spider strolling over his naked skin when he was an infant as "a feeling of utter helplessness, like being explored by an alien thing," almost as if describing sexual abuse—as if the "dirty" spider is also a sexual contaminator of childhood innocence. Ambivalence around sex is also implied as Ross and Molly make love to commemorate their first night in the house: a cut tastefully averts our attention, but to the barn where the exotic spider begins mating with a local female to produce the deadly brood, the film thereby infusing sexuality with danger and disgust.

More generally, pushing past his childhood trauma will allow Ross to restore his imperiled status. Upon first entering their new home, Ross calls his wife inside to deal with a harmless local spider in an embarrassing reversal of anticipated gender roles. His emasculation is compounded by his failure to assume the GP position after his aging predecessor obnoxiously decides he'll hang around for a few more years. After all, Ross's wife has relinquished a lucrative stockbroking career, but now she must resurrect her role as breadwinner. Ross picks up a couple of patients, but when they die unexpectedly from unknown causes, his professional status plummets. The deaths are, of course, from spider bites, but that isn't clear immediately, leaving the new doctor open to charges of malpractice. By overcoming his personal fear, Ross will demonstrate his ability to provide a traditional fatherly protection, and by proving the case against the spidery culprits he'll also rescue his reputation.

The climactic moment of therapeutic breakthrough comes after Ross falls through his floor to the cellar, where he finds an egg sac malevolently pulsating with spider spawn. With Ross knocked to the ground, the big daddy strides ominously over as he lies there petrified. This hairy brute is so large that as it begins crawling up Ross's leg it participates in an up-scaled reenactment of his experience as an infant (Fig. 4.10). It

Figure 4.10. Primal fear: the spider begins creeping up the leg of the arachnophobe Ross Jennings (Jeff Daniels), repeating his childhood trauma, in *Arachnophobia* (Frank Marshall, Hollywood / Amblin, 1990). Digital frame enlargement.

saunters over the recumbent Ross, its creeping, finger-sized limbs again insinuating an immobilizing sexual intrusion. However, this time Ross is able to overcome his paralysis and fight back, and the spider and all its spawn go up in flames.

The film concludes with the Jennings's retreat to more comfortable terrain: in a coda we see Ross and Molly unpacking in a San Francisco apartment. Blissfully free of stealthy countryside critters, they raise a toast to more familiar urban hassles. A minor earthquake rattles the room shortly after, ensuring we know that natural threats can never truly be banished, but still—better the devil you know.

Showing More Leg: *Eight Legged Freaks*

When an inattentive truck driver in a small Arizona town allows a barrel of chemical waste to tumble into a stream in *Eight Legged Freaks* (2002), its contents contaminate the crickets used to feed the stock of a nearby spider farm, causing them to undergo a series of growth spurts. Meanwhile, Chris McCormick (David Arquette) arrives back in town after a long absence. His late father owned much of the land here, and he's racked with guilt that he left town before his father died. Now Chris plans to restore his father's business and rekindle his old flame, Samantha (Kari Wuhrer), the local sheriff. Of course, soon there are arachnids on the loose, ranging in size from cats to cars—formidable obstacles against which the prodigal son can prove himself.

The approach of *Eight Legged Freaks* to animal horror is purposely lighthearted; it doesn't work hard to charge us with suspense, instead offering a pulpy, fast-moving, and often funny rumpus. Early in the film, a spider wrestles a screeching feline up the inside of a drywall, the warring animals' respective outlines embossed into its surface as the cat's owners watch on in confusion—one of numerous slapstick-style encounters. Later, a big spider hooks its many-jointed leg around a victim like a shepherd's crook around a Vaudeville performer, yanking him from the frame. The arachnids also amusingly growl and cackle like the raspy green critters of Joe Dante's *Gremlins* (1984), lending them cartoon villainy in which we can take subversive pleasure. At one point a spider straddles and sinks its fangs into a mounted stag's head, before spitting out the taxidermied tissue in vocal disgust. Murray and Heumann argue that by spoofing eco-disaster, the film allows an environmental message to be communicated without the viewer finding it irksomely didactic: the film, they suggest, "couches a political message in comedy" and presents "as a call to dispose of toxic waste in environmentally safe ways."[28] But the spillage with which the film commences is an accident, and not linked to systematic greed or negligence; the opportunity for a political message is thus bypassed rather than engaged. The film is really interested in whipping up some giant spiders, and chemical waste is an efficient way (within genre traditions) to make that happen. Once those spiders have been achieved, environmental concerns are shuffled out of view, giving center stage to the colossal spiders and the hairy situations they create.

As we might expect, we have a disparate and bickering group of humans who must suppress their intragroup antagonism to defeat a more pressing outside threat. And we also have a reluctant male hero who, by engaging the enemy, can demonstrate leadership and purpose that will restore his tarnished sense of self. Despite the film's comic tone, it engages concerns familiar from more suspenseful spider fare. The arachnids, while very large, are particularly adept jumpers, the film thereby preserving our discomfort with their rapid movement. And the hazards of unmonitored domestic space are also evoked: as the owner of the unlucky cat blindly gropes her hand around cans of cat food on a top shelf of a cupboard, she's unaware of a spider nestled within and waiting to pounce.

More prominently, the signifiers of disgust are thickly present. Spiders don't have red blood like us; their circulatory system differs significantly, and instead of blood they pump a light blue fluid called haemolymph. But green blood is more revolting for its resemblance to mucus (a potential disease hazard), so these spiders bleed green and bleed a lot—spraying slime from their injuries. The little creeps eventually grow too large to threaten oral invasion, yet before that this fear is vividly dramatized: a miner trying to suck clear a hose blockage vacuums in a terrible mouthful, which obscenely reemerges as he dies. In another scene, a man-sized spider creeps through the window of the sheriff's teen daughter, Ashley (Scarlett Johansson), after she emerges from the shower, freshly clean and wrapped only in a towel. Backing her against the wall, the beast brings its fanged face close to hers as if to kiss her but instead begins dousing her in its sticky web, pinning her back (Fig. 4.11). Given Ashley's near nudity and the spider's massive hosing ejaculation, the scene infuses disgust with sexual danger; we should also note that just moments before the spider's attack, the virgin Ashley was tearing up a photo of the boyfriend she dumped for insisting on sex when she wasn't ready. As in *Arachnophobia*, these eight-legged freaks will be conquered through incineration: the most final kind of cleansing, which suggests their status as enemies threatening not just to injure but also to infect.

Under the Skin: *Bug*

The invasive critters of films like *Phase IV* and *Arachnophobia* are real animals that nevertheless come saddled with human emotional resonance. In contrast, the pests of William Friedkin's psychological thriller *Bug* (2006), adapted from a play by Tracy Letts, are entirely psychological projections, but this makes them even more difficult to extract. *Bug* takes place almost entirely within a crummy motel room in rural Oklahoma, where the thirty-something Agnes (Ashley Judd) lives alone. Early in the

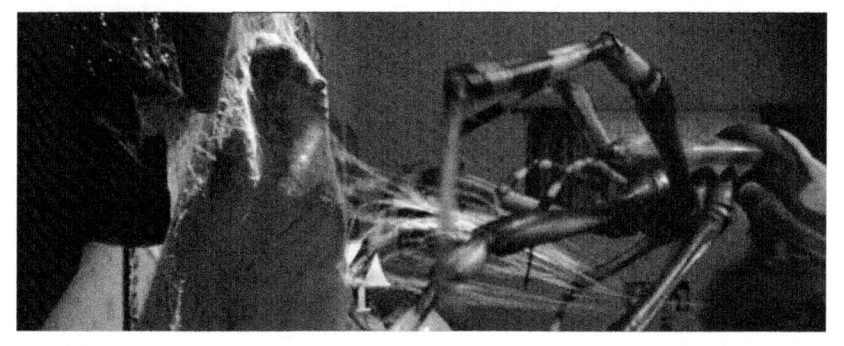

Figure. 4.11. Sex pest: a spider backs the near-naked Ashley (Scarlett Johansson) against a wall and sprays her with web in *Eight Legged Freaks* (Ellory Elkayem, Warner Bros., 2002). Digital frame enlargement.

film, she's unsettled by phone calls with no voice on the other end that she takes to be the work of her abusive ex-partner, Jerry (Harry Connick Jr.). After her shift at the local bar, her only friend R. C. (Lynn Collins) introduces her to a shy drifter, Peter (Michael Shannon), and they begin a relationship. After sex, however, Peter snaps awake, claiming to have been bitten by a bug. He points it out, but Agnes can't see anything (Fig. 4.12). Peter is insistent, the bug is tiny but it's there, and Agnes goes from playing along to falling into her lover's paranoid delusion: the motel is infested with barely visible bugs—bugs that bite and burrow, and even act as transmitters to malign government forces.

As the summary above suggests, the film contaminates human domestic territory by linking arthropod bugs with fears of surveillance through technology: the title "Bug" appears between the phone's persistent ringing, evoking telecommunication "bugs." Peter is an Iraq War veteran, gone AWOL from a hospital after he reacted badly to experimental procedures (or so he claims, anyway). He's terrified of surveillance by his former captors and lies awake watching the ceiling fan which, as in *Apocalypse Now* (1979), audibly melds with the slicing of chopper rotor-blades. Before his supposed bite, the first "bug" Peter detects in Agnes's room turns out to be the insect-like chirp of an expiring smoke detector. He destroys the device, lecturing Agnes on a modern world filled with surveillance. The

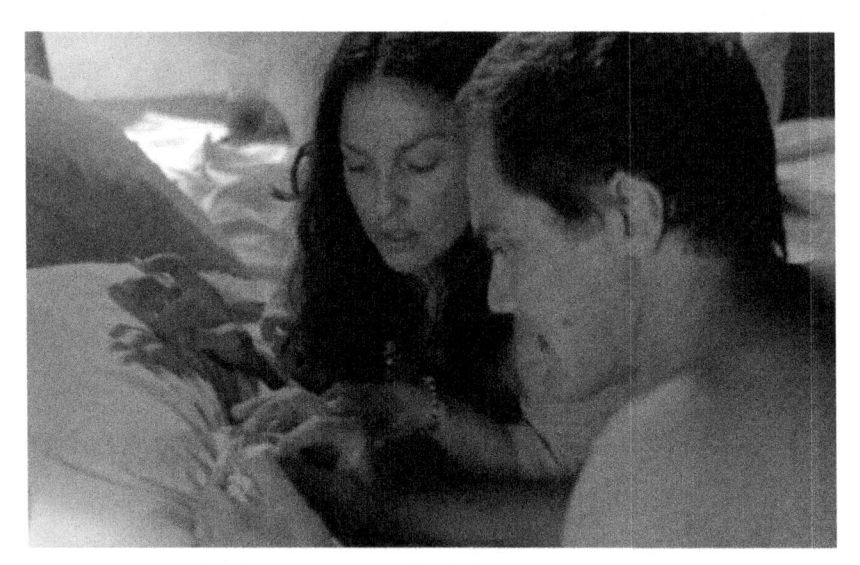

Figure. 4.12. "Right there": Peter (Michael Shannon) tries to show Agnes (Ashley Judd) a nonexistent human-biting bug in William Friedkin's *Bug* (Lionsgate, 2006). Digital frame enlargement.

idea of invisible arthropods sets him on a paranoid slippery slope: if these bugs can't be seen, then they can be anywhere—one should assume they're everywhere. And as his relationship with Agnes proceeds, he redoubles his suspicions that no space is totally private or safe.

While initially without Peter's conspiratorial bent, Agnes's world is one of pervasive insecurity that easily intersects with Peter's delusions. She doesn't live in her own space (the room is rented), and she suspects herself monitored by her abusive ex-partner. Jerry isn't supposed to know where she lives, yet she awakens one morning to find him in the shower in a gross infiltration of her private space. The ease with which Jerry can call her, track her down, and seemingly shake off criminal action manifests Agnes's fears of panoptical patriarchal control. Early on, she pretends she doesn't want a man around, but later admits to Peter that she gets "scared at night": in a world where even her own home doesn't offer security, men's presence and power seem to Agnes unavoidable—better to at least have one of them on your side. She's also haunted by flashbacks, her child having been lost in a supermarket years earlier and never seen again. The event is intolerable in its shock and ambiguity, and Peter's narratives of conspiracy provide at least some answer to life's otherwise idiosyncratic cruelties.

If we can't see where the bugs are, we can't see where they aren't, either, and Agnes and Peter eventually fear the bug's infiltration of not just their living space but their bodies and thoughts too. Peter digs at his arm, convinced that a bug has burrowed under the skin, and examines his own blood under a microscope, hypothesizing that the bugs are implanted robotic mind-control mechanisms. Having made themselves vulnerable to each other, the two allow their paranoias to cross-pollinate and proliferate. As they have sex, we see close-ups of their skin surfaces, hair reactions, sweat, an abstract red spray suggestive of blood. The focus is on fragmentation, on fluids and biological transference—an exchange of one's physical self. It's immediately after this first encounter that Peter will feel his first supposed bug bite. For the vulnerable veteran, who wasn't so much looking for sex, he had said, as for a friend, physical intimacy triggers fears of innermost contamination.

The film concludes with Anges and Pete sealed, naked, in the room they've now entirely insulated with aluminum foil and which glows with the neon blue of bug-zappers. Through a delusional chain of conspiracy thinking, Agnes claims that she must be host to the initial egg-laying "mother bug," and then finally that she is herself the "super mother bug"—self and Other freely switching places now. She decides that "They" (anonymous governmental forces) want to take the bugs away for their own purposes, just as someone took her child: she'll kill herself before she lets that happen, reasserting her motherhood through protection of the bugs she carries. Dousing their naked bodies with gasoline, the couple profess their love for each other before ignition. Their suicide is both an assertion of surrender and a warped act of agency, to serve their bug colonizers and to resist colonization by outside forces.

In all of the films discussed above we've seen dramatized the fear of bugs' capacity to compromise clean distinctions between safe, domestic space and a wilder world beyond. In Friedkin's film the volume on these suspicions is turned right up to psychosis, with Peter and Agnes gripped by fantasies of imperceptible bodily invasion. But it won't stop there: as Lockwood suggests, "once insects get into our bodies, it's a small step to infesting our minds,"[29] and the wounded couple become as deranged and self-destructive as bugs drawn to a zapper.

5

Mad Science Makes for Cranky Creatures

MOST ANIMALS REALLY DO NOT impose on us very much. We're smart enough (mostly) to give the lethal ones a wide berth, and in reality even formidable frighteners like snakes and sharks are not (despite the consternation they provoke) particularly interested in us. But hypothesizing animals' scientific enhancement, either deliberately or by accident—the creation of new, even badder beasts—is a popular way for filmmakers to re-arm animals against us. The idea of deadly designer-animals birthed of human hubris may also be used to relay a moral lesson about the limits of our knowledge, to teach us the foolishness of tampering with what nature has tried and tested. Concern for animals themselves may also be an embedded theme through an implied or explicit critique of animal experimentation. The use of animals as research tools is widespread, but public opposition remains high: a 2014 survey by the Pew Research Center indicated that while 47 percent of the American public supported the practice, 50 percent did not.[1] At a logical level, the use of animals in biomedical experiments is probably more easily defended as an ethical practice than eating animals for food (the number of healthy vegetarians in the world makes it hard to make a plausible claim for the necessity of eating meat). However, something about the high-tech sophistication of biomedical research seems to denaturalize our power over animals, more easily attracting opposition. This chapter tours a variety of cinematic scenarios that splice immoral experimentation with animal antagonism. I'll take us back briefly to the lumbering nuclear brutes of 1950s sci-fi horror, and then move to the environmental effacement wrought by technological "progress" in later decades. We'll take a closer look at the human characters behind the chaos; and conclude by focusing on the prehistorical reptilian rogues of *Jurassic Park* and its sequels, perhaps cinema's most iconic fusion of mad science and fearsome fauna of the past thirty years.

Atom-age Animals

"Horror" attained new dimensions during World War II: on an astonishing scale, the world witnessed extremes of the human capacity for evil and saw new depths to the suffering it precipitates. The systematized murder of millions by the Nazis, in crimes often perpetrated by seemingly ordinary individuals, revealed a darkness to the human mind to trouble and intrigue historians, psychologists, and political scientists for decades to follow. The events of 1945 also showcased the ghastly might of the atomic bomb: a display of human destructive ingenuity so atrociously spectacular that it seemed to challenge comprehension. Horror film scholarship has often linked the preoccupations of 1950s horror cinema to the bomb's cultural aftershock. As David J. Skal explains, after World War II, traditional Gothic foes like Dracula seemed quaint personae compared with what played out in the theater of war: "An enveloping cloak was no longer an image of dread. But a mushroom cloud was. The threat of mass destruction was bigger than ever in America's mind, and so were its monsters."[2] Horror cinema inherited our fears of extravagant atomic havoc, giving us supersized, city-smashing bogies to inflict disaster on a similarly grand scale. If the connection seems tenuous at a distance, several influential films have explicit references to the bomb sutured into them. A key case is Eugène Lourié's *The Beast from 20,000 Fathoms* (1953): top-secret testing of atomic weapons in the blizzard-blown Article Circle revives a (fictional) dinosaur, the Rhedosaurus (the work of stop-motion legend Ray Harryhausen) from its hundred-million-year slumber, and the creature lays a path of destruction toward New York City (Fig. 5.1). Cyndy Hendershot suggests that the dinosaur's attack on the city, after it raises out of the Hudson River "is clearly being used metaphorically to embody 1950s America's worst nightmare/fantasy—the nuclear destruction of its largest city."[3] Before that, a mighty mushroom cloud wafts into the sky from the blast as the polar terrain breaks apart. Back in the control room, miles away, the monitoring scientists admit they don't know what will happen next. As befits such high-tech hubris, another scientist self-regardingly remarks that these tests make him feel

Figure 5.1. Ready to bite the Big Apple: the Rhedosaurus clambers out of the Hudson River in *The Beast from 20,000 Fathoms* (Eugène Lourié, Warner Bros. 1953). Digital frame enlargement.

as if they're "helping to write the first chapter of a new Genesis." However, the film doesn't simplistically view scientific breakthrough as only sacrilege; scientific knowledge is also instrumental in the classification and defeat of the creature, and as Hendershot notes, the film "reaffirm[s] the progress of the Atomic Age" when the beast is fatally wounded with a radioactive bullet.[4]

Inspired by *Beast* and similarly sharing an origin in atomic testing, Japanese sea-monster sensation *Godzilla* (1954) was, as Skal explains, a key transitional text that "grafted atomic trauma onto the *King Kong* formula and launched one of the biggest ritual displays of naïve metaphor the world has ever seen."[5] With its monster awakened by H-bomb testing, *Godzilla* conveys the ambiguous transformative power of atomic energy, which is seemingly able to spawn all manner of fears and wonders "like a technological gypsy curse."[6] We don't see the beast during an opening attack off the coast of fictional Ido Island, in which the big guy incinerates a fishing boat; what we do see is the crew blanketed by a blinding flash like an atomic detonation. And when the monster finally does appear—a fifty-meter-high, striding semi-dragon (Fig. 5.2)—he famously levels all, leaving a landscape indistinguishable from the aftermath of a bombing, complete with countless dead and injured, and water contaminated by radiation.

A paleontologist (Takashi Shimura) picks Godzilla as a two-million-year-old amphibious intermediary between the dinosaurs and the reptiles of today. The influence of *King Kong* is clear, with Ido Island's fictional folklore containing such a creature to whom girls were once sacrificed, and the natives still perform a more sanitized version of the ritual into the present. That won't work, but a young scientist, Dr. Daisuke Serizawa (Akihiko Hirata), has the answer: he's devised an unholy underwater weapon that wipes out oxygen atoms, annihilating all marine life in its vicinity. But he's also racked with fear that his demonic device might fall into the hands of politicians and warmongers. Of course, Serizawa finally agrees to use his weapon, but destroys its written plans and remains behind to perish as it detonates, ensuring that even the instructions stored in his memory are lost forever.[7] Through high-tech weapons Godzilla was made, and through these he will be destroyed. Atomic technology is thus a double-edged sword in the film, with the young scientist a moral authority who safeguards this power with his life against the moral weakness of others.

A heavily edited "Americanized" version was released nearly two years later: *Godzilla: King of the Monsters!* (1956), making extensive use of

Figure 5.2. The eponymous amphibian giant of the original *Godzilla* (Ishirō Honda, Toho, 1954), disturbed from his marine seclusion by thermonuclear bomb tests. Digital frame enlargement.

the original footage, but also integrating Raymond Burr as Steve Martin, an American reporter narrating events in English, thereby providing a cultural foothold for English-speaking audiences. As befits its recycled material, the film is narratively and tonally aligned with the original, yet references to nuclear attack are scaled back. American audiences were not likely to welcome a film that too explicitly depicted the incriminating horror of recent nuclear attack on their wartime opponents. Nevertheless, scenes of widespread devastation remain, and Godzilla's initial attack still happens in a blinding atomic flash, with survivors later dying of shock and unusual burns suggestive of radiation effects. Like the Rhedosaurus, Godzilla manifests contemporary fears of atomic destruction, as the film's post-apocalyptic imagery attests, but he's also a figure that allows that anxiety to be deflected—reprocessed into an attack by a formidable animal predator. A new and terrifyingly technological danger becomes an overblown incarnation of an age-old one, but perhaps also a threat that can more easily be conceptualized and defeated.[8]

Despite the American *Godzilla*'s relative hesitation with its subtext, atomic allusions were radiating through successful American films at the time anyway. In *Them!*, the mutant breed of oversized ants emerge after atomic testing in the New Mexico desert, and, as in *The Beast from 20,000 Fathoms*, there turns out to be something sacrilegious about this kind of power. The senior scientist, Harold Medford (Edmund Gwenn), murmurs that "we may be witnesses to a biblical prophecy come true, and there shall be destruction and darkness come upon creation and the beasts will reign over the earth." Atomic anxiety persisted into Jack Arnold's *Tarantula*: it is a radioactive isotope that supersizes the spider, although the offending scientist's goal was to create a new nutrient to benefit humans. As Hendershot points out, the positive possibilities of atomic discovery, as well as its destructive power, were very much part of the cultural vocabulary of the 1950s. And in this case, just below the wobbly high wire of utopia is the risk of terrifying destruction. The director's later film *The Incredible Shrinking Man* also entertains the unforeseen effects of atomic advance, with a radioactive cloud leading to the diminution of the film's title. *The Black Scorpion* (1957) lets loose scaly arachnid terrors not through atomic but a volcanic explosion, yet these eruptions are so cataclysmic they nevertheless evoke recent wartime destruction, as does the revival of the screeching insect titan of *The Deadly Mantis* from the same year. In the latter, volcanic blasts in the South Pole trigger a glacial collapse on the other side of the world, unthawing the insect from its timeless tomb. This unlikely outcome is entertaining in its novelty, but it also implies the ultimate unpredictability of the earth we inhabit. Detected first by the continental swoop of radar, the mantis emerges to try our

Cold War security measures, and will soon be chased by jet fighters like an enemy aircraft. Not quite so big, although equally alarming, is the deformity at the center of Kurt Neumann's *The Fly* (1958), a mutation explicitly influenced by the wonders of atomic advance (or decline).

As we can see, throughout this era, horror cinema is immersed in the insecurities inherent in scientific breakthroughs and the political purposes to which they might be put. The bomb was the most disorientating high technology of the atomic age, and its framing in films like *Them!* and *The Beast from 20,000 Fathoms* hypothesizes further conceptual confusion, giving us narratives in which "lower" lifeforms are jolted to primacy. Most of us know that radiation exposure can cause genetic damage, but the idea of its creating humongous human-eating animals seems bizarrely arbitrary. However, the dedication to imagining atomic concerns in such a way is suggestive of the lingering influence of our species' history of predation. Perhaps, such films seem to imply, if our hubris continues unchecked we'll blow our lead on this planet, and our rivals will come storming back.

Eco Transgression, Planetary Payback

The ecological reconfigurations of films such as *Them!* and *The Beast from 20,000 Fathoms* were again emphasized throughout 1970s horror as they intertwined with contemporary environmental concern. In early 1969, over three million tons of oil were spilled into the ocean off the coast of Santa Barbara, California, covering thirty-five miles of beach and over eight hundred square miles of ocean,[9] decimating wildlife and instilling deep environmental worry; as a consequence, the first Earth Day was declared in 1970 to push for awareness and policy reform. As Wheeling and Ufberg point out, widespread reporting of the spill's degradation of the picturesque American landscape "got people thinking about how to balance their desires for economic progress (and cheap energy) with the emerging idea that humans have a moral obligation to protect the environment."[10] The same year, protests developed around U.S. nuclear weapons testing on the island of Amchitka in southwest Alaska, and Greenpeace was formed in 1970 in Vancouver before developing a worldwide presence throughout the 1970s. In 1972, the United Nations General Assembly gathered in Stockholm for the first Conference on the Human Environment to specifically address environmental issues, including resource renewability, wildlife protection, and pollution management; and World Environment Day was held for the first time in 1974 as a consciousness-raising initiative. It was also in the 1970s that scientists first realized that human-produced chemical emissions had the ability to cause ozone depletion,[11] with the increase in ultraviolet light expected to produce a rise in the rate of skin cancers as well as broader ecological and agricultural effects.

Several contemporary films engaged hot-button environmental issues, or at least used them to springboard or underwrite otherwise unlikely stories in which technology has taken us too far. In *Day of the Animals*, discussed earlier, a hole in the ozone layer induces aggression in the animals of a high-plains area of the United States, while *Frogs* (1972) claimed itself a tale of a time "when Nature strikes back." Despite the film's poster featuring a large frog with a human hand dangling from its chops, the majority of the human hunting is performed by other swamp creatures, especially snakes (and no humans are devoured by anyone). Nevertheless, the cinematography certainly favors the squat and pudgy frogs (actually South American toads), and scene changes are often punctuated by low-angle shots of them that confer a cryptic sense of menace.[12]

Callous environmental destruction is pointedly at issue in *Frogs*, as nature photographer Pickett Smith (Sam Elliott) cruises his canoe down the littered waterways of an island owned and occupied by wealthy patriarch Jason Crockett (Ray Milland). Once the photographer meets Crockett, it becomes clear that this old scoundrel has been spraying chemicals onto local wildlife to silence the frogs' annoying "ribbit" sound, and his similarly selfish family lament their taxes being spent on anti-pollution initiatives. It isn't long before the nonhuman natives begin their insurrection, with frogs waggling and slapping against the French doors. As Jennifer Schell points out, the film "represents natural ecosystems as possessing innate self-correcting mechanisms. When the Crocketts throw the environment out of equilibrium with their pesticides and pollution, the animals provide balance and restore order to the world."[13] The amphibian threat is also reflective of human tension. Crockett reveals that his family is gathered to celebrate a number of their birthdays that roughly coincide with the Fourth of July holiday. Despite the patriarch's plans, the Crockett clan are clearly disintegrating: one son is a drunk whose wife can't stand him, both of them hanging around only for the Crockett inheritance. Another son brings along his African American girlfriend, who befriends the Crockett family's black servants, testing traditional boundaries of class and race. The vision of a stratified society that Jason Crockett clings to is in decline, with the wheelchair-bound old man symbolizing its waning power. The Fourth of July setting (and the surname "Crockett") position the family as a metaphoric microcosm of the tensions of American society more broadly, and their struggle against the local wildlife is also symbolic of their struggle against the "natural" tide of social change.[14]

The cinematic apex predator of the 1970s was of course *Jaws*; while that film featured little environmental subtext (its serial-killing shark attacking without incitement or motive), it provided the influence and bankability of animal horror for films that did. While often cited as a mere *Jaws* clone, *Orca* absorbed the environmental consciousness of the era, though manifesting it not through techno-anxiety but rather through the egregious indifference to wildlife of its rogue captain. And in *Sssssss* (also from 1977), Dr. Stoner (Strother Martin), a herpetologist obsessed with his serpentine pets, experiments on his assistant to create a human-reptile superspecies that will outlive the catastrophes wrought by civilization's advance. In admiration of reptilian hardiness, Stoner strives to realize a new race, inoculated against the looming perils of progress, which seemed to many at the time of the film's production to be a genuine threat.

Nutty Professors and Zany Zoology

As *Sssssss* suggests, wayward scientific endeavors involving animals are regularly the tainted fruit of a single figure, a stock "mad scientist" type that predates (but may interact with) contemporary environmental concerns. Given that our culture typically speaks of animals as "irrational," the alliance is nicely ironic: an out-of-control creature birthed in the backfire of hyper-rationalism. The figure's most archetypal incarnation is of course Victor Frankenstein, the lone genius who transgresses known science and nature, alienated from society by his ambition but enthralled by his ability to author life itself. Although, as Ina Rae Hark points out, we may go so far as to say that "the scientist's quest for knowledge [also] suggests the forbidden fruit of the tree of knowledge and the first cause of the entry of evil into the world."[15]

The eight-legged freak at the center of Jack Arnold's *Tarantula* is the work of an overly ambitious scientist: biologist Professor Deemer (Leo G. Carroll) injecting a menagerie of caged animals with his special super-nutrient. The tarantula is roughly man-sized before it escapes, but the professor views his creation with scientific dispassion, overlooking the monstrousness obvious to the rest of us, and from which we know only trouble will come (Fig. 5.3). His obsession has also insulated him from concern for his fellow human, and he hides the body of one of his victims to prevent the law meddling in his (to him) all-important work. Another isolated experimenter is Dr. Moreau, H. G. Wells's madman from *The Island of Doctor Moreau*, realized in a number of films but most prominently in Don Taylor's 1977 version. Moreau (Burt Lancaster) attempts to mutate wild animals into humans to unlock the secrets of

Figure 5.3. Professor Deemer (Leo G. Carroll) inspects the oversized arachnid he has created in his lab in Jack Arnold's *Tarantula* (Universal, 1955). Soon it will escape, its growth continuing unabated. Digital frame enlargement.

genetic influence, but produces only hideous half-breeds. In *Piranha*, a reclusive scientist on a decommissioned military base has clung to his work enhancing aquatic carnivores as bioweapons for use in Vietnam. Similarly, in *Spiders*, arachnids have their DNA spliced with that of extraterrestrials in an attempt to engineer the ideal wartime attacker, although they of course escape to wreak havoc in the familiar fashion. However, here the blame is deflected away from the creators themselves and onto the government for which they work, demonstrating the vulnerability of scientific enterprise to corrupt commissioners.

The perennial controversy of animal research often injects these characters with moral repugnance as they toil on their volatile animal inventions. In *Man's Best Friend* (1993), Dr. Jarrett (Lance Henriksen), having been ejected from the mainstream scientific community for his experiments on endangered species, sets up a private research corporation to persist with much of the same behavior. His prized yet secret project is a Tibetan mastiff into which he has spliced the characteristics of various apex predators: the speed of the cheetah, the climbing ability of the jaguar, the strength of a bear, but also the chameleon's ability for camouflage (all of these exotic animals and more kept caged in the miserable menagerie of his lab). Journalist Lori Tanner (Ally Sheedy) breaks into his facility after hours and films the horrors she finds, including rabbits with ears cut off and a young orangutan with its brain exposed, snagging the kind of undercover footage we associate with animal rights groups. The range of captives and their horrific injuries suggest not a measured and sober scientific process but one descended into sadistic extravagance. Lori rescues the mastiff, who's faithful to her but potentially lethal to everyone else. The choice of animal in this film additionally underscores the scientist's inhumanity, since dogs are often linked with family life: this cynical and isolated scientist has not only eschewed domestic pleasures but also implicitly sought to corrupt them.

Hark notes that the mad scientist trope is often suggestive of anti-intellectualism. The uncomfortable awareness that some people may possess greater cognitive ability is dealt with through stories that denigrate their capacity to make benevolent, emotionally intelligent decisions.[16] If they hold better cards than us, we fear they'll play them to our detriment. In *Tarantula*, Hastings, the doctor who investigates the strange events, is for the viewer a more familiar and amiable form of intellectual authority, someone knowledgeable enough to outmaneuver the scientist's unhinged intellect, but not intimidatingly so. He's also distinguished by his attitude of awe and humility toward the natural world; he accepts that there is much beyond his abilities, while his professorial opponent is an arrogant meddler in creation. The theme of scientific vanity is also clear at the conclusion of *Piranha*, as a researcher (Barbara Steele) tells the media that the threat is contained because the ravening fishy horde cannot survive in the saltwater of the wider ocean. Despite the massacre that has just taken place, the scientist lies to perpetuate secrecy for her own reasons: "There's nothing left to fear." Moreover, she gives this phony assurance directly to the camera, a gesture that chills us with the calm deliberation of her dishonesty.

In light of these elitist intentions, such films regularly seek to remind us of a divine superiority over all. Christopher Tourney suggests that the philosophical and scientific boom of the Age of Enlightenment, which, beginning in the early 1700s, profoundly challenged traditional religious worldviews, was "shadowed by a strong antirationalism that remains powerful. Its manifestations include the feelings that science is downright dangerous to one's spiritual well-being and that science is too secular, in the sense that scientists have escaped the restraints of Judeo-Christian morality."[17] In *Werewolf of London* (1935), scientist Wilfred Glendon (Henry Hull) is infected on an expedition in Tibet to retrieve a rare flower despite the religious apprehension of his local guides. As Wilfred dies, the once-atheist werewolf speaks humbly of now meeting his maker. Similarly, in *Sssssss*, the mad scientist's degenerate atheism is explicit, but given the film's snake theme, accelerated into the satanically perverse. With the slyness of the serpents he so admires, Dr. Stoner hijacks and reconfigures creation toward his own agenda, his form of "reproduction" tied to his sacrilegious idolization of the snake as creation's true masterpiece. In *The Island of Dr. Moreau*, the doctor's own description of the island as "paradise" early in the film implies the corruption of a preexisting Eden, and he makes his mutants pledge to a set of commandments delivered from a ledge. This scientist has established for himself a godly position while demonstrating neither real godly power (his creations are all botched), nor divine compassion. Much later, in *Deep Blue Sea* (1999), one of the only survivors of genetically engineered sharks will be the film's cook (LL Cool J), nicknamed "Preacher," a character distinguished by his Christianity. In the end, reverence and humility are better rewarded than the hubris of Preacher's troublemaking high-IQ coworkers.

The nature of science is to breach the boundaries of current knowledge, and it has obviously brought us innumerable benefits. The occasional malfunction may be morally confronting, even despicable, but it's not enough to inspire us to renounce the whole enterprise: we understand, at some level, that mistakes and progress come hand in hand. And indeed, occasionally these characters have noble (if naïve) intentions. In *Deep Blue Sea*, for instance, the lead scientist (Saffron Burrows) seeks a cure for Alzheimer's, the disease that affected her father, by mining the cerebral fluid of sharks for therapeutic application. While differing markedly in tone, *Rise of the Planet of the Apes* also depicts well-intentioned experimentation. Although his profit-hungry colleagues might not share his deep motives, Will Rodman (James Franco) develops treatments tested on chimps to find a cure for his father's dementia. The drug stimulates the apes to super-intelligence, enabling them to confront human tormentors, but prior to this the film provides a moving portrayal of the father's mental degeneration. Yet, ultimately, as the chimps' righteous rebellion indicates, *Rise* admonishes us for stepping on those within our power in order to reach what we see as the higher peaks of progress.

Creative Minds and Contaminated Bodies: *The Fly*

Among the most celebrated monster movies of their respective eras, Kurt Neumann's *The Fly* from 1958, as well as David Cronenberg's loose 1986 remake, both dealing with the beastly effects of haywire science, deserve special focus. If we self-flatteringly take the human animal as the apex of cognitive sophistication and moral value, the fly seems representative of its indigent nadir. Of all the creatures to transform a man into, a fly seems dramatic not so much for the qualities that man might gain (like the heightened senses of the werewolf) as for the extent of his demotion in a hierarchy of life forms. The transformation of man into insect has perhaps its most prominent precursor in Franz Kafka's 1915 novella *The Metamorphosis*, in which a diligent young salesman, Gregor Samsa, awakens to find that he is now a giant insect, something like a beetle or cockroach, with the cause of the bizarre change never revealed. While the scenario would suggest hysterical alarm to most minds, Kafka's idiosyncratic treatment depicts Gregor as troubled foremost by the deep inconvenience to his ability to fulfill his socially expected role. The young man frets over missing the early train to work and ticking off his fastidious employers, and he dreads the burden he now presents to the parents who rely on him for financial support. Accordingly, for this hyper-attentive and intensely responsible character, the sudden transformation into such a lowly yet cumbersome creature seems at least partly a surreal expression of his self-effacing nature and pathological fear of dependence. Both versions of *The Fly* take a somewhat different approach: their science-fiction framing warns of the radical imprecision of scientific progress, and their focus on the bodily horror of man-insect transformation spotlights the deep repugnance of contamination, as well as (in Cronenberg's version especially) obscenely metaphorizing the primitive priorities of human organisms themselves.

The catalyst for this alarming creation in the 1958 version is the experimental work of André (David Hedison), a scientist working out of a lab in the basement of the home he shares with his doting wife Hélène (Patricia Owens) and young son, Philippe (Charles Herbert). Nauseated by travel, André creates a teleportation device that demolishes and reconstitutes one's physical form at the atomic level. But one day he accidentally splices himself with a fly that intrudes into the machine. The result is a man with a fly's head and a clawlike arm, and—somewhere buzzing around the house—a fly with a human head and one human limb. The tale of transformation is told in flashback, with André's wife under suspicion for her husband's death. Yet, as we discover, the murder was really an act of assisted suicide to end her lover's misery and eradicate evidence of the man-monster forever.

André's laboratory within the house indicates the scientist's inability to keep intellectual obsession and family life separate. After a bout of reclusion, he better lives up to his spousal role by taking his wife to the ballet, but during the show he can't help but begin scribbling equations on the program. His divided persona eventually culminates in his body becoming literally separated into opposing creatures: one confined to the basement for fear of exposure, the other too mobile, flying freely around and unable to be located. With his fly-head, the previously quixotic and restless—yet hardly unlikeable—André becomes explicitly repellent. When the cloth used to hide his visage is finally torn away, we see a bulbous black cranium embedded with oversized, goggle-like eyes and twitching mouthparts (Fig. 5.4). A shot from André's perspective, a multiple lensed fly's-eye-view of his hysterical wife, entrenches the new division between traumatized wife and transformed husband.

The choice of a fly clearly evokes the strangeness of insects, denizens of a world that encroaches upon and yet so little resembles our own. Houseflies specifically are alien in appearance (as macro photography confirms and André's fly-noggin approximates) but also highly familiar, even if unwanted. The confusion of man and fly is at once a horrible confusion of polar opposites but also a recognition of our uncomfortably shared existence. As we know, flies are also a disease hazard, and accordingly objects of human repulsion. When André's wife provides him with food, he eats it with his head covered by the cloth, but cannot help but use his hairy fly-hand to help break the meal into edible portions, pressing down disgustingly onto his steak. Later, he approaches Hélène as if for a kiss, but stops himself, surely aware that (his intentions aside) what he now offers is not the intimacy of the lover but the touch of disease.

André's transformation is prefigured by changes in his personality stereotypical of the mad scientist's waning compassion and humility.

Figure 5.4. Fly in the face of reason: Hélène (Patricia Owens) shrieks in terror as she sees her husband André (David Hedison) in his mutated form in *The Fly* (Kurt Neumann, 20th Century Fox, 1958). Digital frame enlargement.

The first living thing tested for teleportation is the family cat, which doesn't make the return trip—disseminated as a series of signals never to re-cohere as a flesh-and-blood being. We might be tempted to think that any ethical unease inspired in modern viewers by André's animal testing is unintended by a film from 1958, produced in a culture that did not much concern itself with animal welfare. However, it's clear that this represents a moral decline for André given that he'd earlier instructed his son to "play gently" with this same puss. Hélène is the voice of the film's future-shock hesitations, and this subtext pushes through pointedly when she discourses on "the suddenness of our age—electronics, rockets, Earth satellites, supersonic flight—and now this." Yet in defending his work before he accidentally metamorphoses, André compares it with television (the way a signal becomes disintegrated and re-integrated), locating the film amid numerous technological advances that revolutionized American life in the 1950s. The film's message is ultimately one of moderation: Hélène is too uncomfortable with the acceleration of technological advance, while André isn't uncomfortable enough. After his change, he writes a note to his wife conceding his error: "There are things man should never experiment with."

In body-horror maestro David Cronenberg's remake, the family man is replaced by an ambitious young scientific entrepreneur, Seth Brundle (Jeff Goldblum), craving opposite-sex attention (Fig. 5.5). Brundle woos

Figure 5.5. Ambitious young inventor Seth Brundle (Jeff Goldblum) tries to woo science journalist Ronnie Quaife (Geena Davis) by boasting of his big discovery in David Cronenberg's *The Fly* (Brooksfilms, 1986). Digital frame enlargement.

glamorous science reporter Ronnie (Geena Davis) back to his apartment with the promise of a private viewing of his great breakthrough, and they commence an affair as she documents his refinement of the teleportation machine toward the goal of carrying human cargo. When Brundle subjects himself to the device, the remake abjures the immediate appendage exchange of the earlier film: at first glance, all is normal. A few changes gradually appear, but they offer positive outcomes: increased sexual drive, strength, and athleticism. Yet Brundle's body gradually begins decaying, and his increasingly snappy temper drives Ronnie from the relationship. The bodily breakdown culminates in Brundle's metamorphosis into a rancid, staggering, and man-sized fly-beast, his human skin sloughing away as his ex-lover tries to squirm free of his hideous grasp.

Brundle shares André's inability to separate work and home, with living and lab space combined in his open-plan apartment. Yet the film's switch from a married father to a nerdy single guy is significant in driving the story. Seth's attempt to woo Ronnie with his invention is obviously a pickup strategy: as soon as he gets her back to the apartment, he seats himself behind a piano and ostentatiously batters out a melody, hoping to impress. After their relationship commences, Ronnie is hassled by her ex-boyfriend and current boss at the magazine, Stathis Borans (John Getz), who's jealous of the attention she affords her new subject. Ronnie wants nothing to do with Stathis, yet Brundle's insecurity is pricked hard by the perceived rival. The young man swigs from a bottle of scotch back at his apartment, ranting jealously to a baboon pet/test-subject as he worries that his girl is out doing God-knows-what with her former flame. That's when it happens: he teleports himself from one side of the room to the other in a mixture of jealous disregard for his own safety and desire to outdo a mate-rival. For all his intelligence, Brundle is unbalanced by his primitive emotional reactions—he will be undone by his primate desires, as the presence of his monkey listener implies.

The changes Brundle initially experiences after teleporting underscore the film's focus on male insecurity and rivalry, since they take the form of hypermasculine traits he previously lacked. When Ronnie notices new hairs on her lover's body, Brundle expresses delight in his new manliness: "I've been looking forward to a hairy body." Yet the giddy science nerd soon becomes the bullying macho-man, and he insists that Ronnie also try the teleporter. When she refuses, he walks out in a rage and into a local bar. Here he snaps a man's wrist in an arm-wrestling contest in which the winner gets to take home a woman who watches on. In this scene, we see that the young geek's masculinity has become so primitive that he eagerly embraces a brutal dominance contest for mating rights.

In line with its director's body-horror pedigree, the remake ratchets up the evocation of flies as a source of bacterial contamination. Despite Brundle's macho energy after teleporting, Ronnie notices her lover's sweaty and blemished skin: "There's something wrong with you, Seth, you're sick," she pleads. There's worse to come: fingernails pop out in creamy ooze and sores open on Brundle's face as the human cedes biological ground to the genetic intruder. In Cronenberg's version, hybridization does not manifest as simply mutation (the emergence of phenotypic fly traits), but as widespread infection. Indeed, barring the ultimate stage of transformation, there is little that is overtly "fly-like" about Brundle; what we see is closer to a rampant and disfiguring series of infections. The impression of disease hazard becomes feverishly heightened when Ronnie discovers that she's pregnant by this human genetic meltdown. She arranges an abortion, but dreams before the procedure of doctors removing from her uterus a gigantic squirming maggot. Obviously, Brundle is not such an attractive male candidate with whom to be reproducing right now—an unprecedented human compost of maladaptive mutations—but he is also a walking avatar of disease.

Our sympathy for the volatile and bad-tempered Brundle strengthens toward the film's conclusion. Recognizing that his personality is increasingly corrupted by the primitive priorities of the insect, he fears for Ronnie's safety and advises her, with the few remaining vestiges of his humanity, to stay well away (Fig. 5.6). We recognize in the young

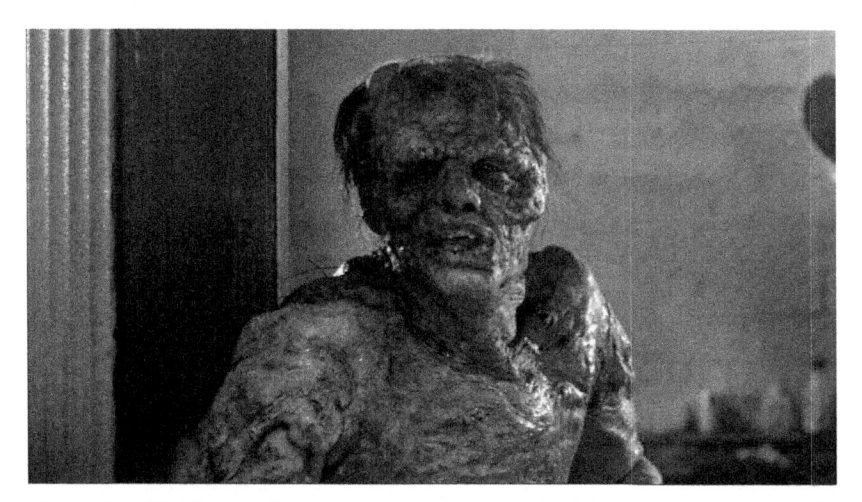

Figure 5.6. "You have to leave now, and never come back here": Seth Brundle (Jeff Goldblum), already substantially mutated, warns his lover Ronnie (Geena Davis, out of frame) away before he reaches the peak of his terrifying transformation in *The Fly* (David Cronenberg, Brooksfilms, 1986). Digital frame enlargement.

scientist one tamed and shamed by his own hubris. But it's too late, and Brundle's decay proceeds toward an outcome that, however reckless he may have been, he could not have foreseen and hardly deserves.

Big Dreams and Big Problems:
From *Jurassic Park* to *Jurassic World*

Steven Spielberg's *Jurassic Park* (1993) contains surely one of the most commercially successful and culturally resonant depictions of animal predators rejuvenated by techno-wizardry. And those predators are formidable indeed: dinosaurs, the extinction of which circa 65 million years ago, as paleontologists postulate, allowed mammals like us to prosper.[18] Now they're back, thanks to the eager and enterprising mind of John Hammond (Richard Attenborough), another scientific meddler unable to clearly contemplate the limits of his knowledge and control (Fig. 5.7). While not a scientific genius himself, the affable and mega-rich Hammond has in his employ scientists at the vanguard of DNA manipulation. They will help him realize his vision of an island theme park of real dino attractions, before system and security failures famously unleash the animals' carnivorous and human-inclusive appetites. A romantic entrepreneur, Hammond walks with a bamboo stick suggestive of an enthusiasm for jungle adventure, and topped with a polished stone of petrified amber from which his scientists extract the eons-old dinosaur DNA—an item

Figure 5.7. "Welcome to Jurassic Park": having revealed a majestic brachiosaurus to his guests, John Hammond (Richard Attenborough) proudly announces his creation in Steven Spielberg's *Jurassic Park* (Universal, 1993). Digital frame enlargement.

outwardly archaic yet in reality a modern gem of scientific progress. Clad in a white, short-sleeved shirt and pressed pants, a safari suit–like combo, Hammond is nevertheless too pristine, a man who enjoys the image of adventure but who's unprepared for the grime. As befits this cultivated image, in his dealings with the park's early visitors, Hammond's desire to please is overwhelmingly apparent. He performs hammily in a child-friendly educational film included on the tour, stresses his desire to keep prices reasonable to appeal to all classes, and repeats as a catchphrase his assurance that even on trivial park features he has "spared no expense." When his grandchildren join a tour of the park, he embraces them with genuine and touching excitement, a doting grandfather eager to indulge and entertain young visitors.

Hammond is the enterprise's proud patriarch but not the lone mastermind behind it, and on a tour of the park's laboratory he reveals his scientific coalface crew. The chief geneticist is Henry Wu (BD Wong), who leans nonchalantly against a table as the tour group arrives in time to witness a tiny raptor neonate breach its shell. With his pencil eraser Wu scrubs an error from whatever he was writing on a clipboard as he greets the group. What was it? A misspelling—perhaps a miscalculation? No matter: as his explanation of the genetic process indicates, Mr. Wu is quite confident of all final results. Hammond tenderly coaxes the raptor baby from its cracked egg. He oversees all the births, he says, reinforcing his pampering and parental role. But he's also babying one of the creatures that, at full-size, made traumatically short work of a park employee in the film's opening scene. "What species is this," asks visiting paleontologist Alan Grant (Sam Neill) uneasily, already recognizing its budding menace. From early in the film, we know all about Grant's ambivalence toward children: his character arc repairs this through his protection of Hammond's grandchildren. Yet here is one situation in which his apprehension toward an infant is well placed.

Hammond's foil comes in the form of Ian Malcolm, a black-clad, self-styled academic rockstar played by Jeff Goldblum (by now a veteran of mad-science cinema). Malcolm is an expert in Chaos Theory, a consultant brought in at Hammond's lawyers' behest to diagnose potential problems. And diagnose he does—the ostentatious goof revealing himself to be the unlikely voice of moral reason. Malcolm comes hard after Hammond, critiquing both his disrespect for the cycles of nature that struck dinosaurs dead long ago and his cavalier attitude to genetic power. While *Jurassic Park* is without the explicit religious subtext of films like *Werewolf of London* or *Sssssss*, it still promotes deference toward a mysterious and abstract Nature, genetic interference with which is similarly sacrilegious.

As Malcolm tells Hammond, "The lack of humility that's being displayed before nature here staggers me." In reality, while its successful manipulation may require knowledge of our limits, Nature does not ask us to display humility before it—it isn't a deity. But Malcolm's words insinuate the importance of a traditional Christian modesty. Accordingly, Malcolm doesn't isolate any particular systemic fault to which he objects: the whole thing is a problem, and we're encouraged to feel that Hammond's error, like that of Satan in *Paradise Lost*, is his general pride and audacity.

Nevertheless, a particular fault or two does emerge: spontaneous genetic mutation and the compromise of key security systems by a money-grubbing employee engaged in corporate espionage. If greed doesn't figure in the idealistic Hammond's vision, it might figure in the visions of those on whom he relies. Hammond finally concedes to the naysayers after chaos hits, although not before being lectured by paleobotanist Ellie Sattler (Laura Dern) as he eats alone in the park's restaurant, the shelves of the nearby gift shop already stocked with merchandise to please eager visitors. Reminiscing on his ambitions, the aging inventor explains to Ellie his first creation, a motorized flea circus, describing the delight and family interaction it inspired in its audience. The park, he explains, was intended to show them "something real, not devoid of merit." In a harsh self-assessment, denigrating his past work, Hammond casts himself as a charlatan whose earlier efforts only simulated creation—not like the literally reproductive park. But it isn't all ego: we can see a man delighted by his inventions' capacity for family fun and excitement. Moreover, given the film's early mention of his daughter's divorce, his desire for the success of this supercharged flea circus might well be wrapped up in a grandfather's desire to restore an idealized family unity.

As the helicopter swoops away from the island to safety at the end of the film, and the film's once-triumphal theme tinkles softly, Hammond stares forlornly at the amber top of his cane, slowly rotating this wondrous yet now-thwarted seed of discovery (Fig. 5.8 on page 132). Alan Grant sits with Hammond's sleeping grandchildren snuggled against him, finally accustomed to the potential joys of reproduction as his lover Ellie, seated opposite, smilingly approves. From Grant's perspective, we see pelicans cruise gracefully above sun-kissed water outside the helicopter, a sublime shot suggestive of the wonder of the world (and of the animals) already around them—a wonder that doesn't need complicated genetic resurrection. Hammond stays fixated on his flawed vision. He thereby misses the spectacle of natural creation outside the window, as well as the family unity right beside him. As the film closes, he remains a man obsessively attuned to possibility—or to the past—but not to the present.

Figure 5.8. What might have been: with the survivors ferried out of harm's way in *Jurassic Park* (Steven Spielberg, Universal, 1993), and thankful for their safety, John Hammond (Richard Attenborough) rests his eyes sadly on the genesis of his now-botched dream of Creation. Digital frame enlargement.

The prehistoric havoc returns in the sequel, *The Lost World: Jurassic Park* (1997), set primarily on a neighboring island used as a breeding facility, where dinosaurs have now been living for four years unattended. InGen, the genetics company founded by Hammond, has sent a militarized team of experts to round up the dinosaurs with the intention of creating a new theme park in San Diego. Hammond, apparently having learned something from the previous panic, wants his creations left alone without human interference, his paternal streak now nicely uncorrupted by vanity. But he's been ousted from the board of the company, so he hires a team of naturalists, filmmakers, and experts to film the dinos in order to court public sympathy and sabotage InGen's attempts to remove them. With the science fiction groundwork having been laid by the earlier film, *The Lost World* places further emphasis on jungle adventure and the attempts of Hammond's crew to stymy the InGen exploiters. Yet the company's actions tap into and expand the original film's concern with the corporatization of science: Hammond may have had a change of heart, but the market will always produce more opportunistic predators, striving to wring from these expensive creations every dollar they can. As we expect, the company crew have all of the power and none of the wisdom, and the dinos are soon back to shredding corporate plans, and personnel.

The franchise's adventure elements continued in Joe Johnston's *Jurassic Park III* (2001), structured around a rescue mission for a young boy who drifts onto the dino isle after a parasailing mishap. But an emphasis on mad science, specifically, returned with a vengeance in Colin Trevorrow's *Jurassic World* (2015), some fourteen years afterward. As *World* opens, we see a close-up of baby dinos breaking out of their eggs, and as the shot gently withdraws we can distinguish a laboratory environment around them: the hard-learned lessons of the previous films have obviously been forgotten and new dinosaurs concocted. We soon learn that Hammond's work has been extravagantly commercialized into a lavish new park, "Jurassic World," already open for young and old. Claire Dearing (Bryce Dallas Howard) is the park's hyper-attentive operations manager, and early in the film she leads a trio of corporate execs on a tour of the business side, explaining the demand that drives innovation: "Consumers want them bigger, louder, more teeth." Advances in genetic modification have been able to oblige, and the park now offers corporate sponsorship for new attractions. The latest investment opportunity is the newly created forty-foot carnivore "Indominus rex," which will also become the film's central terror. The Indominus is a brute bigger than T. rex, with overhanging teeth like a crocodile and cadaverously pale skin that befits its Frankensteinian nature, for the Indominus is a genetic grab-bag of super-predator features. This hybrid makeup means a greater chance of unforeseen mutations, and thus consequences: the animal escapes its enclosure with its velociraptor-like problem-solving intelligence, its ability to control its own body temperature to elude infrared scanners, and its unexpected power to self-camouflage. This monster is like no predator that ever was, and when it gets loose it acts that way, laying waste to everything it comes across, slaughtering staff, tourists, and other dinosaurs alike—leaving enormous Apatosaurs scattered dead over the park's plains.

Hammond's head scientist Mr. Wu returns to become the amoral face of corporatized science. Clad in a black turtleneck like Steve Jobs and sipping Jasmine tea in his private office, Wu is now a rich and refined overseer of his lab-coated colleagues. His manner is professional and dispassionate, in calm contrast to the negligent science he authorizes. When the park's new owner, Simon Masrani (Irrfan Khan), informs him of the Indominus's trail of butchery, Wu expresses disappointment but shows no great alarm. And when Masrani asks him who approved such unstable modifications, the genetic wizard puts the blame back onto his boss Masrani, citing his request for "bigger, scarier, cooler" beasts, and casting himself as merely a hardworking conduit to the wishes handed down from superiors, without any ethical responsibility himself. Masrani is no scientist; he's concerned primarily with presenting visitors with a thrilling product. His requests may indeed be foolish; but the film makes clear that Mr. Wu knows better and grants dangerous dreams anyway.

The film's focus on this new genetic monstrosity has the intriguing effect of naturalizing the creatures with which we're already familiar, and which at least existed in prehistory. While we know that all of the dinosaurs have some degree of genetic modification to correct genome gaps, the Indominus is an abominable concoction that thrusts the others back into verisimilitude. The emblematic showdown between the natural and acceptable and the freakish and ungodly forms the film's climax. Attempting to detain the Indominus so humans can flee, Claire runs to the pen containing the Tyrannosaurus, the main monster of the original film, and using a flare leads the unknowing dino into combat against the larger and deadlier Indominus. We know the Tyrannosaurus is a tough beast from a tough world, but this fight is hardly fair. The rex is at least a "real" animal, but now it faces a supernormal predator with no ecological precedent. The Tyrannosaur fights with admirable tenacity, but takes a savage and bloody beating from its enhanced opponent. Yet the rex still manages (only just, and with some assistance) to conquer its bigger rival, through which turn the film also signals the triumph of the "natural." As *Jurassic World* closes, we see the battle-scarred Tyrannosaur stride atop one of the park's elevated helipads to survey the island. The setting sun casts the horizon in a golden glow as the rex emits a mighty roar, thundering far across its domain (Fig. 5.9). The terrible abnormal alpha

Figure 5.9. Having vanquished the cruel and freakish Indominus rex, a concoction of mad science and marketing, the Tyrannosaurus rules again in Colin Trevorrow's *Jurassic World* (Universal, 2015). Digital frame enlargement.

that terrorized the ecosystem, indiscriminately killing all in its path, has fallen, and the Tyrannosaur's natural dominance is proudly and properly restored: the once and future Tyrant King.

For all their animal havoc, the films discussed in this chapter give us only ourselves to blame—for creatures foolishly placed back into ecological circulation, or tormentors constructed anew. Whether framed by an explicitly religious sense of order or not, these films assume a natural hierarchy of creation with which it is taboo to tamper, accidentally or otherwise. Science has been responsible for human advances too numerous and beneficial to list or even easily comprehend. However, these techno-horrors suggest an ongoing suspicion of promethean intellectual feats, with their questionable power, their corrupted ethics, or their susceptibility to too-human ideologies, accidents, or self-interests.

6

In Their Sights

The Gaze of the Predator

JAWS: THE REVENGE (1987), the franchise's final installment, begins as Spielberg's original film did by showing us the roaming point-of-view attached to the perilous "jaws" at issue. The shark scans the ocean bottom as Michael Small's score (incorporating John Williams's iconic motif) churns ominously away, even sticking its head above the surface near a jetty to eyeball the human world above. At the sequence's conclusion, however, we see a still shot of an unblinking eye—a cold pool of black—the camera having apparently now turned back on the silent undersea starer. Here is the ocean fiend out of whose eyes we were just watching. A fraction of a second later, we realize, no—this eye belongs to something dead (and deathly still). The menacing mood evaporates as we hear a sizzling. There's another cut, and we grasp the reality: we're elsewhere, and this is the eye of a harmless fish, simmering away in Ellen Brody's pan as she cooks dinner in her home. We thought we glimpsed it, the marine monster preparing to strike, but we didn't, and that means it's still out there—the far bigger fish to fry. The implicit matching, then mismatching, of these shots taunts us with a kind of false seeing, denying us the sense of control implicit in at least getting a look at this creature: the ability to objectify the predator, gauge its size, proximity, and threat. The shark will remain hidden from our view, its autonomous point-of-view (and evasion of our own) linked to the violence it is poised to inflict.

This deceptive play around predatory point-of-view, a central motif in the *Jaws* films, is also exemplary of a broader fascination with "seeing" in animal horror: the power of animals to take us in their sights, and to evade or refuse our own visual control. The imagery of staring, glowing, or generally menacing eyes abounds. As Kong pushes his growling head through the trees to confront the manacled Ann Darrow in *King Kong* (1933), we witness the ape's empowered appraisal of the sacrifice the tribesmen have left chained in front of him. Later, and on the loose in Manhattan, the ape clambers up Ann's apartment building in search of his runaway bride and peers through the window behind her, at this great height, and with surprising stealth, his visual power seeming almost omnipotent (Fig. 6.1).

Many years later, in *The Grey*, when John Ottway waves a flaming torch at the blackness beyond his crew's campfire, he sees only the burning eyes of their pursuers, a constellation of malign stars. As the *Jaws* franchise suggests, a potent manifestation of this theme is the first-person simulation of an animal's gaze, especially as it takes humans in its sights, as enemy, edible, or both. In Spielberg's original, of course, while naked Chrissie's male admirer is passed out uselessly on the sand, she's

Figure 6.1. Peeping Kong: Jack Driscoll (Bruce Cabot) assures Ann Darrow (Fay Wray) of her safety in her upstairs apartment in *King Kong* (Merian C. Cooper & Earnest B. Schoedsack, RKO, 1933). But Kong, by peering through windows, has located her almost immediately. Digital frame enlargement.

appraised from the shark's perspective not as a mate but as a morsel. Since Spielberg's film, depictions of animals' predatory focus became especially widespread. The opening credit sequence of *Day of the Animals*, released shortly after *Jaws*, includes cryptic close-ups of animal eyes—an owl, puma, and hawk gaze directly into the lens. In *Orca*, the eye is the key symbol of the animal's power: at one point the Captain is reflected in its lens, centered and locked for vengeance like the target of a missile.

Movies, of course, are not produced by nonhumans. Animal point-of-view shots don't manifest the autonomous behavior or intentions of real animals, nor are such shots likely very faithful representations of what appears visually for them. In a famous 1974 essay, "What is it like to be a bat?," philosopher Thomas Nagel explains that while we probably all accept that bats do have experiences, their vastly differing sensory equipment—namely, their ability to "see" via echolocation—means we're simply without the biological equipment to accurately understand that experience. Even if we might imagine to some extent what it would be like to possess bat biology, we are only imagining what it is like for us: the bat's own experience of being a bat remains inaccessible. Nagel acknowledges that to some extent this problem can exist between individual humans (especially, for instance, if one of them is deaf or blind); yet the animal suggests a more insuperable division.[1] Although bats obviously differ from sharks, wolves, lions, and spiders, the bat example vividly illustrates the problem of accurately experiencing animal perspectives broadly. Even if through rigorous scientific analysis and application we could cinematically reconstruct (for example) how a shark sees the world, the fidelity would be illusory: we'd still process the images in our own way—we can't feel what visual stimuli mean to the shark. Accordingly, through these point-of-view shots we immerse ourselves in human interpretations of what the animal might see. Such shots are necessarily "analogies," ones structured around human visual systems, but in the moment of viewing they are intended to be understood narratively as faithful to their animal subjects. As Gregersdotter and Hållén summarize, "Just as the modernist literary technique of stream of consciousness is not so much a mimetic representation of a psychological reality as a rhetorical technique, these filmic techniques are nothing more or less than signs that signify the phenomena that constitute subjectivity."[2]

In some instances, these point-of-view shots, in their color, clarity, or movement, are not very different from those of a human, and any difference comes in the animal behavior the shot suggests (flying or swimming or scurrying). Yet more often the animal's predatory gaze will be marked out somehow: in *Anaconda*, shots from the creature's point-of-view employ cranes and canted framing intended to simulate a serpent's tilting and twisting diagonally through space (its vision is "crooked," both literally and morally). Or a qualitative in-camera or post-production effect might be used: in *Snakes on a Plane* (2006) the serpents see with smeary thermal vision; in *Bad Moon* (1996) images from lupine points-of-view are stretched along the horizontal axis; *The Ghost and the Darkness* attributes its feline man-eaters with monochrome night vision (Fig. 6.2).

Predatory first-person perspectives are not unique to animal horror. Notable outside examples including slasher films such as *Deep Red* (1975) and *Halloween* (1978). *Murder by Decree* (1978) and *Friday the 13th* (1980) engage the technique as well. In these examples we experience a disorientating, unstoppable, and perhaps even voyeuristic view of transgression, but also one accompanied by the concealment of the culprit for dramatic and narrative purposes. Both types of film elicit anxiety by withholding their culprits from the familiarizing power of our vision—we don't get even the minor sense of awareness that comes with seeing our attacker. Yet whereas the standard cinematic serial killer, however monstrous, is a fellow human, the animal point-of-view implies that which is alien in physical, moral, and experiential terms, and is thus arguably the apex of the technique's uncanny effect. Over and over again in animal horror we discover ourselves to be targets, physically imperiled by an autonomous force able to enforce its brutal interpretation of us. Through other eyes, we see ourselves as prey, as lunch—as subject to a foreign translation of our value in which our essential humanity is lost.

Figure 6.2. John Patterson (Val Kilmer) tries to aim his rifle atop a hunting platform at night in *The Ghost and the Darkness* (Stephen Hopkins, Paramount, 1996). The human can't see his prey, but we know the lion can as the film immerses us in its night vision. Digital frame enlargement.

Taking a Look at Ourselves

Animal horror's emphasis on the animal's gaze is perhaps usefully considered in the context of the pervasiveness of the human tendency to look at animals. Art critic John Berger wrote of what he saw as the disappearance of animals from everyday life: whereas once humans lived in a sort of organic "parallelism" with animals, he suggests, real animals are now relatively absent. In their place, he sees a vast vocabulary of images and associations through which they have become caricatured. Foremost, he argues, animals are now things to look at, their objectification furthering our distance from them.[3] The institutions that reinforce the normalcy of looking at animals for pleasure are of course numerous. Perhaps most obviously, zoos, while touting conservation and educational value, exist for the public for this purpose. Cinema, too, has long been such an institution. Since Eadweard Muybridge's experimental motion photography of the running racehorse "Sallie Gardner" and rider in 1878, animals have never been far from cinematic spectacle.[4] Accordingly, it's not surprising that animal attacks be cinematically staged with such persistent reference to their points-of-view, intervening into so many one-way projections onto the animal.[5]

The sight of the animal looking permits our identification with the creature, at least to some extent, because it's a behavior we understand. Gregersdotter, Hållén, and Höglund point out that "close-ups of animals' eyes are used in many animal horror films to signal a psychological connection between human and animal adversaries, which likewise implies the presence of a human-like internal world in the animal."[6] As per Nagel, the animal's embodied experience may remain cryptic to us, but our acceptance of an internal world generally (what psychologists call a "theory of mind") is important. Studies of visual cognition indicate that humans are highly sensitive to gaze-direction in others, and it's probable that this is linked with the engagement of anti-predator responses.[7] We know that we look at dangerous animals because it makes good survival sense to be interested in potential threats.[8] We're smart enough to intuit that if looking allows us to size up our predators, it also allows them to size up their prey. I mentioned in the introduction to this book that locals boating in the Sundarbans delta of India and Bangladesh will wear facemasks on the backs of their heads to deter man-eating tigers because big cats prefer stalking prey that hasn't spotted them.[9] Through such an example we can see eye-gaze as an important cue across species, for predators and prey, in terms of calculating the intention of the other. Barrett points out that the difference between predators and other environmental hazards like cliffs or toxins is their intentionality: "They are animate, sentient beings that process information and behave in the service of goals that they are well-adapted to achieve and that are in opposition to those of humans."[10] We can't afford not to care what they think or do. The gaze of the predator compels us to recognize the presence of another mind, and to do the best we can to predict its intentions. However, in the case of horror cinema's first-person predatory perspectives, we don't have that chance. Seeing only ourselves, we're deprived of one of the few predictive cues that we have, and the only thing left to feel is fear.

Cover Your Eyes from *The Birds*

Birds haven't had a prolific career in horror cinema: Hitchcock's film thronging with angry avians is largely an outlier. Most of us don't recognize the world's feathered beasts as too much to worry about compared with their toothier terrestrial cousins. Eagles are of course formidable hunters, often of prey larger than themselves; golden eagles, for instance, will sometimes drag mountain goats over cliffs to kill them. While humans have little to fear these days, our ancestors would not have been so complacent. The famous fossil skull of a two-million-year-old Australopithecus africanus child discovered in 1924 bore markings consistent with those left by birds of prey, indicating that he or she was snatched by the head and carried off by a prehistoric eagle.[11] British bird expert Leslie Hilton Brown comments: "Even today I would not put it past an eagle to take and kill an infant left out in the open, perhaps uncovered and wriggling. . . . And though I will not nowadays believe that a swaddled baby in a pram in Switzerland will be snatched up into the air by a non-existent Lammergeier [bearded vulture], I will accept that at some distant time in human memory some such thing may have happened as a factual basis for fable."[12] In an excellent essay, Mary Ellen Bellanca has connected such threats to Daphne du Maurier's original story "The Birds," on which Hitchcock's film was loosely based, while also making reference to its adaptation.[13] If we retain somewhere the archaic apprehension that animals may strike from above, it may be that Hitchcock's film is able to "unsettle our complacency" in an otherwise comfortable modern environment.[14]

The story itself begins harmlessly enough. A self-possessed young socialite, Melanie Daniels (Tippi Hedren), meets handsome lawyer Mitch Brenner (Rod Taylor) in a San Francisco bird store, where he apparently mistakes her for an attendant and asks after a pair of lovebirds for his young sister. With an appetite for mischief, Melanie plays along, although Mitch is wise to her ruse; he knows very well who she is, having glimpsed her in court defending against some minor scandal. After smugly exposing Melanie's gag, Mitch departs, leaving Melanie intrigued by the stranger. An entitled prankster, she discovers this mystery man's name and plans to bring a pair of lovebirds to him at his home in Bodega Bay, where he lives with his possessive mother, Lydia (Jessica Tandy), and younger sister, Cathy (Veronica Cartwright). Having cheekily delivered the gift into the very living room while Mitch and family are absent, Melanie is spotted by Mitch anyway—just as a gull incongruously swoops at her, scratching her head (Fig. 6.3). Mitch comes to her aid and, back at the house, she meets Cathy and his mother, from whom she receives a frosty greeting. The birds get a lot battier from this point on, and the Brenners and their visitor, as well as the townsfolk at large, are soon besieged by the hostile birds of Bodega Bay.

The threat posed by the creatures is frequently ocular: "Cover your faces—cover your eyes!" Mitch shouts as birds cascade down the chimney to hurtle around the living room. As the children flee from the schoolyard, a ponytailed girl in a red jumper is knocked over, leaving

Figure 6.3. Large Hedren collider: a gull careens down on Melanie Daniels (Tippi Hedren), scratching her forehead in the first move by the eponymous antagonists of *The Birds* (Alfred Hitchcock, Universal, 1963). Digital frame enlargement.

her prey for the pecking pests. Her eyeglasses are flung to the ground and crack, her vulnerability thereby highlighted through this visual symbol. The film's opening credits, in which bird silhouettes flit and flap hectically across the screen, uses the boundaries of the frame to make anticipation of their approach impossible, linking the animals with visual panic. The most shocking manifestation of this motif, however, is Lydia's discovery of the corpse of her farmer neighbor, Dan Fawcett, slumped against a bedroom wall with its eyes pecked out (Fig. 6.4). The revelation of Dan's gruesome injury comes through an advancing triple jump cut, then a further cut that quickly averts our gaze. While this moment is unusually graphic for Hitchcock, in seeing this man, who has been violently deprived of his own ability to see, we're nevertheless barred from a stable shot that would allow us to adjust to the sight. In practical terms, the cinematography here preserves the effect of the gory make-up, since looking longer would allow us time to spot the illusion. Yet also, as Slavoj Žižek writes, in terms of our emotional response, "these quickly advancing shots . . . frustrate us even as they indulge our desire to view the terrifying object more closely: we approach it too quickly, skipping over the 'time for understanding,' the pause needed to 'digest,' to integrate the brute perception of the object."[15]

Figure 6.4. Don't look now: erratic cutting allows us only a quick yet gruesome glance at the corpse of the Brenner family's neighbor, found with his eyes pecked out, in *The Birds* (Alfred Hitchcock, Universal, 1963). Digital frame enlargement.

Let's say that Hitchcock's tale of a screeching sky-borne menace owes some of its uncanny resonance to a hazy ancestral suspicion of what might swoop from above. The birds' rebellion is still weird enough that even casual viewers are harassed by the question of why they're doing it—the question the film never properly answers. Perhaps the most popular historically among scholars are interpretations centering on the film's familial and romantic turmoil as a Freudian drama in which the animals express Lydia's anger and possessiveness. Margaret Horowitz writes that the birds "function as a kind of malevolent superego, an indirect revelation of Lydia's character. She is a possessive mother intent upon furthering a symbiotic, oedipal relationship with her son."[16] Yet this interpretation is undermined by the birds' attack on irrelevant targets, like school children or Lydia's neighbor, Dan. Žižek's broader approach, through the lens of Lacanian psychoanalysis, can account to some extent for this problem: the birds aren't so much "symbols" as they are explosive and incoherent manifestations of unconscious oedipal turmoil.[17] In his documentary *The Pervert's Guide to Cinema* (2006), Žižek refers to the birds as an outburst of "raw, incestuous energy" that cannot be reconciled with—that instead rip through—"the natural set-up of reality."[18] They don't make sense because inarticulate primal energy doesn't translate neatly into a stable reality; it disrupts it. This analysis is somewhat dissatisfying since it's broadly unfalsifiable; any inconsistencies we notice can be dismissed because "inconsistency" itself is the interpretation's defining characteristic. But the idea of a destabilized reality does seem to capture something of the effect of those pecked-out eyes: the three quick still shots that bring us closer to empty sockets without letting us truly grasp what we see. The moment seems to insinuate a horrifying hollow in the world of meaning.[19] In a sensitive reading, Murray Pomerance views this moment a little differently, linking the spectacle not so much to an emptiness of all meaning as to what forever eludes human comprehension. For him, Dan's eyes manifest like "portals into the dark abyss" hinting at a kind of terrible supernatural sight that understands the otherwise cryptic nature of the film's attackers: "The dead Fawcett . . . sees the birds for what they are and credits them with an identity that Melanie Daniels only fears and suspects. . . ."[20] The quickly advancing shots hit us with the initial shock of mutilation, yet the lingering effect of those dark sockets is something more, a sense that, on the other side of death, Dan "finally really does see, and see what we have been blinded to all along."[21] However, to us, the mystery of the birds' intentions must remain something blackly and ungraspably beyond our own sight.

With her focus on the birds as evocations of ancestral threats, Bellanca sees the brutal yet confusing assault (of which Dan's emptied eye sockets are a particularly trenchant symbol, however interpreted) as part of the disorientation of being prey: "In the unreadable mystery of the birds' attacks, the story also regresses humans into an epistemologically primitive state in which they cannot understand the fate that befalls them and, like unwary hominids plucked from the gene pool, run out of time to figure it out."[22] Our confusion about the animals' motive, she argues, is part and parcel of immersing us in the panic of predation, at one time a feature of our existence. The various interpretations touched on above can be aligned at least in that they emphasize the subversion of humans' ability to make direct sense of the world around them. And it is through an assault on our primary "meaning making" sense—vision—that this subversion is evoked.

In the final scene, the amassed avians watch the human protagonists leave while curiously withholding attack, their unexpected and eerie abatement causing them to further recede into unknowability. As Mitch, Melanie, Lydia, and Cathy shuffle nervously into the car, they do so under the view of all these birds; yet no individual stare is identified. At this point they are thoroughly under the communal gaze of the creatures—something intolerably threatening but unable to be met, pinpointed, or understood.

The Eyes of *Jaws*

Although we don't see the shark of *Jaws* directly until about forty minutes into the film, its iconic initial attack centralizes notions of seeing and of being seen. Having at least heard of the film or seen the poster, we already know that the underwater first-person perspective depicted in the credits is that of a killer shark, but the choice to leave it unframed by any human perspective underscores the animal's worrying autonomy and stealth. From the predator's perspective we'll see the naked Chrissie as she frolics, framed for slaughter. She never sees her aggressor coming, and her dopey admirer (passed out on the sand) not only doesn't help her but, later, can't even provide an account of what happened.

Looking (and failing to look) is centralized in *Jaws* in several ways. Previously possessed of an empowered sense of her naked self, Chrissie, through the gaze of the creature, becomes starkly vulnerable. In a famous contemplation of being stared at while naked by his pet cat, philosopher Jacques Derrida suggests that in the experience of nakedness before an animal (even a cat) the threat of attack is somehow evoked—it seems "on the [the animal's] lips or on the tip of the tongue."[23] Derrida focuses on the "shame" of such an encounter, the shame "of being naked as a beast." Of course, the animal is also naked, but it doesn't know or feel that it is naked, and in that sense it is not naked: "Because it is naked," Derrida writes, "without existing in its nakedness, the animal neither feels nor sees itself naked."[24] Although a shark is very different from a cat, perhaps some of these feelings of vulnerability through nakedness overlap when we see the nude Chrissie taken in the sights of the more confidently and organically naked animal predator.

More obviously, the animal's gaze also occurs in the context of the male trying to take Chrissie in his own sights (and arms). Not the passive loner she seems, Chrissie quickly seizes control of the encounter, allowing her admirer a lot more to look at (even putting on a kind of graceful "performance" in the water). Yet at the moment the young man disqualifies himself, the girl is taken as the object of an unwanted and more menacing "admirer"—a creature who will, in its own way, visually appraise and pursue her. In an outcome depicted in the following scene, the shark eventually transforms the girl into something to repel the gaze: the lifeguard who finds Chrissie's corpse blows his whistle to alert those around him but then averts his eyes in nausea. Peter Biskind, writing in *Jump Cut* in 1975, felt that the shark was itself a symbol of the same male's desire: "The shark, all too obviously, can only be the young man's sexual passion, a greatly enlarged, marauding penis." I think most viewers would probably question how "obvious" that truly is. Rather, the shark seems to emerge in the space of the boy's inattention, demonstrating his failure as a sexual and protective force. As the girl waits naked and ready, in rushes the predator to seize that which has been framed for (but relinquished by) male sexual desire.

Male control is of course contested by the shark in the narrative more broadly through the challenge it lays down to the town's new policeman. Indeed, animal horror more generally often stages tests of male protection by jeopardizing romantic interests, clear in *King Kong* but also a theme stretching right back to myths of princesses guarded by dragons. *Piranha* (1978) opens very similarly to *Jaws*, with the fearsome fish targeting a topless swimmer. When Sue Charlton bends dangerously down in a thong swimsuit by a pond in *Crocodile Dundee* (1986), she does so under the voyeuristic gaze of Mick, secretly watching from behind nearby trees: again, the animal's brutal culinary "objectification" will intrude on male sexual intentions. Point-of-view animal attacks on humans affront our distinctive "humanity"; when we're taken as prey it strips us of our perceived specialness. But their staging also often tends toward an implicitly male and heterosexual valuing of the victim prior to attack—what the animal takes is not just a life but a potential mate.

While I've focused primarily on the shark's initial gory gambit in *Jaws*, the link between vision and power is implied at several points throughout the film. In Quint's famous USS *Indianapolis* speech, the grizzled mariner tells his companions, "You know the thing about a shark: he's got lifeless eyes. Black eyes, like a doll's eyes." Pragmatically, this description helps mitigate any dissatisfaction with the realism of the mechanical shark—"Bruce"—used in the making of the film (which experienced frequent breakdowns during production). Should Bruce seem to the viewer too lifeless, Quint has already flagged inanimate eyes as a demonic feature of sharks. But also, since his story describes the trauma of his shipmates bobbing in the cold water at night, "waiting their turn to be eaten," the lifeless eyes suggest horrifying and inscrutable moral vacancy.

Since a takeover of visual power has been inherent in the creature's attack, it seems appropriate that an anthropocentric takeback is implicit in its defeat. The mast upon which Brody is perched slips closer to the surface of the water, and an air tank becomes lodged in the crevice of the "jaws" steaming toward him. As Brody fires the shot that detonates his foe into a red geyser of fishy offal, he snarls: "Smile, you son of a bitch." He wants a clear shot at the explosive canister, but the request also evokes a photographer's request to a subject to smile for a "shot." Having substantially eluded human view, and "looked" with a ravenous intentionality of its own, the shark becomes open to annihilation at the same time as it's able to be clearly framed by an avenging human gaze.

In Their Eyes: *Wolfen*

Michael Wadleigh's supernatural crime-thriller *Wolfen* (1980), based on a novel by Whitley Strieber, makes extensive use of the ocular theme, using it to symbolize conflicting human/animal understandings of the world around us. Troubled NYC detective Dewey Wilson (Albert Finney) is called to investigate a series of gory kills, beginning with the mutilation murder of a wealthy real-estate developer and his wife. Big money has plenty of enemies of course, and possibly connected is a militant Native American activist, Eddie Holt (Edward James Olmos). But what we see of the attacks, and police examination of the mess left behind, suggests some hairier happenings. Indeed, the film's slayings are prefigured by long sequences depicting a mysterious animal's point-of-view as it roams the city, an in-camera combination of reduced color and amplified contrast distinguishing its perspective from our own. Wilson eventually discovers that the creaturely culprits are "wolfen," ancient spirit-wolves revered by the Native Americans. Banished to the fringes of civilization by western industrial advance, the wolfen attack the vulnerable whom society has left similarly on the outskirts, preying primarily on the homeless who inhabit abandoned city blocks; yet they've made an exception for the developer, who was poised to overhaul one of their final hunting grounds.

We don't see any of the creatures who are doing this mysterious looking until relatively late in the film. They are first glimpsed as two bright eyes in the darkness on the staircase of a derelict building, and later as massive black wolves. Their eyes radiate a forbidding and powerful glow, confirming their visual power. The unusual amount of time devoted to depicting the world through the creatures' points-of-view, rather than exposing the animals to our contextualizing gaze, conjures the sense of a truly alternative perspective, threatening to permanently destabilize the order and normality Wilson seeks to restore.

Wolfen's theme of competing perspectives is borne out by linking the creatures with Native Americans. When Wilson consults an animal expert on lupine hairs found at the crime scene, the latter tells him that the wolves of the local area "went the way of the Indian and the buffalo—the genocide express." The Native activists kept under watch by Wilson make these links more explicit; feeling stunned and hopeless after the wolfen kill one of his colleagues, Dewey seeks out the activists, who fill him in on what he hasn't yet grasped. For generations the wolfen lived alongside the Indians, until white man's disruption, after which these great hunters were relegated to preying off the rejects of human society. "In their eyes," one of Eddie Holt's crew explains, continuing the film's ocular emphasis, "you're the savages." Eddie summarizes: "You got your technology, but you lost. You lost your senses." Colonialism and capitalism are linked by the film with repression of a spiritual and natural world around us, and the overlapping Native/wolfen perspective presents a critical counternarrative to technological progress. The resulting impression is that this particular threat is not merely some aberration of civilized life to be corrected by good policing, but instead an ever-present rival reality.

When the Sights Come to See You: *Jurassic Park*

Having centralized a visual poetics of villainy in *Jaws*, Spielberg again linked animal aggression to visual power in *Jurassic Park*. Very early in this film, a mythology is created around the park's prize monster, the Tyrannosaurus rex, whose vision (the film postulates) is based on movement: stay utterly still and you might evade detection—knowledge that later becomes pressingly relevant. The group embark on their tour through a set of promisingly *King Kong*–esque gates as John Williams's heroic score scales to a triumphal peak. But the dinosaurs are nowhere to be seen. Inside their Jeeps, the visitors crane and gawk, but see nothing. As it turns out, this magical mystery tour has all the frustrations of an average zoo visit, in which animals on exhibit often elude clear view. Later, after park systems go haywire and dinosaurs escape, the tour group is spectacularly spooked by the Tyrannosaurus. The rex stalks from behind the once-electrified fence, emitting a series of shudder-inducing roars, and when this overwhelming attraction finally moves into sight of its human viewers, it looks at them. The children squabble in one of the cars as the carnivore king, attracted by their waving torchlight, lowers its monstrous eyeball to the glass of the passenger-side window (Fig. 6.5). The animal that evaded the tourists' and our own eager gaze now imposes a malevolent gaze of its own.

As the cranky Tyrannosaur begins demolishing the Jeep with the screaming children inside, Alan Grant jumps from his own vehicle, lights a flare—a type of dazzling visual effect—to ensnare the animal's attention, casting the fizzing device away from the cars. The distraction works, but then (not to be outdone in the hero stakes) Malcolm gives the same trick a whirl. The rex won't fall for it a second time: the beast seems to have "seen through" the illusion, demonstrating an ability to load learning onto its raw instincts, and it maintains pursuit of Malcolm instead of the flashy prop. The rex returns to the Jeep as Grant snatches one of the children, Lex (Ariana Richards) from within, but they don't get far, and come face to face with the monster, the rain dripping off its colossal snout. Grant's earlier comment about the vision of the rex being based on movement now becomes urgently relevant, as the creature pauses to inspect these

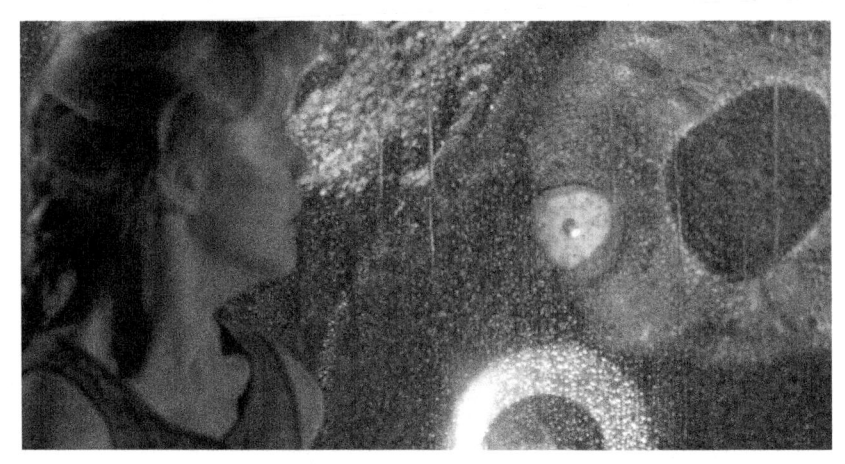

Figure 6.5. The Tyrannosaurus rex refused to make an appearance during the park tour, but, having escaped its enclosure, it looks directly into one of the cars at the human within (Ariana Richards), in *Jurassic Park* (Steven Spielberg, Universal, 1993). Digital frame enlargement.

human morsels, who must by all means remain utterly still. Taken as a whole, this scene immerses us in a fearsome yet complex consideration of the animal's visual power, forcing us to imagine how we are seen by it. The visual effect in Spielberg's film (the dinosaur) has become so real that it not only looks back at us, but can also be misdirected by effects and illusions, just as we can.

A more direct assault on the human gaze comes through the fate of treacherous park programmer Dennis Nedry (Wayne Knight) in his encounter with the seemingly playful Dilophosaurus. Upon breeding this particular specimen, Hammond's scientists have discovered that the reptile has not only an eye-catching neck frill but also the ability to spit black globs of blinding venom into the eyes of its victims. It is thus, as the tour's recorded narrator earlier remarked, a "beautiful but deadly addition" to the park—a sight that may both entice and punish its spectators. In his attempt to smuggle embryos out of the park for a rival company, Nedry bogs his Jeep and is accosted, while struggling to winch the vehicle out, by this modestly-sized, cheeping, and fairly cute creature. He loses his glasses in the bushes, his vision compromised, but even if he could see clearly, Nedry wouldn't know what this is—he has no actual interest in the park's creations. He initially takes the reptile for a harmless, dog-like dino variant, but this is no pet: the beast suddenly pops its frill with a livid screech and shoots a tarry blast into Nedry's exposed eyes, before devouring its screaming victim (Fig. 6.6).

Figure 6.6. Dennis Nedry (Wayne Knight) is blinded by the venom of the seemingly cute Dilophosaurus in *Jurassic Park* (Steven Spielberg, Universal, 1993). Digital frame enlargement.

Empowered animal perspectives have remained a crucial motif in stories of animal rebellion. In *Rise of the Planet of the Apes*, for instance, the pharmacological enhancement that lends the apes their uncanny intelligence also causes their eyes to turn green, their gaze thus positioned as the sign of their independence. In a film series that critiques human oppression of animals, the apes' opposing "view" of us is elevated to primacy. Given the importance of eye-gaze to predator–prey interactions, the motif has had the strongest currency in horror. These films show us imagined points-of-view that defy and disrupt our perceptions of the animal; they allow animals to evade our usually empowered gaze, ascribing them autonomy in action and thought. But they also disrupt our perceptions of ourselves, regularly reducing us to meat in a more brutal world that isn't as far behind us as we thought.

7

Snakes Alive

SNAKES PREFER TO KEEP CLEAR of us, which is fortunate, as they provoke considerable discomfort and, for many, utter terror when they do appear. "What is there in snakes anyway," asks biologist Edward O. Wilson, "that makes them so repellent and fascinating? The answer in retrospect is deceptively simple: their ability to remain hidden, the power in their sinuous limbless bodies, and the threat from venom injected hypodermically through sharp hollow teeth."[1] Of all the animal phobias, that of snakes—ophidiophobia—is the most common. Recent research suggests that fear of snakes is powerful enough in 2.6 percent of the population to legitimately meet the diagnostic criteria for ophidiophobia.[2] As we've already heard, humans' snake-fear is rooted in evolutionary psychology, given that snakes were a long-running co-evolutionary threat for our ancestors, and accordingly we share our snake aversion with primate cousins.[3] In fact, snakes remain a serious risk in many hunter-gatherer cultures; among the Aché of Paraguay, for example, snakebite accounts for 14 percent of all adult male deaths.[4] Some research suggests that it is not quite true to say that we are "innately" afraid of snakes so much as that we have an innately hyper-sensitive capacity for developing snake-fear.[5] However, as noted earlier, more recent study has observed stress-responses toward snakes in infants who are too young to have learned fear of the reptiles, tipping the evidence further toward innateness.[6]

As I mentioned in the context of spiders, fear in humans is marked not only by physiological reactions but also irregularities in the way we process information: our attention becomes biased in favor of threat-related stimuli. Interestingly, whereas attentional bias toward spiders is enhanced in those who self-report fear of spiders, bias toward snakes remains consistent despite people's level of fear.[7] Van Strien and Isbell suggest that snakes are subject to "automatic first-stage visual processing of emotional cues"[8]—that it is in our fundamental cognitive design to always notice snakes as the top priority. Subjects will easily spot snakes even when experimenters embed them in complex visual displays, and we're wary enough that our snake-detection alarm can be tripped merely by snake-like shapes that enter our field of awareness.[9] Wilson explains: "It pays in elementary survival to . . . go beyond ordinary caution and fear. The rule built into the brain in the form of a learning bias is: become alert quickly to any object with the serpentine gestalt. Overlearn this particular response in order to keep safe."[10]

Although we may fear snakes to greater or lesser degrees,[11] and snake-fear can certainly be overcome, snake-fear is part of our evolutionary heritage as homo sapiens. In fact, the impact of snakes on our development may be more profound than just inherited apprehension: Lynne A. Isbell has presented a cohesive theory according to which humans' high visual acuity is indebted to evolutionary pressure from snakes, given that detecting venomous snakes, and pointing them out to others, was vital to protohumans' survival. Your possession of vision keen enough to distinguish the individual letters that make up the words on this page may very well be thanks to snakes. In any case, while the forms in which horror antagonists appear might sometimes seem puzzling (mummies, birds, dolls, and so on), snakes shouldn't be a surprise to anyone: they've been scaring us for a long time. And so they slither menacing through numerous films: *Rattlers* (1976), *Venom* (1981), *The Exorcist III* (1990), *Anaconda* (1997), *King Cobra* (1999), *Snake Island* (2002), and *Vipers* (2008), to name but a few. The sufficiently self-evident threat of snakes is implied in title of tongue-in-cheek thriller *Snakes on a Plane* (2006), which delivers on its dreadful promise of snakes against which evasive action is suddenly stratospherically difficult.

Given that snake-fear is more or less wired into us, perhaps there isn't much to say about cinematic serpents? We can already see why they're there, after all. However, as much as the snake repels, as Wilson has noted, it also gives rise to fascination; we tell stories about snakes, even integrate them into religious myths.[12] Our adapted suspicion of snakes has been developed by a legacy of Judeo-Christian mythology in which the Devil is depicted in the form of a snake. Drake Stutesman explains that prior to this, many earlier mythologies (Egyptian, Greek, Babylonian) situated the serpent as part of a "combat myth" in which it plays a broader role as a "life force" and a representation of the "undivided cosmos." In these traditions, a hero's conflict with the serpent triggers a restructuring of the world.[13] In ancient Egyptian mythology, for example, the snake "is not permanently defeated but is half of the ever-functioning world."[14] The combat myth was incorporated into Christianity (via Judaism) through the tempting snake of the Garden of Eden, as well as Christ's battle with the serpent (as the Devil) in the Nicene Creed. Yet the translation into Christianity tended to cast the snake in a more distinctly negative role, a villain in "Manichean allegories, where the hero, such as St. George or Jesus, conquers the snake-shaped Devil, or a ninth-century St. Patrick drives the bad snakes from Ireland."[15] It seems safe to say that, in the West at least, we've been surrounded by depictions of snakes inflected by Christianity as either implicitly or explicitly satanic, exemplified cinematically in films such as *Jaws of Satan* (1981), *The Last Temptation of Christ* (1988), and *The Exorcist III*.

The snake's suspiciousness, both physically and morally, is complemented in film and literature by a dangerous geographic exoticism. Snakes are frequently foreign to the characters they threaten, arising in locations unfamiliar to Western audiences, as in *Raiders of the Lost Ark*, *Anaconda*, *Snake Island*, or *Lockjaw* (2008), or even the venomous asps that the Egyptian queen entices to end her own life in Shakespeare's *Antony and Cleopatra*. Alternatively, they are imported from faraway, as in *Venom* or *Snakes on a Plane*. In Rudyard Kipling's *The Jungle Book* story "Rikki-Tikki-Tavi," a mongoose defends an English family against the native Indian cobras trying to repel the foreigners; and in Arthur Conan Doyle's tale "The Speckled Band," an Englishman is killed by an asp imported from the Indian colonies. Sune Borkfelt suggests that tales of dangerous fauna implicitly reinforced colonial ideologies: "pointing to the need for 'protection' of native peoples from uncivilized nature and its creatures was among the most common ways of providing justification for imperialism during this era."[16] Native to Australia are the two most venomous snakes in the world, the inland taipan and the eastern brown snake, yet curiously enough, Australia has produced no killer snake movies of note. However if we delve into the nation's literary history, prominent is Henry Lawson's short-story "The Drover's Wife" from 1892, in which a housewife left alone struggles to protect her children from a snake that invades their rickety outback home. In this colonial context, the snake is again the exotic challenge to domestic life in a landscape still regarded as hostile, unforgiving, and ultimately foreign.

Bed Snakes: *Conan the Barbarian, Sssssss,* and *Venom*

In addition to its exoticism, the snake's presentation in cinema is often sinisterly erotic, and there's a fascination with imagining serpents in sexually intrusive or suggestive scenarios. In *Blade Runner* (1982), escaped criminal cyborg Zhora (Joanna Cassidy) works as a stripper, her routine focused around a Burmese python with which, the film implies, she performs sexually. The poster for *Sssssss* depicts a cobra surrounded by the frame of a woman's parted and painted lips. Similarly, the promotion for *Vipers* shows a horned viper winding its way up a woman's naked torso. This snaky sexuality is played out in the film itself: a pack of vipers sets on young couple as they make out in a tent, biting them all over their naked bodies. Later, another couple, Jack (Aaron Pearl) and Georgie (Mercedes McNab), finish having sex, and Jack moves down his lover's body, nibbling playfully at her leg as she relaxes. But then he jumps into the shower: the snake will take it from here. The sleepy woman assumes her lover is trying to reignite her interest, but those aren't Jack's caresses as the snake begins sliding up her leg (Fig. 7.1).

In *Blade Runner*, the sleazy emcee introduces the stripper's act with reference to Adam and Eve: "Watch her take pleasure from the serpent that once corrupted man." Accordingly, this eroticization of movie snakes is likely traceable to a Judeo-Christian cultural inheritance prioritizing sexual chastity. Snakes are the nominated animal villain within that tradition, with general malevolence overlapping with the sexually sinful. Also on the erotic theme, Freud, considering the snake-haired figure of Medusa, thought of serpents as phallic, the gorgon symbolic of castration fears

Figure 7.1. An oversexed serpent glides up the naked Georgie's (Mercedes McNab's) leg in *Vipers* (Bill Corcoran, VP Productions, 2008). Digital frame enlargement.

associated with women.[17] Joseph Campbell thought along similar lines: the snake as phallic, but he saw its mouth as vaginal.[18] Do snakes really resemble penises, though?—surely only superficially. Stutesman offers that since creatures like earthworms are shaped similarly yet attributed no corresponding mythology, the idea of the "phallic snake" is probably more suggestive of male "wishes rather than fears"[19]—men wanting their equipment to be more "snake-like." It's also possible that the snake's movement (already provoking our alertness through our attentional bias) complements these erotic associations, involving a seeming surplus of contact and traction: snakes seem to caress everything they move over.

Yet as its bestial incarnation implies, sexuality linked to snakes is always somehow troublingly outside cultural normativity. John Milius's *Conan the Barbarian* (1982) repeatedly links snakes with sexual perversity through the snake-cult against which its muscular hero (Arnold Schwarzenegger) strives. While not a horror film per se, *Conan* draws considerably on the genre through its use of animalized villains. The snake-cult is headed by the bewitching Thulsa Doom (James Earl Jones), murderer of Conan's mother, who uses snakes in all of his rituals and insignia and keeps a giant snake as a pet, later slain by Conan as he breaches Doom's stronghold. Inside the cult's inner sanctum, Conan witnesses his nemesis metamorphose into a man-sized serpent as he oversees the ritual orgy of his followers.

Conan's sexual life is consistently abnormal or troubled. After he's sold into slavery as a young man, he's bred to whomever his masters desire; following his escape, he's nearly killed by a witch who transforms into a shrieking ghoul mid-coitus. Things settle down sexually for the hero after he meets female brigand Valeria (Sandahl Bergman)—until Thulsa Doom kills her too. In contrast to Conan's sexual struggles, the villain's erotic life is controlling and extravagant, as his cult's orgies suggest. *Conan* was released following the decline of the 1960s and 1970s counterculture, during a conservative turn in American filmmaking.[20] Doom and his numerous brainwashed followers seem to present a reactionary fantasy of sexual liberation, with snake imagery complementing the idea of a threatening—yet ambivalently alluring—sexual decadence.

Sssssss, which also features a man transforming into a snake (albeit via mad science instead of sorcery), also intertwines the snake with sexuality outside dominant norms. Snake specialist Dr. Karl Stoner (Strother Martin) experiments on his naive assistant, David (Dirk Benedict), under the pretense of immunizing his understudy against future snakebites while actually trying to create a human–snake hybrid. The professor spends a great deal of time with the shirtless David, attending to him with his mysterious injections, and he's incensed when his subject begins a romance with his daughter (Heather Menzies). Although he's probably afraid that his genetic meddling will somehow contaminate his daughter, Stoner's desire to stymy this sexual union works to highlight the possessiveness and eroticism of his relationship to his assistant. For the snake-obsessed Stoner, the heterosexual couple's procreative acts threaten the "procreation" the scientist is attempting with David himself.

A more erotically suggestive—and more directly snaky—scene comes after the school bully Steve (Reb Brown) kills the beloved python pet of Stoner's daughter. Dad stuffs a deadly black mamba into a satchel and drives to Steve's house. The brawny jock has just finished having sex with a female admirer; she wants more, but Steve has a big game tomorrow and kicks her out. Stoner creeps in on the showering Steve, the athlete's naked body visible through the mist-covered shower curtain, and tosses his weapon of choice into the stall. The staging of Stoner's attack around the younger man's naked body (a body recently framed as sexually active and desirable) insinuates the professor as an intrusive voyeur while again inserting the snake into a sexually evocative scenario.

The American-British co-production *Venom* gives us just one snake (again the deadly African black mamba), this time in a suburban house full of crooks and their hostages, and again links the snake to sex. English maid Louise (Susan George) and chauffeur Dave (Oliver Reed) conspire to kidnap the son of the wealthy family for which they work, with a little help from foreign criminal creep, Jacques (Klaus Kinski). With his parents away, the boy (Lance Holcomb) has been left in the care of his grandfather (Sterling Hayden), an aging safari photographer. A precocious animal enthusiast, this kid keeps a miniature zoo in an upstairs room, including a number of reptiles. The morning of the plot against him, a mix-up at the local animal importer means he's given the lethal mamba (intended for a toxicology lab) instead of the more subdued species he'd requested. Back at the house, the box is opened and the little villain let loose, quickly snapping Louise fatally on the face. The police are alerted to the snake mix-up, a constable arrives at the house to inquire, and the situation soon becomes a full-scale siege. For the crooks, the danger inside the house matches or surpasses that of the armed police horde outside.

As the early attack on the maid suggests, the snake punishes these servant-class crooks for their transgression of the status quo. We might say the creature manifests the threat of an exotic natural world of which only the upper-middle class have expertise (the safari grandfather and his snake-enthusiast grandson understand this danger better than their upstart kidnappers). But wrapped up in that punitive subtext is still the snake's sexual menace. Louise seduces the reluctant Dave into the conspiracy, undressing in front of him and promising her sexual attention as an

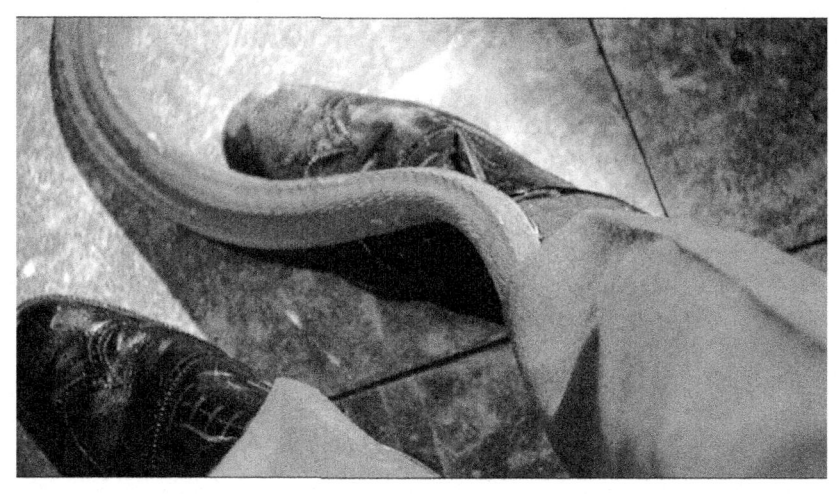

Figure 7.2. Trouser snake: a black mamba wriggles toward the sensitive flesh of criminal Steve (Oliver Reed), in *Venom* (Piers Haggard, Paramount, 1981). Digital frame enlargement.

additional reward. Accordingly, Dave's death is punitively sexual: injured on the ground, he watches as the snake slowly slides up one trouser leg, inching closer and closer to his crotch, where it will fatally bite him on the penis that led him astray (Fig. 7.2).

Male Snakes in the Grass in *Anaconda* and *Anacondas*

In a year that James Cameron's *Titanic* (1997) dominated the box office, Peruvian director Luis Llosa's own film tracking an imperiled boat—a rather smaller affair threatened by a monstrous jungle serpent—performed quite adequately for its size.[21] At the center of the film is Terri Flores (Jennifer Lopez), a first-time director trying to get her big break with a documentary on the elusive Shirishama Indians of the Amazon. She brings with her a disparate crew of characters typical of animal horror, and the atmosphere becomes more discordant when they accept aboard Paul Sarone (Jon Voight), a stranded Paraguayan ex-priest who traps snakes for zoos and collectors, and who offers to guide the crew on their journey.

A series of mishaps befall the explorers after Sarone's arrival. Gary (Owen Wilson), the sound man, and Denise (Kari Wuhrer), the producer, are charged by a boar during a sexual escapade on shore, and the intrepid anthropologist advising the mission (Eric Stoltz) sustains a near-fatal injury when freeing the tangled boat propeller. Of course, things only get worse when a scaly, beady-eyed gargantuan snake (adept at traversing both land and sea) begins tracking the boat's crew, snatching, squeezing, and gobbling their party one by one. The flustered crew are much at Sarone's mercy, and it becomes clear that the cunning trapper is exploiting them to track the giant anaconda for profit.

The snake, conjured variously through animatronics and digital effects, is both colossal and infinitely swift. Far more than its real-life counterpart, the animal's eyes are set in a fiendish scowl and its head embellished with red-orange flecks that exaggerate its satanic malevolence. The brute's body is roughly the width of a human's trunk, and before it devours its prey it coils around them, cinching its massive weight. In one scene, we hear the victim's bones crack before the snake's gaping maw, pink and slimy, looms down upon him. Snakes are not dramatically vocal, so as well as an acid-sizzle hiss, this anaconda howls and screeches in aggression or outrage as the situation requires. And, as in *Jaws* (by which the film is much inspired), the creature of *Anaconda* shows extraordinary dedication to the human hunt, having nothing better to do than remain locked in relentless pursuit of these specific people.

Llosa's film attributes a wild sexual energy to the Amazonian environment, but simultaneously laces it with threat. As Gary flirts with Denise, he asks, "Is it just me, or does the jungle make you really, really horny?" The attack on the couple by a wild boar comes when she takes him up on his offer, as they canoodle in the sultry wilderness. Before things get too perilous, Terri the director and Steven, the anthropologist who hired her, share a romantic moment on the boat's deck at dusk. Steven remarks on the courtship rituals of the fireflies around them, based on the duration and frequency of their "flashes" (suggestive of nudity). Terri endorses the bugs' sexual candor: "I like that, no pick-up lines, no misunderstandings. Just instinct and nature." As the couple kiss, we see a more aggressive display of animal "instinct" somewhere on shore as the anaconda stalks and strikes a panther. As the wildest thing in the wild jungle, the snake embodies this fusion of sexuality and danger, a mixture evoked by snake-trapper Sarone's dialogue: when this serpent coils around you, he tells the crew, it "hold[s] you tighter than your true love." The film implies that we cannot appreciate "animal" sexuality without also recognizing that violence is a similarly animal instinct. The jungle might seem sexually liberating, but it's also a world free of the moral rules that preserve our safety.

The snake isn't the only villain in *Anaconda*, as Sarone is presented to us as a human incarnation of what he hunts. The trapper is slippery and manipulative, certainly metaphorically "snake-like." After the anaconda constricts and consumes the boat's driver during a salvage excursion organized by Sarone, the trapper bats back criticism, reasoning with a sly smile, "Don't make me out a monster: I didn't eat the captain Mateo." Later, Denise mutters to the others: "I'm not so sure he didn't eat the captain; he sure looks satiated." After the crew discover his manipulations, they tie him to the mast by his wrists, but he manages to seize hold of Denise with his legs, constricting her throat much like his serpentine counterpart. The snake-hunter also models something sexually "animal," and in his case undesired. With her lover underwater, engaged in the hazardous task of trying to free the boat propeller, the stressed-out Terri massages her neck, then looks up to notice the much older Sarone gazing lecherously at her. Numerous times throughout the film, we see shots from the anaconda's point of view as it appraises its human targets. Now Terri is subject to another type of predatory objectification from the snake-like Sarone (Fig. 7.3).

Figure 7.3. The snake-like Sarone (Jon Voight) openly eyes-off Terri (Jennifer Lopez) in *Anaconda* (Luis Llosa, Columbia, 1997). Digital frame enlargement.

The film also suggests the poacher's ability to almost magically and satanically "tempt" several shipmates. As the boat collects him toward the beginning of the film, he looks cryptically to the driver, Mateo, who will henceforth act as his accomplice. Similarly, the mellow-natured Gary is wooed to the hunter's side during conflict, mystifying his colleagues with his out-of-character aggression. Sarone's snakiness is enhanced by Christian allusions: Sarone claims he initially trained as a priest before abandoning his vocation. In short, while the crew try to keep the snake antagonist at a distance, they are kept busy and imperiled by a snake-like antagonist among them. Clearly inspired by Quint of *Jaws*, Sarone is also (and even more than his forerunner) too morally close to his fierce and amoral prey, and he too will be consumed by the animal world he too much embraced. The hunter's consumption is clearly the most impressive death within the film ("jaw-dropping" in more ways than one): devoured head-first, legs flailing desperately in the air as the snake stretches to accommodate its man-sized meal (Fig. 7.4).

Anaconda's lower-budget sequel, *Anacondas: The Hunt for the Blood Orchid* (2004), directed by Dwight H. Little, shifts the snake-terror from South America to Borneo. There are no anacondas in Borneo, but that's just a technicality—what's important is that the setting is exotic enough to plausibly harbor such a hazard. In this installment, a team of corporate scientists hire a boat in quest of a rare orchid with the ability to replenish its cells infinitely, a discovery that holds the key to eternal youth. As the film's title suggests, the snake menace is multiplied, and team members are picked off one by one, having wandered into the anacondas' high-traffic zone in mating season.

Figure 7.4. The snake devours its human double, Sarone (Jon Voight), in *Anaconda* (Luis Llosa, Columbia, 1997). Digital frame enlargement.

Anacondas reproduces many aspects of the original film. Again, we have a female protagonist entering a location linked with intrusive male sexuality. Amid a host of mostly whiny co-researchers and pharmaceutical reps is Sam Rogers (KaDee Strickland), a young scientist and former student of the expedition's leader, Jack Byron (Matthew Marsden). As soon as the boat embarks, the expedition's young doctor makes a pass at Sam: "We're young, we're single, we're in Borneo." She brushes off the flirtation, although of more concern will be her mentor, Jack, who suggests that his professional favors might be reciprocated sexually. She politely declines, and he takes the hint (for now anyway), but leaves her wondering whether her value on this trip is meant to be scientific or sexual. While Jack isn't linked to snakes as assiduously as Sarone in Llosa's original film, he's still the subject of allusions to the "animal" within, especially after Sam develops a romantic affection for the expedition's muscular guide, Bill (Johnny Messner). When snakes start picking off members of the crew, Bill explains to the group the territoriality of male snakes during mating season. As he does so, we see a reverse shot of Jack, glowering at his dashing rival—a quick shot of another territorial male.

The obsessive Jack spearheads the quest beyond safety or sanity. Eventually he forces Sam at gunpoint to retrieve the orchids for him by walking along a log above a muddy, squirming snake orgy. Fear of falling here isn't just about death, but suggestive of Sam's fear of falling into a metaphoric abyss of sexual degradation. Moreover, the focus on an exchange of flowers is symbolic of Jack's aggressive desire for "romance" between him and his unwilling protégé. Like Sarone, Jack will die for his obsession, and he's eventually knocked into the pit to be devoured. But before this moral reckoning comes, the climactic snake-pit sequence is a feverish adventure-film metaphor for a smart young woman's fear that she is not more than the dehumanized sexual resource of her snake-like male superior.

Mile-High Anxiety: *Snakes on a Plane*

David R. Ellis's *Snakes on a Plane* (2006) deployed serpents, and a lot of them, with cheeky B-movie simplicity. The film's blunt title implicitly advises viewers to engage with the film without critical reflections on its logic, plausibility, social comment, or artistic value—as pure and proud escapism. *Snakes* oscillates between horror and comedy, allowing enough shudders to sustain the suspense while encouraging laughter at its titular scenario's creative absurdities. That scenario is brought about when carefree surfer Sean Jones (Nathan Phillips) witnesses vicious drug lord Eddie Kim (Byron Lawson) bludgeon to death a U.S. District Attorney in Hawaii. Sean is swiftly assigned FBI tough-guy Neville Flynn (Samuel L. Jackson) for protection, and arrangements are made to fly him to Los Angeles to testify. Despite a boost to security, Kim's inside man at the airport hoses pheromones over the Hawaiian leis distributed to aircraft passengers, intended to entice and agitate a multitude of venomous snakes stored for transport in the plane's cargo hold. A rigged cargo-door ensures the riled-up reptiles find their way through the plane's nooks and crannies into the fuselage, where they dangle, jump, and snap at passengers every chance they get. Neville, the crew, and a few frightened passengers must work together to try to save the wounded and retake control of what has become a flying pandemonium of serpentine predators.

The drug lord's silly plan—intended to bring down the whole plane—is of course simply a way to realize the film's title and dramatic possibilities therein. Sean survives the flight, but we never see him make his testimony because we don't care that much: the snakes are the real draw here. Nevertheless, the relatively graver importance placed on Sean's survival allows the film to maintain tension as it fosters our perverse enjoyment of attacks on numerous more ancillary characters. *Snakes* extensively exploits our attentional bias toward the reptiles by threading them through an environment cluttered with seats, bodies, baggage, low ceilings, and little chance to escape. At one point the cabin's oxygen masks are deployed, the descending tubes interwoven with numerous snakes, rudely offering death rather than life support. As passengers attempt to make it from one end of the snake-infested plane to the other, we're drawn into a game of spot-the-snake, given the visually confusing array of aircraft fixtures and accessories. In such moments, the film becomes a kind of "tunnel of terror," in which threats might strike at any moment and we ready ourselves by seeking to identify them in advance.

Unlike *Anaconda* or its sequel, *Snakes* has no real interest in its human villain, but it still attributes to the serpents habits of sexual intrusion: in fact they're more sex-obsessed than ever. The reptiles' first strike is on a glamorous young couple (Samantha McLeod and Taylor Kitsch) who retreat to the plane's bathroom for sex. Cross-cutting warns of the approach of two snakes through the ventilation system, and they emerge through a hole in the ceiling (Fig. 7.5). One snake sinks its fangs into the young man's throat while the other, failing a strike at the girl's screaming face, leaps and latches onto her nipple, its irreverence provoking a fusion of horror and humor as we see a close-up of this wriggling, macabre tassel.

Perhaps the attack is moralistic: the snakes emerge through the hold left by a smoke-detector the couple removed so they could smoke pot. More interesting, however, is the way the film uses the snakes to elicit dark humor by not simply ending the couple's sex but more so

Figure 7.5. A snake prepares to strike a nude couple (Samantha McLeod and Taylor Kitsch) having sex in the plane's bathroom in *Snakes on a Plane* (David R. Ellis, New Line, 2006). Digital frame enlargement.

making a mockery of it. The nature of the victims is important here. Young, blonde, tanned, trim: the couple are conspicuous stereotypes of bodily perfection. Their bronzed figures are emphasized by the cool blue of the cubicle interior, and as they undress the shot scans both the male's muscular physique and the toned and bare-breasted torso of his lover. We don't know anything about them, but we already know their "types": bimbo and himbo. The snake attack vandalizes the sex of these aspirational bodies, and if we find humor here it arises (as humor so often does) through a sudden loss of status—in this case the status of the seamlessly attractive. As the snake dangles from the girl's breast, it transforms her glamorous body into something ridiculous, demeaning the sexual mystique of a few moments before.

Snakes on a Plane has plenty of random attacks more typical of animal horror. A snake pops out of a barf bag, for example; and as mentioned above, the film delights in the ease with which snakes might furtively steal through the confined and visually cluttered space of an airplane fuselage. But its obsession with sexualizing snake attack can't possibly be overlooked. Another early attack sees a snake launch itself from a toilet bowl to snap onto the penis of a urinating man, who whips and thrashes his unwanted extension while shrieking absurdly, "Fucking snake, get off my dick!"

In an even more perverse episode, we see a heavily overweight woman soundly sleeping, but who then smiles and moans as a snake wriggles up her dress. The crude humor of the scene depends not only on the snake's outrageous invasion, but also the unexpected sexualization of such an obese body. Prior to this scene, as this large woman made her way down the aisle to take her seat, she was approvingly watched by a young man, Troy (Kenan Thompson), whose buddy then leaned in to tease him about his unconventional sexual tastes: "You like that," he'd grinned mockingly. The snake follows up the joke, sleazily enacting sexual urges unable to be openly admitted. Later, the friend of the fat-fancier is bitten on his behind, and an effeminate male flight attendant is a little too quick to offer to suck out the poison: "There will be no sucking!" the wounded man protests. Immediately afterward, an attractive young female passenger pierces a swollen bite on the arm of a young boy, draws the poison out with her mouth, and spits it into a cup. The guy with the bitten butt watches on, his erotic interest absurdly piqued: "That's what I'm talking about," he breathily whispers. His buddy saw it as well: "Ah, I got bit too," he claims. First the act of sucking venom is played as implied fellatio for a homophobic gag, but then the joke turns onto the warped sexual perspective of two straight men who see as "sexy" a woman sucking a wound on a boy's arm ("bad taste" indeed). Through the equation of venom and semen, we see snakes again used to provide opportunities for the comical rupturing of polite, approved, or decorous versions of sexuality. Mainstream cinema sex is generally fairly routinized, and these impishly sex-curious snakes invite us to enjoy the knowingly "gross" and transgressive humor of sexual extremity.

As we conclude our engagement with cinematic snakes, we might find it curious that the fear of animals onscreen is so often intertwined with sexuality. After all, in various *King Kong* films, Ann Darrow is abducted to be a "bride of Kong": the anxiety is not that she will be eaten by the beast but rather stolen and somehow enslaved to sexual molestation. The shark of *Jaws* makes its most potent and visible attack on the body of a naked teen girl, with the formula repeated in *Grizzly* (1976) and *Piranha* (1978). Men don't escape unwelcome attention either, as we've seen, with snapping snakes choosing tender cuts of male meat in two of the films discussed above. An explanation for this might come with reference to bestiality taboos; after all, sexuality is certainly a point at which the distinction between humans and other animals is stringently maintained. But are we constantly terrified of being implicated in cross-species sex?—does that really bubble just below the surface of our culture or consciousness? It seems unlikely. I think a simpler explanation will serve. Not just survival, but sex, has been an evolutionarily crucial domain of human interest and activity; it's logical that it be frequently implicated in threats to our bodily integrity or existence. From oversexed vampires and succubi to the forced impregnation depicted in the *Alien* series, horror monsters that compromise, hijack, undermine, or appall our sexual and reproductive efforts are really nothing new. When we weave horror tales of animal attack, it's not surprising that they too are willing to hit us "where it hurts." In the case of snakes, their deviousness in Christian mythology more easily aligns them with fears of sinful seduction, as in *Venom* and *Conan*, and sexual coercion, as in the *Anaconda* films. But as we see in *Snakes on a Plane*, this symbolic sexual baggage may be accelerated into the absurd. Given our evolutionary inheritance of snake-alarm, and the visual nature of cinema as a medium, snakes are handy horror film villains. But since they make us jump so instinctively, they're also ideal villains with which to play some very silly games.

8

Bad Dog!

The Rogue Hounds of Horror

TAKEN GENERALLY, THE ANIMALS who rise to confront us in horror cinema are a forbidding array ideally exotic to, and absent from, our everyday lives: sharks, lions, giant snakes, crocodiles, wolves, and so on. They're creatures often regarded with fear and wonder via television sets, on guided tours, or behind screens and barriers in zoos or aquaria. That is to say: they're animals held at some definite distance from us—either literal or virtual—that are then narratively brought unnervingly too close. We know when we swim in the ocean that somewhere in that water there are sharks. The important thing is that they're "over there." But on Amity Island the shark is constantly and maliciously "too close"; and because the ocean typically renders it invisible, its lethal closeness is undetectable until it's too late. However, horror can be engendered by animals whose proximity to us, both physical and emotional, has by contrast a considerable intimacy—animals whose closeness is both commonplace and desired. Associated with fidelity, affection, and love without the sometimes exhausting conditions of human bonds, and also associated with being cute, domestic dogs seem implausible candidates for horror monsters. Yet several films, including *The Exorcist* (1973), *Dogs* (1976), *Suspiria* (1977), *The Thing* (1983), *Cujo* (1983), *Man's Best Friend* (1993), and *Rottweiler* (2004), have positioned the dog—briefly or centrally—in such a way as to destabilize our way of viewing these creatures, inverting their comforting associations and imagining them, in various configurations, as fundamentally antagonistic to the human society that welcomes them (Fig. 8.1).

As we know, animal horror generally represents a striking challenge to human dominance; animal attacks present us with radical upheavals of an imagined human–animal hierarchy. We're intrigued by—can hardly look away from—situations in which they might have power over us. With dog-horror this doesn't seem to quite fit. Most of us like dogs; we're not typically afraid of them (their "closeness" isn't an issue). Unlike our relationships with snakes or big cats, we haven't only co-evolved with dogs over many thousands of years, but also controlled their evolution ourselves through selective breeding, emphasizing in them the traits that make them compatible with human company. Edward O. Wilson explains that dogs are particularly favored "because they live by humanlike rituals of greeting and subservience. The family to whom they belong is part of their pack. They treat us like giant dogs, automatically alpha in rank, and clamor to be near us. We in turn respond warmly to their joyous greetings. . . ."[1] Dogs seem most emblematic of our view of ourselves as "animal lovers" (if we consider ourselves as such), and we presume that we treat them well—and many of us do. Yet the everyday lives of domestic dogs are still structured by us in ways that certainly manifest, enact, and naturalize our power over them: through training that ensures appropriately domestic behavior; through whether they reside indoors or outdoors at any given time; through where and how they are exercised (if

Figure 8.1. When good boys turn bad: the deranged dog of *Cujo* (Lewis Teague, Warner Bros., 1983). Digital frame enlargement.

they are exercised at all); through the company we provide or withhold from them; through their reliance on us to provide food and water; and so on. Their relationship to us is generally one of extraordinary dependence. It may not be fearful or antagonistic, but it is hierarchical; we are their "masters." We have only to visit shelters to see the fate of dogs nobody wants, to grasp truly how much they're within our power—to see the very rawest end of that hierarchy.

Enmeshed with these domestic rituals that confirm our power is, for many, a tremendous affection, and a deep enjoyment of the role of provider. Indeed, so dutiful in our care are many of us that we imagine the power hierarchy is really the other way around: we idealize dogs' dependence on us. The phrase "a dog's life" traditionally referred to a wretched existence,[2] drawing on a working-dog's lot of sleeping outside and eating scraps; now it more often conveys admiration for a canine life of leisure. And accordingly, our relationship with dogs seems to represent the human–animal hierarchy in its most apparently benign, reciprocal, and consensual form. At the same time as we affirm dogs' "belonging" in Western societies and the ways in which they enrich and complement our lives, we also understand that they are animals; we appreciate that they are distinct from us. For instance, opinions often differ on what level of "human" treatment is acceptable, normative, or desirable for canine companions—at what point an especially doting dog "owner" ought to be reminded that a dog is not a human being. And unlike the humans some may occasionally treat them as, dogs have no legal rights anywhere (although anticruelty statutes place some restrictions on their treatment). We acknowledge their animality, and yet we also have them cordoned off from their "wild" animal counterparts, given that they have been bred by and effectively designed for us. Neither belonging totally to "animal" nor "human" realms, the dog is able to become a figure of some ambiguity, to attract uncertainty around its nature and the legitimacy of its closeness to us—in essence, uncertainty over what the dog is.

The unique relationship between humans and domestic dogs has long been represented in narrative screen productions, prominent examples of which include TV's *Lassie* (1954–1973) and *Inspector Rex* (*Kommissar Rex*, 1994–2004) and, at the cinema, *Lassie Come Home* (1943), *Old Yeller* (1957), *Benji* (1974), *Turner and Hooch* (1989), the *Beethoven* series (1992–2014), Disney's *Air Bud* series (1997–2013), *Red Dog* (2011), *The Adventures of Tintin* (2011), and numerous other animated productions with more anthropomorphic canine characters. At the forefront of human–canine relationships in cinema are those that reinforce the complementary relationship between us and them. They may be gallant family protectors, as in *Beethoven* (1992); loveable strays waiting to be redeemed, as in *Old*

Yeller; or pooches who strive to get back to the domesticity from which they have been somehow displaced, as in *Bingo* (1991) and *Homeward Bound: The Incredible Journey* (1993). It may be that through such (often fanciful) representations, our connection to dogs is not merely depicted but also promoted. McLean speculates that our "relationships with animals are . . . potently shaped by the uses to which animals are put in reality-based narrative media such as film."[3] In any case, onscreen dogs tend to affirm real-world dogs' position of belonging in the society on which they are dependent, and to reinforce (even exaggerate) their intersection with human lives. Given cinema's role in portraying—and perhaps bestowing—idealized images of the dog, it has also, through the horror film, become a potent ground for the disquieting contestation of expected and desired dog behavior.

From Defenseless Dog to Controlled Killer

Horror's bad dogs need to be considered in relation not just to dogs in our culture more broadly, but also to their more conventional position amid cinematic darkness. In *The Wizard of Oz* (1939), surely worse even than the famous threat by the Wicked Witch of the West (Margaret Hamilton) to Dorothy (Judy Garland)—"I'll get you, my pretty!"—is its gratuitously malevolent addendum, "And your little dog, too!" The warning is from a familiar "horror" figure, a witch, albeit one dislocated from her native genre; nevertheless, even in the context of this family fantasy, her threat to harm a helpless little dog is a powerful attribution of absolute moral badness entirely befitting horror villainy. Indeed, dogs are recognizable within horror cinema as early victims of violent attack. Much like that of a child, the dog's vulnerability always powerfully enhances the despicability of those who would abuse it.

Hitchcock's *Rear Window* (1954) provides an important example of the Defenseless Dog trope in a thriller context that intersects with horror cinema. Lars Thorwald (Raymond Burr) has killed his wife. Well, probably: according to L. B. "Jeff" Jeffries (James Stewart) anyway, the temporarily disabled and chronically bored photographer who uses a long-focus lens and binoculars to spy on his neighbors in a sealed-off apartment complex in Lower Manhattan. Despite the initial skepticism of those around him, it turns out Jeff is on to something. So is the Norwich terrier belonging to one of Thorwald's upper-floor neighbors, a creature dotingly ferried from his owners' balcony to the courtyard below via a pulley and a basket. Thorwald has buried some part of his hapless wife in the garden, and the dog has been taking a curious interest in just that spot. One morning the innocent meddler is found in the yard with his neck broken. Upon discovering his little body, his female owner announces with heartbroken rage to the entire complex around her: "You don't know the meaning of the word neighbors! Did you kill him because he liked you?" Narratively, the dog is killed because he senses something beyond human ken, threatening to give the game away (albeit innocently so). Yet given the doggy cuteness of this little sleuth, and the shared affection for him also encouraged by his amusing mode of transport, his murder works to compound the malevolence of his killer. Indeed, the dog's death, and his owner's damning address (met with silence from her auditors), strikes an oddly harrowing note in the film, breaching an otherwise hardboiled tone (even Thorwald's dismembered wife is not granted such poignant sympathy). The accusation also underscores the dog as a manifestation of communal domesticity, grossly insulted by his murder. The little Norwich roams freely around the courtyard, implicitly connecting the otherwise separate inhabitants whose apartments skirt the area. Murray Pomerance writes that "when the neighbors seem unmoved by his death, they become through this cold inattentiveness prototypes of the disconnected modern personality."[4] This cute little dog emphasizes by his contrast "the brutalizing, monumental, spiritually vacuous superstructure of modernity's skin."[5] The dog is a "natural" (yet infinitely tame and charming) counterpoint to a mechanized, urban apathy that surrounds him. The canine's killer is an appalling attacker of innocence, but he's also a heartless modern stranger within the community the dog fostered through a shared sense of affection and caring.

Four years after Hitchcock's film, in Irvin Yeaworth's *The Blob* (1958) two teenagers, Steve and Jane (Steve McQueen and Aneta Corsaut in their debut roles), blockaded inside a movie theater, are forced to leave a small dog outside to be annexed by the gelatinous space invader. The adorable pet's demise obviously underscores the danger of the eponymous Blob, but it also inscribes the moral evil of this otherwise rather indistinct attacker. Our perception of the Blob as something "low" and "mean" is amplified by its soulless victimization of the adorable and no doubt faithful (and thus morally virtuous) pup. Steve's decision to leave the dog outside to be devoured enacts the human/animal hierarchy in practical terms: the dog is considered too insignificant to risk human life in rescuing. Yet the scene is suffused with ambivalence given that it also invokes a human duty of protection to an animal so vulnerable, so ill-equipped to face or understand such a threat. As in *Rear Window*, the dog's victimization spotlights the villain's ruthlessness, but it also does so by stressing the human/animal hierarchy powerfully enough to provoke guilt around our failure to live up to our pseudo-parental power.

Today the Defenseless Dog has become something of a horror/thriller cliché. Horror viewers are familiar with the dog as first victim in

Funny Games (1997 and 2007), *The Conjuring* (2013), *Preservation* (2014), and *The Babadook* (2014), and many other films. A dog isn't quite the first victim in *Jaws* (1975), given Chrissie's death in the prologue, yet a dog's disappearance on the beach is the prelude to more extensive human carnage. Typically in modern horror, as in *The Conjuring* or *Preservation*, the Defenseless Dog allows writers to communicate deadly threat without sacrificing a main (human) character through whom the narrative can advance. In *The Conjuring* the worried dog is the first victim of hostile spirits in a haunted house, a bleak warning to the house's human occupants. Similarly, if less supernaturally, the faithful dog of a hardy hunter and outdoorsman is the first victim in *Preservation*, amplifying the threat presented to his person. In these instances, our sympathy for the dog is assumed, as is our duty to protect it, and thus, implicitly, our hierarchical power over it. Defenseless Dogs indicate that when it comes to canines, the human/animal hierarchy is highly emotionally invested, a fact rendered dramatically potent in the anxiety-producing domain of the horror film.

Rebellious dogs will often appear in movies to assist in malevolent human schemes, representations that play upon the animals' image as servile to our interests, and suggest that they might follow us further than they should. In *The Most Dangerous Game* (1932), the diabolical Russian Count Zaroff (Leslie Banks) uses dogs to aid him as he hunts travelers who find themselves shipwrecked on his remote island. In the popular 1959 adaptation of the Sherlock Holmes mystery *The Hound of the Baskervilles*, an apparently demonic hound terrorizes the descendants of a cruel aristocrat, mauling Baskervilles who venture onto the wild moor at night. Again, the dog performs ultimately in ruthless obedience to a mad master. The hound of the Baskervilles turns out to be a flesh-and-blood (if large, hungry, and particularly belligerent) domestic dog, hunting at the behest of an obscure and deformed descendant of the Baskerville line (Ewen Solon) who stands to inherent the family fortune—if only he can get Sir Henry Baskerville (Christopher Lee) out of the way. The moors, where the attacks are staged, contrast with the civility of Baskerville Hall, presenting a "wild" landscape in which the sundry poor hunt for their dinner as best they can, linking the grim and swampy wilderness with the similarly "uncivilized" lower classes. The mischievous missing Baskerville may claim a blood connection, but through his grotesque webbed hand the film ensures we recognize that he lacks the genteel characteristics of the status to which he strives—he has instead a malformed "animal" feature.

The dog in Richard Donner's eschatological horror *The Omen* (1976) is similarly imbued with both demonic menace and class tension, albeit more implicitly. In this case a family nanny (Billie Whitelaw) brings a hulking Rottweiler into the house to help guard young Damien

(Harvey Stephens), the adopted son of a wealthy family who is in fact the budding antichrist. Late in the film, and having learned the terrible truth about his son, Damien's father Robert (Gregory Peck) must tiptoe around his house to avoid the dog, now clearly no ordinary canine but rather some kind of hellhound set to maul anyone who interferes in its master's apocalyptic designs. In Sam Fuller's *White Dog* (1982), a stray White Shepherd adopted by a Californian woman turns out to be a so-called "white dog": a dog deliberately trained to viciously attack black people. The film focuses on the dangerous and possibly fruitless attempts of a black trainer to cure the dog of the lessons deeply instilled by its previous owner. Again, we see the same pattern: this dog isn't just spontaneously "racist"; it is enforcing a particular human's ideological program. The film's focus is on whether the animal can be re-inscribed with a different worldview.

Similarly, Spanish science-fiction/horror hybrid *Rottweiler* deploys a dog who is again faithful to a terrifying fault: a cyborg Rottweiler tracks the innocent escapee of a futuristic prison, enacting the will of its dead prison-guard master. We are aware of the dog's willingness to take our instruction, and the figure of the "cyborg dog" is an exaggeration of the dog's perceived "programmability." All of these films evoke the dog's potential to perform as a powerful tool of human villainy. However, I want to now turn from those films to films that destabilize, rather than implicitly reinforce, the hierarchy between humans and dogs—films that dispute in a more profound way the idea of the dog as "man's best friend."

"Who's there!": *Suspiria*

Dario Argento's cult classic *Suspiria* (1977) is set in and around a German dance academy secretly run by a coven of witches, where people—young women, mainly—turn up dead. However, one of the victims is a blind piano player, Daniel (Flavio Bucci), employed to provide music for rehearsals and recitals, and who leaves his seeing-eye dog, a German Shepherd, tethered to a handrail outside while he works. Daniel plays for the troupe inside, but meanwhile outside the school the stone-faced cook (Franca Scagnetti), with a small and silent boy by her side, walks toward Daniel's dog, tied up and waiting patiently for its master. The cook stares strangely at the sitting animal as she approaches, but a cut to inside the building obscures what happens next. We see an instructor (Alida Valli) stride down a hallway and into the room where the dancers rehearse. Inside, she viciously berates Daniel, telling him that the little boy has been rushed to hospital after the dog bit him. Daniel is both distressed and incredulous, and responds in passionate defense of his companion—"a peaceful, faithful animal!"—before he's aggressively fired and turned out by his employer.

That night, guided by his dog, Daniel goes to a bar for a while, and then walks home through the eerily empty Königsplatz square. The film's score begins chiming a music box–style melody, increasingly overlaid by breathy whispering that suggests some cryptic and unseen presence around the blind man. In the center of this vast empty area, Daniel's dog suddenly begins barking in hysterical concern, swiveling in various directions—yet no threat (nor even fellow creature) is visible. "Who's there?!" the blind man nervously shouts. We see shadows on the buildings around him, but an aerial shot confirms—even compounds—that these two are all alone. The dog continues to bark nervously, raising the alarm. The music stops. Then the attacker manifests: Daniel's own dog lunges at his throat, toppling him to the ground. Bright blood spills profusely from his mouth and neck as the Shepherd, somehow converted to villainy, ruthlessly mauls its helpless master. Daniel now lies dead, and the Shepherd begins calmly eating from the blind man's face and neck, before the grisly scene is spotted by two pedestrians across the street, who run over to chase the animal away.

When Daniel is verbally abused by the instructor over his dog's alleged misdeed, we strongly suspect that no such thing occurred. Even though their villainy hasn't yet manifested overtly, these dance academy people are obviously weirdos. Yet the poor dog can't contest the damning accusation against it. As he's fired, Daniel himself is frustratingly powerless before his scheming employers, the bond between blind man and pet implicitly reinforced through shared vulnerability. In the attack scene, it initially seems the dog is again proving his faithfulness by raising alarm. There's clearly nothing visible: the scene suggests that dogs have some psychic senses beyond our own, and are able to detect hidden forces of evil. This trope surely arises from our observance of dogs' heightened olfactory sense, and their ability to hear sounds within a greater frequency range than we can,[6] powers that can certainly make dogs appear "psychic." The dog has senses beyond our own, but senses thankfully in our service—and the disabled Daniel of course needs those abilities more than most people do. But the dog overturns any such role, demonstrating a disturbing independence. Daniel is the dog's "owner," its caregiver and "master," yet as the one guided by the animal, he's also in a position of unusual reliance. The dog's role as an assistance animal is used to darkly play with the notion of who is dependent on whom. With the soundtrack's spooky whispering and rattling, the scene intends to imply that the dog is now somehow "possessed," under the influence of the dance academy's murderous occult owners. Yet the horror and surprise really depend on articulating that vague supernatural threat through a more earthly sense of the uncanny: the subversion of an especially invested human/animal relationship. Daniel's repeated cries of "Who's there?!" a few moments earlier might now be applied to his closest companion: questioning how much he can truly "know" the creature with whom he shares his life.

A Demonic Bark: *The Exorcist*

Several of these films additionally invoke our uncertainty by playing on what we might term the dog's "categorical ambiguity." Dogs are a familiar sight in Western societies but, as I mentioned earlier, we still recognize them as categorically distinct from us, as "animals"—albeit not "wild" ones. William Friedkin's *The Exorcist* plays on this categorical confusion; the film does not focus on an animal antagonist, but dogs feature specifically in a powerful moment early on. The demonic evil that notably inhabits and corrupts the body of twelve-year-old Regan MacNeil (Linda Blair) is first cryptically heralded in the film's prologue, set in Northern Iraq, where an elderly priest, Father Merrin (Max von Sydow), is participating in an archaeological dig. From under a rocky mound, he retrieves the head-fragment of an idol of the Assyrian demon Pazuzu. Intuiting some particular import to the relic, he later climbs to a rocky outcrop to confront an intact and supersized statue of the spirit. The statue has various animal characteristics: it's winged, toothy, and clawfooted. Moreover, we see—and hear—two feral dogs in combat rearing and ripping at each other over the barren earth below (Fig. 8.2 on page 178). As Merrin faces what will become his nemesis, the fierce sound of the beasts battling each other is elongated and amplified; it fills the soundtrack as the scene transitions to Georgetown, where the demonic possession will actually occur.

Animal imagery occurs elsewhere in the film. The demon roars at Merrin that the girl under his control is a "sow," her degraded innocence phrased in animal terms. In a scene absent from the theatrical issue but re-integrated into the popular 2000 re-release, the younger priest attending the ritual, Father Karras (Jason Miller), questions Merrin on why the demon has targeted this girl in particular. Merrin answers: "I think the point is to make us despair: to make us see ourselves as animal and ugly, to reject the possibility that God could love us." In this moment the film partakes in Christianity's traditional attribution of an immortal soul to humanity exclusively.[7] The "animal" slides into place as the negative term in a dualism of sacred/profane, loaded with a host of other associations. In her survey of Christian art, Rowena Loverance points out that while animals may sometimes stand in for virtues, "they are more likely to stand

178 Brute Force

Figure 8.2. As Father Merrin (Max von Sydow) faces the looming status of the demon Pazuzu in *The Exorcist*, we see two feral dogs fighting viciously on the ground below (William Friedkin, Warner Bros.,1973). Digital frame enlargements.

for vices, both individually and corporately. . . . What is more, they have been made to bear a great deal of anti-Christian imagery, carrying the sins of the whole faith, as it were."[8] Val Plumwood writes that Christianity "seek[s] narrative continuity for the individual in the idea of an authentic self that is nonbodily and above the earth," one in which the body is "inessential, devalued and animal."[9] In *The Exorcist*, as in *The Grey* and *The Shallows* (although with a more spiritual vocabulary), animality is representative of a state of existence without redemptive meaning or purpose. The animal evoked here is not merely spiritually lacking, but—as dramatized by the possessed Regan—profoundly licentious, uncontrolled, and unclean. While there are virtually no animals in Friedkin's film, a specific idea of "the animal" is powerfully central.

Feral dogs are noteworthy for being on a conceptual or categorical boundary. Despite their "wildness," they evoke their domesticated cousins with which Western viewers are familiar. Prowling the outskirts of the city of Mosul, the dogs early on in *The Exorcist* are conceptually and literally "on the border" of civilization. Since they are not properly "wild" creatures, they suggest the uncanny breakdown of familiarity and a primitive violence beneath. It's fitting then that these evocations of domestic decay mark the transition to a domestic setting that will undergo a profound breakdown. The film uses these warring dogs to provide an overpowering visual and auditory symbol of defamiliarization and regression.

Canine Confusions in *The Thing*

John Carpenter's *The Thing* (1982) takes place at a remote U.S. scientific base in Antarctica, after an extraterrestrial is unearthed from deep within the ice by a Norwegian rival camp. The "Thing" is a shape-shifting creature that absorbs its prey, colonizing their entire biology with visibly identical cells of its own. The Thing is thus the most paranoia-inducing of monsters: it can look, sound, and behave like any organic lifeform, human or animal. The first incarnation of the Thing we see is at the very start of the film, in the form of a husky dog, escaping the Norwegians, who've now grasped its nature. A helicopter appears over the snowy landscape, its occupants in violent pursuit of the dog as it bounds toward the American base. The helicopter passenger fires shots at the creature with a rifle from above, and when that fails he begins dropping grenades, which the dog also evades. The aircraft is landed near the American base, and the pilot tries to throw a grenade himself but fumbles it, detonating the helicopter and killing himself. Even after this disaster, the rifleman continues his seemingly mad course to shoot the dog until he hits one of the Americans, Bennings (Peter Maloney), in the leg and is shot dead in self-defense.

The film has not provided sufficient information for the viewer to recognize any fault in this desperate dog, and thus easily enlists our sympathy for the animal, positioning it within a traditional and sympathetic frame of domesticity. To all appearances these men are irrationally "hunting" an animal that one does not legitimately hunt. In embracing and offering safety to the persecuted dog, the Americans enact our own sympathy as viewers, recognizing the hunted dog's "proper" domestic nature and attendant right to protection from senseless attack. Afterward, life in the camp goes on, with the addition of this lucky and apparently ordinary working dog. Yet, to the accompaniment of the sinisterly minimal pulsing of Ennio Morricone's score, the dog begins quietly eroding our earlier impressions of vulnerability. It stealthily pushes a door ajar and paces quietly down a hallway, stopping to press its head to a closed door and assess the activity within. When the men bring a bizarrely mangled corpse back from the destroyed Norwegian camp, the dog watches from a doorway, the shot attentively registering the animal's interest. In none of these scenes is there anything explicitly nefarious about the camp's new canine charge. Nevertheless, the dog's behavior, and the camera's interest in it, gradually works to attribute a distinctly private life to the animal, suggesting interests and intentions not coordinated, prescribed, or even known by human masters.

Later, as the men play cards, Bennings criticizes the dog's presence after it brushes against his injured leg under the table: "Clark will you put this mutt with the others where he belongs?" Clark (Richard Masur) obeys, and it's at this point that the dog's curious behavior spectacularly escalates. The other snowdogs laze around inside the pen, but this new one sits carefully down in a sphinx pose, drawing further attention to its mysteriously calculating behavior (Fig. 8.3).

Clark leaves, and together in the darkness the other dogs begin to bark at the new inmate, barking that feverishly escalates as the animal's entire cranium gorily ruptures and blooms open like the petals of a flower. A lashing tentacle spits out—one of numerous now also writhing from the dog-Thing's body. As further mutations begin to sprout, a terrified dog tries to chew through the wire mesh of the pen to escape,

Figure 8.3. No ordinary mutt: the calculating and uncanny dog-Thing (played by wolf-malamute hybrid "Jed") in John Carpenter's *The Thing* (Universal, 1982). Digital frame enlargement.

thereby demonstrating with dire earnestness the vulnerability so faultlessly mimicked earlier by the dog-Thing. When the barking raises alarm, the men rush in to confront a slimy, furless, hound-faced miscreation that confounds clear description. With a flamethrower the men incinerate this still-transforming Thing, yet, as they'll soon realize, this strange creature has already extended its biological influence by taking possession of at least one of these men. But which one? Who is still human, and who (despite his assurances) is secretly a Thing?—and how can this be determined? Considerable suspicion and strife will be stirred up among the men on these questions throughout the remainder of the film, as the insidious alien (in various guises) advances its plot to absorb and simulate everyone it can.

Inherent in the horror of the Thing's revelation here is its deep challenge to our automatic attribution of a particular nature to the fleeing dog: that it is persecuted, distressed, domestic, and terrestrial. Yet, as it turns out, whatever this dog appears to be thinking or feeling at any moment, whatever the dog looks like it is—it isn't. With this in mind, I think the minor human exchange that precedes the shocking canine transformation assumes greater significance. Up until Bennings's complaint at the card table, the dog was essentially a perfect domesticate: a harmless house dog, left to its own devices and permitted autonomy within the base. Bennings's impatient demand that the dog-handler Clark "put this mutt with the others where he belongs" implies a kind of trespass. He disputes the dog's right of way and, in effect, the domesticity that has been attributed to it. While others are content for the dog to inhabit human living and even sleeping quarters, to Bennings it "belongs" with its own kind. We might say that a minor crisis of definition is created over the dog's social status and, ultimately, what a dog is.

Elizabeth Leane and Guinevere Narraway zoom in on the dog in Carpenter's film as a figure that uncomfortably blurs the boundaries between "nature/culture" and "wildness/domesticity"—binaries through which we define ourselves as humans. On the one hand, the dog, as an animal, is representative of "nature" in any nature/culture split, although it remains, they write, an "(imported) part . . . to which humans have historically most related."[10] For them, the dog's unique definitional in-betweenness means it is perfectly positioned to provoke a deeper and more sinister sense of ambiguity—able to give rise to the ultimate boundary-blurring paranoia of the Thing. The transgression of a nature-culture/wild-domestic boundary is particularly potent here given this dog's irrepressibly wolflike appearance, which underscores its latent "wildness." Indeed, the dog-Thing was played by animal actor "Jed," actually a wolf-malamute hybrid. Leane and Narraway highlight the tension this creates when combined with the dog-Thing's almost over-performed domesticity—for instance, as it paces the hallway, pressing its ear calculatingly to each door: "This animal," they write, "is both more and less than a dog—more knowing, arguably more 'human,' than one would expect, yet also more wolflike, and therefore more wild, than a dog."[11] This explanation is suggestive of Noël Carroll's hypothesis of threat posed by horror monsters. Carroll emphasizes many monsters' confusion of stable and accepted cultural categories: monsters that are somehow both alive and dead, animate and inanimate, half-creature, half-man, and so on. For Carroll, our sense of cultural order is dependent on familiar systems of classification, and these horror creatures that defy stable categories provoke for us a sense of "impurity" and cognitive dissonance. Horror monsters, he writes, "are un-natural relative to a culture's conceptual scheme of nature. They do not fit the scheme; they violate it. Thus, monsters are not only physically threatening; they are cognitively threatening."[12] Similarly, the spectacular Thing arises following a creeping sense of this animal's contradictory nature as something both wild and calculatingly "too civilized." Before the dog becomes obviously a monster, we're made more and more uncomfortable with it as a dog.

Straying Too Far: *Cujo*

Lewis Teague's *Cujo* (1983) also evokes a tension between "civilized" and "wild" identities. The eponymous Cujo is a harmless Saint Bernard turned mankiller after contracting rabies, thus thoroughly inverting the breed's historical associations with human rescue. The film begins with a curious dramatization of the dog's position in between human and animal worlds. We see a wild brown rabbit scouting the scenic countryside around it, but then into this pastoral idyll enters the similarly "animal" yet awkwardly contrasting Saint Bernard. As this dog, whom we will come to know as Cujo, pursues his newfound prey, he's clearly enthralled by the freedom and stimulation of this natural environment. In challenging the forest critter, the dog initially strikes a mildly threatening presence. Yet pleasure in this dog's chase is permitted by the suggestion of his inadequacy as a domestic animal attempting to match (and catch) a wild counterpart—the dog probably won't kill this rabbit anyway. Indeed, as the rabbit sprints into a hollow log to exit out of the other side, the dog wastes time staring into a space he clearly cannot fit. Only "playing" the wild predator, the dog is without a wild thing's instinctive sense of strategy, and poorly aware of the limitations of his own body.

This scenario is repeated as the rabbit darts into another hole with Cujo in hot pursuit. But this time the hole leads to a deep cave. The rabbit is safely tucked away and undisturbed, but Cujo's frustrated barking disturbs innumerable black bats, who swarm screeching around the dog's head, with one of the creatures sinking its contaminated fangs into his too-curious nose. The dog, his head still stuck, is shot from behind as he struggles and howls, his body clumsily vulnerable (Fig. 8.4).

In this scene we see a contrast between wilderness, with its connotations of freedom—but also volatility and danger—and the more civilized associations of domesticity. While large and potentially imposing, this purebred dog is clearly no wild animal, yet there's also real delight in his exploration beyond the domestic, in his irrepressible natural instinct to wander and chase. Yet pursuing the rabbit into the cave is a bridge too far, and leads to a more permanent infection of the straying dog by an uncivilized wildness through the disease he contracts. Later in the film, as Cujo reaches the peak of his rabid transformation, he's glimpsed through a gloomy mesh of trees, the once-cuddly dog now a creature of the darkest wilderness, his change evoking the uncertainty (and the potential reversal) of the dog's domestication.

After Cujo's fateful wounding, we meet some human characters, the Trenton family: Tad Trenton (Danny Pintauro), a young boy who shivers in fear of the monster in his closet, and his parents Vic (Daniel Hugh Kelly) and Donna (Dee Wallace). Cujo isn't the Trenton family dog but rather the dog of a working-class family, the Cambers. The father, Joe

Figure 8.4. Sticking your nose where it doesn't belong: the playful Saint Bernard is contaminated by the dark side of the wilderness he enjoys in *Cujo* (Lewis Teague, Warner Bros., 1983). Digital frame enlargement.

Camber (Ed Lauter), is a mechanic, and eventually Donna, accompanied by her son Tad, will drive her dying car out to the Camber property for repair. The Cambers aren't home but the by-now thoroughly rabid Cujo is. In this the film's climax, mother and child are besieged in their car by the crazed canine, whom Tad interprets as his bedtime monster incarnate. Escape for the two seems impossible, but there's a discarded baseball bat on the ground nearby: Donna must summon the courage to leave the safety of the car and confront the slobbery and deranged predator.

In the contamination of the domestic creature with a volatile wildness Teague's film recalls Disney's *Old Yeller*, albeit framing the animal's transformation as one of horror rather than tragedy. In *Old Yeller*, the beloved farm dog, once an annoying stray, is bitten while gallantly defending his adopted family from a rabid wolf. The closeness of the family's oldest child, Travis (Tommy Kirk), to his canine companion means Yeller's decline achieves famously harrowing tenor when, in his father's absence, Travis steps up to put down his rabid best friend. Yeller's admirable fighting allegiance to his family ironically leads to a terrible inversion as, once infected, Yeller presents an untenable danger to the family—the dog is transformed totally by the pathogen of his dark and savage opponent/counterpart. In *Cujo*, however, the dog is left essentially unlinked to any human companion, interacting little with his family prior to infection. This means the film can position the dog on the periphery of society (and the narrative), permitting his gradual transformation into a "monster" without human characters noticing until they're under attack. Complementing this, Tad's monster-fear allows the film to invest the increasingly deranged dog with a more superstitious sense of dread.

However, not merely a spooky reminder of childhood fears, the increasingly savage Cujo comes to manifest a more fundamental structural tension within the Trenton home. The Trentons' life has all the signifiers of bourgeois bliss: clearly wealthy, the family occupy a spacious double-story house, the spoils of the father's job in the advertising business, to which he drives his Jaguar convertible. During his hard-earned leisure time, Vic sometimes plays tennis with Steve Kemp (Christopher Stone), a local carpenter. Early in the film, the duo play a match in which Vic bests his opponent, as is apparently his habit. When the loser offers a rematch, Vic can't help but note his partner's seeming eagerness to lose again: "Whatever turns you on." As it happens, Vic is the real loser here, and what turns on Steve is Vic's wife—the following scene shows him in bed with Donna. The hint of some hidden corruption of domestic normalcy is additionally suggested by TV commercials for cereal we see playing on the Trenton family's TV (and produced by Vic Trenton's company), featuring a professor character who tastes the product, telling viewers, "Nope—nothing wrong here!" The professor's weirdly minimalist endorsement is about as comforting as Donna Trenton's evasive assurances when her husband gently asks about the state of their marriage. Vic knows there's something wrong, but it will take him till later in the film to figure it out. By contrast, the Camber family, to which Cujo belongs, manifests domestic tension overtly. Joe Camber is an abusive alcoholic, and Cujo's overlapping into the richer family's life implies their contamination by a similar domestic upheaval. All throughout the film, incidents of domestic conflict are matched by shots of Cujo sulking somewhere and groaning; as in *The Exorcist*, the dog becomes a symbol of decaying domesticity. The film reaches its hectic climax after Vic discovers the affair (just as Donna was calling it off—bad luck), and he's called away on work business; hence, Donna is alone with her son, ready for particular punishment, when the monstrous dog attacks.

Curiously, the film seems careful to show what a caring husband and father Vic is. The family's house is huge, and he is obviously an excellent provider, but it's also he who primarily attends to their son when he has bad dreams, and Donna praises his parenting. When Vic feels he's getting the cold shoulder in the bedroom, he tactfully asks about it. What is perhaps most interesting about Donna's affair is how seemingly random it is. When her lover Steve asks her why she wants to call it all off, she replies as if she has been mystified by her own conduct: "Well, gee," she says, "I've got this great husband at home, great kid, and here I am fooling around with the local stud." The affair seems conspicuous by its pointlessness beyond novel sexual gratification—that Steve is indeed a "stud." Consequently, the film seems to position Donna's "straying" to echo that of Cujo at the start of the film. The opening scene shows us a creature gripped by his own innate sense of play and attraction beyond his domestic environment, reveling as if he were a wild thing. In her affair, Donna too has pursued an instinctive desire beyond the civilized world she usually inhabits. And indeed, the macho working-class Steve is a "wilder" man than her husband. His house is a shambles, and after she rejects him he reveals a volatile temper. Donna won't leave her husband; she obviously isn't interested in Steve as a long-term prospect, but she wanted some wild play in the meantime. In short, her otherwise pointless affair suggests her usually suppressed "animal" instincts, evoking a "wildness" within the human.

In the opening of *Jaws*, Chrissie seems to embrace a playful spontaneity, frolicking in the natural environment as she lures her would-be lover on—that is, before her attempt to embrace a utopian "wild" freedom is violently canceled by the brutal wildness of the shark. In *Cujo*, too, a female character feels the pull of something primal and faces terrifying animal opposition. We know that several films feature male characters overtaken by their own wildness and then fatally punished for letting their civility slip away. For female characters, the "wildness" seems more likely to manifest sexually, probably because of the greater moral importance placed on female sexual "civility" in the rather paternalistic world of the films concerned.[13] Donna isn't killed off immediately like Chrissie, and she doesn't lose herself to her instincts like her male counterparts; instead she remains troubled by this part of herself that she cannot easily reconcile with her everyday life. It's unsurprising, then, that it is Donna Trenton specifically who must face up to Cujo in the film's climax: the dog manifests as a hideous incarnation of the worst extreme of domestic defection, terrorizing Donna with the "wild" impulses she has entertained. Most obviously, *Cujo* is a film about a dog who becomes radically undomesticated after straying too far from domestic life, but through his connection to Donna the film hints at the perils for humans of transgressing the "proper" limits of domesticity. Donna must face the animal threat without the male help she has offended through her infidelity. Moreover, by defending her son, she must prove her maternal chops after the affair that destabilized her family and (given the film's conservative milieu) undermined her motherly competence. Donna will survive—will defeat the monster that has been "dogging" her. However, through her bloody and traumatic ordeal, the film also suggests that she will have been sufficiently shocked back into the world of domesticity for good.

9

Beast Mode

Becoming the Wolf Man

MYTHS OF HUMAN–ANIMAL hybrids have circulated throughout many cultures; the most cinematically prominent, however, have been tales of those cursed with fur and fangs, contorted not only into wolfish form but also held in thrall to the impulses of a wild thing. Wolves have been a long-running threat to humans (and protohumans) in some regions, including Europe, where werewolf legend proliferated (Fig. 9.1 on page 188). The fairytale "Little Red Riding Hood," as Hart and Sussman point out, would have had some origin in the fear and frequency of wolf attacks, given that "the power of life and death was on the wolves' side for most of the evolutionary expanse of wolf–human interactions in Eurasia."[1] Accordingly, early werewolf lore depicts these beasts as agents of terror and evil. Moreover, as "Little Red Riding Hood" suggests, the werewolf trope frighteningly speculates a feared predator's disguised infiltration of otherwise safe society.

What is it like to become a wolf? To suddenly bristle with fur as the mystical pull of the full moon takes hold and fangs protrude from your salivary maw? What is it like to be given over to the rapacious instincts of the predator? Some thought they knew: "lycanthropy" has been applied clinically to mental disturbances in those who believed themselves to be wolves, and acted the part too—growling, gnawing furniture, howling at the moon. However, lycanthropy is not considered a distinct pathology, but rather an idiosyncratic expression of other conditions such as schizophrenia or the effects of drug abuse.[2] Aside from the delusional among

Figure 9.1. Detail from *Werewolf* (1512), woodcut by Lucas Cranach the Elder (1472–1553). Herzogliches Museum.

us, we don't claim to know what lupine life is like, and the mentally ill don't know, either—such episodes are extreme manifestations of human imaginative power. Horror movies are such manifestations too, and the genre has immersed us in numerous accounts of variously liberating, painful, feverish, and enraged man-wolf metamorphoses.

The modern werewolf's transformation is almost always involuntary, with the condition shown to be evaporating its subject's feelings of free will. While werewolfism typically confers great physical strength, it subtracts psychological control. This process often attracts our empathy as viewers: if a wolf man can't help what he becomes, then deep down he's not truly as morally monstrous as his appearance and behavior imply. This suggestion isn't new: as Leslie Sconduto notes, treatments of the werewolf in the medieval era began to frame werewolves through more complicated and sometimes understanding lenses.[3] An essential and morally upright "human" often remains inside, evoking the possibility of cure, redemption, or simply sympathy.

We often look to animals to describe seemingly aberrant human conduct, describing wrongdoers as acting like "pigs," "rats," "worms," and as behaving "like animals." Such vocabulary projects onto animals impulses and behaviors that we have trouble accepting as part of the human. This chapter tracks several cinematic werewolves to explore what kinds of dark desires are reflected by them. The title here refers to wolf men in particular because becoming a werewolf has been predominantly a male problem. Male werewolves are at the heart of classic werewolf films, while female werewolves are typically marginal figures. In Neil Marshall's *Dog Soldiers* (2002) a female werewolf makes an unexpected and late appearance, but unlike her male brethren she's put down before she hits her rabid peak. Even in the action-horror franchise *Underworld* (2002–2016), which depicts the gang war of vampires against "lycans," and thus contains multitudes of both creatures, we see that while the vampire crew are diversely gendered, the werewolves are overwhelmingly male. We've so far seen several cases of conceptual overlap between men and animality in animal horror, especially through concerns that a useful level of animal energy might tip over into something more troubling. As we'll see, many werewolf films might be thought of as this theme's apotheosis. Male-focused though the subgenre may be, I'll still include a few she-beasts, considering how they intersect with the standard laid down by their male counterparts. The werewolf is clearly a long-running trope: I don't intend to negate the various particular, idiosyncratic, and creative ways writers and filmmakers have used it, but I think we can still chow down on a few key preoccupations of films that sensationally let loose the animal within.

"He kills what he loves best": *Werewolf of London*

An eminent London botanist, Wilfred Glendon is an early victim of cinema's full-moon fever in *Werewolf of London* (1935). The dedicated researcher treks up a Tibetan mountain to locate a fabled flower specimen that blooms only in the light of the moon, foolishly ignoring local legend of a curse. Wilfred secures the sample, but at a high price: a wolf man sneaks up and gnaws into his arm, transmitting to him the terrible affliction. Years later, we learn that Wilfred has endured periodic transformation into the same sort of man-beast (Fig. 9.2 on page 190). He neglects his young wife Lisa (Valerie Hobson) to work busily in his lab, trying to coax a bloom from his hard-won flower in the hope of generating a cure for his secret syndrome. One evening the crabby recluse reluctantly attends a party where a mysterious guest, Dr. Yogami (Warner Oland), fills Wilfred in on the specifics of werewolf lore, specifically that such a creature will "kill what it loves best," thereby instilling further anxiety in the secretive scientist. His beastly outbursts aren't Wilfred's only problem. Bored and dejected by her workaholic husband, Lisa flits around town with an old school chum and former fiancé, Paul (Lester Matthews), provoking Wilfred's jealousy and thus steering him toward Yogami's grim prophecy.

Figure 9.2. Wilfred Glendon (Henry Hull) lurks in his laboratory as his change takes hold in *Werewolf of London* (Stuart Walker, Universal, 1935). Digital frame enlargement.

I noted in chapter 5 that *Werewolf* is undergirded by a subtext of Christian humility: with Wilfred worn out and at wits' end, he appeals to the Almighty as he again awaits his transformation. Yogami explicitly refers to the creature as a satanic creation—the half-man, half-wolf is a beast of the ungodly in-between, and indeed, to be a werewolf, theologians once thought, was to be suffering under the spell of Satan.[4] Moving past this more explicit theme, we also need to be alert to the romantic turmoil that parallels Wilfred's transformation. He has been working for a cure for some time, yet the story we see begins when the romantic rival steps onto the scene. Lisa's one-time lover is a dashing adventurer, a man contrasting in youth, excitement, and personality to the surly and isolated Wilfred (habitually holed up in his lab). The scientist's disdain for his competitor is undisguised from the outset, and he later bitterly refuses to join the former lovers for dinner (Fig. 9.3). Eventually Paul makes his move, and Lisa confesses the misery of her marriage. In this context, the physical transformation of Wilfred is highly suggestive of a psychological change induced by sexual jealousy, an emotional response strongly linked to mate-murder—just the kind of murder alluded to by Yogami.

Figure 9.3. Lisa Glendon (Valerie Hobson, center) introduces her suspicious husband Wilfred (Henry Hull, left) to her former lover Paul (Lester Matthews, right), of whom Wilfred is correct to be suspicious, in *Werewolf of London* (Stuart Walker, Universal, 1935). Digital frame enlargement.

Research into the evolutionary psychology of jealousy, especially the work of David Buss and colleagues, provides disturbing insights that resonate uncannily with werewolf cinema. Romantic jealousy exists in all human cultures, and is a highly significant cause of violence and homicide between spouses, as well as between mate-rivals.[5] There is by now extensive evidence that jealousy in both sexes is an evolved response to the problems of human mating throughout deep history—namely, the pressure to retain a valued mate. For heterosexual men, specifically, a central problem of human mating has been paternity uncertainty. A female can always be certain that a child is her own, but a male cannot: male sexual jealousy (and attendant mate-guarding behavior) is an adaptation against the threat of cuckoldry.[6] Successful gene reproduction is the underlying biological "program" of all organisms, and failure to reproduce left males at a genetic dead end. In the ancestral environment, mistaken paternity was a devastating blow, as it meant that resources of both time and labor had been squandered in the service of another male's offspring.[7] Accordingly, studies consistently show that relative to heterosexual women, heterosexual men are more incensed by sexual infidelity, particularly.[8] Today, of course, we might not have the slightest intention of having children (and have even taken precautions against it); but this is a highly novel situation to which our emotions are not adapted. Our rational computations may be in the twenty-first century, but our emotions are still running a stone-age program. Similarly, this is not to say that any man who discovers his partner having an affair consciously thinks in that moment about his "jeopardized paternity": the point is that the possessive impulses of jealousy evolved to guard against that threat. Accordingly, it's little surprise that in *Werewolf of London* we see the wolfish transformation of Wilfred linked to an obvious trigger of jealousy. As the young wife flirts with the younger rival, ever more threateningly, the ugliness and aggression of the werewolf arise to metaphorize the rage of losing sexual possession.

We know that the jealous Wilfred will eventually try to "kill what he loves best," but why would he? Jealousy motivates mate-guarding behavior, sometimes involving intimidation, but it isn't intuitively clear why this might result in murder—except perhaps as the accidental by-product of hostile jealousy. Here things get even darker. Buss has provided alarming evidence that more than simply the slip-up of an over-jealous mind, evolved adaptations for mate-murder likely exist in us as well. He suggests the existence of a psychological module the function of which is "not threat or deterrence, but rather the literal death of a mate," that may be activated under particular circumstances.[9] But how could murdering a cheating mate ever have been reproductively "beneficial," fostering such a disturbing psychological adaptation over evolutionary time? In every culture, cuckolds are objects of disrespect and ridicule. To be cuckolded would have inflicted profound damage on a male's reputation and meant a drop in his social status.[10] Given that women tend to mate across and up social dominance hierarchies, the humiliation of cuckoldry also meant loss of future mating potential—it had disastrous flow-on genetic effects, in addition to the initial threat of mistaken paternity.[11] In the small tribal groups in which humans have historically lived, murdering a defecting mate could have gone some way to maintaining male prestige and social standing, effectively recovering one's future mating potential. The murderer would have announced himself as one not to be trifled with by future mates, as well as intimidating any future mate poachers.[12] In polygynous societies, where a male might have had more than one female, murder would have struck fear into the remaining females, reducing the chance of further desertions.[13] The death of the female would also have eradicated the constant reminder of the male's humiliation. Most of us are familiar with the dark and seemingly illogical sentiment of many jilted and jealous lovers: "If I can't have her, no one can." This is clearly despicable morally, but in evolutionary terms it is (disturbingly) logical. Again, given that humans have spent their natural history living in small communities, in the ruthless game of natural selection mate-murder also worked to handicap the genetic competition. If a male murders a defecting mate, his loss will not become another's gain: murder denies rivals access to a mate that one has personally lost anyway.[14]

Mate-murder would have been a net reproductive benefit only under quite particular conditions; if the victim had nearby kin who could retaliate, for example, the option would become too costly for him. Killing a mate would also have to not jeopardize any of the male's existing children by taking away a crucial caregiver.[15] Nevertheless, given that it provided a last-ditch means of salvaging the male's future mating potential, as Buss summarizes, "As disturbing as the idea is, mate killing under certain circumstances would have been reproductively advantageous, leading to the evolution of psychological circuits for mate murder."[16] Under this lens, the relationship between sexual jealousy and werewolfism becomes clearer: in Wilfred's tale we see a folk dramatization of alarmingly dark impulses, a way of explaining why a man might "transform," and feel compelled to, specifically, "kill what he loves best." Cultural evidence suggests that at some level we understand that a normal man may transform into something beast-like under such circumstances. Buss notes that "in Texas, until 1974, a husband who killed a wife and her lover when he caught them in flagrante delicto was not judged criminal. In fact, a law held that a 'reasonable man' would respond to such extreme provocation with acts of violence."[17] Similarly, until the 1970s, in New Mexico and Utah, murder in these circumstances was also not considered a crime, and there have been similar legal exemptions worldwide.[18] Among the Yapese of Micronesia, for example, "a husband who caught his wife in bed with another man 'had the right to kill her and the adulterer or to burn them in the house.'"[19] These allowances imply a disquieting portrait of a "reasonable man," from whom extreme violence may still arise. However ethically unsettling, numerous cultures have understood that, on rare occasion, otherwise sane men may absent themselves and become something more brutal: an alarming scenario for which the transformation of a well-to-do husband into a ferocious beast seems a particularly apt metaphor.

Wolf-man Wilfred's sexual jealousy, with a final goal of mate-murder, is reflected in his victims, who are clearly proxies for his wife. Warned by Yogami, we already know that Lisa is the ultimate target, yet this can't happen immediately because it would force the narrative to a resolution too soon. Before he goes after his spouse, Wilfred crawls through a window in downtown London to pounce on an inebriated female party guest, who nevertheless manages to holler for help before the wolf man strikes. Quite sure that the very Devil had come to get her, she loudly laments her "worldly wickedness" as having brought on such a fate. Having failed here, in a pinch Wilfred falls on a young blonde woman in the street instead, a person credited as a "streetwalker"—again suggestive of transgressive sexual morality. Later, stalking around the London Zoo, he strikes the drunken mistress of a night-watchman (Jeanne Bartlett), who moments ago embraced her paramour in a passionate display before he guiltily tried to shrug her off: "I've got a wife and kids." These victims are not random: in the world of the film, they're women diminished in sexual virtue—a series of deflections that foreshadow Wilfred's true target, as Lisa's betrayal builds.

Finally, the interloper Paul confesses his enduring love, and the stage is properly set. Despite moaning about her marriage and having given Paul every sign of reciprocating his attraction, Lisa surprisingly declines: "We've been through it all before," she huffs. Wilfred, however, doesn't know about her rebuff, and in wolfish form dashes in to throttle his wife. She gets away, but Wilfred later strikes again at his own home. He knocks Paul unconscious and smashes his way inside to get at his wife in an attack evocative of real-world intimate partner violence (Fig. 9.4). Shot by the

Figure 9.4. Kill what he loves best: Wilfred (Henry Hull), having broken into his own house, reaches for his wife Lisa (Valerie Hobson) at the climax of *Werewolf of London* (Stuart Walker, Universal, 1935). Digital frame enlargement.

police in the nick of time, Wilfred dies, his human appearance returning as he does so. Those left behind resolve to lie about what they've seen to preserve his honor: Wilfred was killed accidentally while defending his wife against an intruder, they say. This conceptual separation between the man and beast decontaminates Wilfred's identity, divesting him of responsibility. This provides a mythic analogue to the kind of laws that excused jealousy-related spousal homicide: here is a man, the film implies, inherently noble, who became a monster uncharacteristically.

Literary werewolves have been used in a variety of ways, but it's worth noting that the theme of cuckoldry and male honor violence is clear in one of werewolf fiction's early landmarks, "Bisclavret," a short story composed in the twelfth century by the medieval poet Marie de France. The eponymous Bisclavret is a noble knight and loving husband, yet one who worries his wife by mysteriously vanishing for three days of the week before returning home in high spirits, apparently thankful to be back. The husband refuses his wife's questions, fearing he will lose her love. But she wears him down eventually, and he confesses that he absconds to transform into a wolf, and lives in the forest until the condition passes. Bisclavret's fears were well founded, it turns out: his wife sends for a local knight who has long sought after her, and starts an affair with him: "I offer you my love and my body; make me your mistress."[20] She instructs her new lover to steal her husband's clothes from their hiding place while he's on his wolfish sojourn, thereby depriving him of the ability to be changed back. A year passes, and the King encounters the wolf on a hunting expedition. When the creature graciously pleads with its royal would-be killer, it shows itself to be no ordinary beast. This strange, well-mannered wolf becomes a favorite of King and court alike, yet when the knight who took Bisclavret's wife comes to call there, Bisclavret attacks, dragging him to the ground. Bisclavret has the respect of the court, so they assume that there must be some reason for this strange outburst. Later, Bisclavret's wife is subject to an even more brutal assault: "When Bisclavret saw her approach, no one could restrain him. He dashed towards her like a madman. Just hear how successfully he took his revenge. He tore the nose right off her face."[21] The King again suspects some mystery motive, and interrogates the wife into a confession. In the end, Bisclavret's clothes are returned to him, allowing his restoration to human form, and his wife and her lover are banished.

As Sconduto points out, "Neither the rightness of Bisclavret's action nor the sympathy of the narrator is left in doubt,"[22] ensuring that we read in the tale an aggressive punishment of sexual betrayal. Bisclavret's mutilation of his wife, while nonfatal, is a devastating attack on her attractiveness; she was introduced as "worthy and attractive in appearance."[23]

Her value in the mating arena has been profoundly degraded through honor violence aimed at ruining her mate-value for other men: if he can't have her, no one can. The stories of both Bisclavret and Wilfred imply jealousy-motivated aggression so violent and out of character that it can be explained only through the metaphor of physical—and bestial—transformation.

The Hairiest Heir: *The Wolf Man*

In George Waggner's *The Wolf Man*, lycanthropy is similarly linked with male violence, although in this case it's more closely tied to social status and sexual aggression. Larry Talbot (Lon Chaney Jr.) is a cordial and charming young gentleman returning to the family estate after the unfortunate death of his brother. In the village, he chats up local girl Gwen Conliffe (Evelyn Ankers), while inspecting a cane inscribed with the sign of the werewolf. "What big eyes you have," he jokes, working wolfishness into his flirtation, and he tells Gwen that he'll pick her up that evening for a date. Out with Gwen that night at the town's edge, Talbot must dash to the rescue of her friend Jenny (Fay Helm), as she's attacked by a wolf. He kills the beast, bludgeoning it with his new cane, but not in time to prevent Jenny's death and not before he incurs a deep bite. Talbot claims he killed a wolf in self-defense; the police say he killed a local gypsy (Bela Lugosi)—the werewolf having reverted off-camera to his human form, leaving everyone confused. Talbot's wound heals almost immediately, but he soon develops the telltale symptoms and escapes into the night to go human hunting.

The timing of Talbot's infection is important. After he successfully persuades Gwen to meet him for a moonlight stroll, she annoyingly arrives with the ill-fated Jenny in tow. The trio walk through the woods, where they encounter the gypsy's wagon. Talbot knows an opening when he sees one, and urges Jenny to go inside and have her fortune told, thereby allowing him some unchaperoned time with the lovely Gwen. Yet as this industrious suitor leans his would-be lover against a tree, ready to express his affection physically, Gwen makes a confession: she's engaged to be married. The admission has been almost absurdly delayed, but it's a definitive rejection: "In fact, I really shouldn't be here." Talbot isn't so easily deterred: "Oh, but you *are* here . . ." He still has Gwen leaning up against the tree when he hears Jenny's screams and runs to her aid (Fig. 9.5). The attack does not simply provide a narrative mechanism through which Talbot contracts lycanthropy; it seems to channel into werewolfism his sexual frustration after he learns that his energetic efforts have been a waste of time. Becoming a werewolf, the film insinuates, is effectively

Figure 9.5. On an evening walk in *The Wolf Man* (George Waggner, Universal, 1941), Gwen Conliffe (Evelyn Ankers) admits to her admirer Larry Talbot (Lon Chaney Jr.) that her heart belongs to another: "I really shouldn't be here." "Oh, but you *are* here," Larry responds. Digital frame enlargement.

to be possessed by a more brutal temper, to see sex as something to be taken by force.

Yet Larry Talbot's distressing lupine state isn't only a metaphor for sexual violence: becoming the wolf man also badly damages his social currency and confidence. His wealthy family have quite a standing in the village, and the son's homecoming represents a further promotion given that the death of the brother has left him the sole heir. Once respected and upwardly mobile, Talbot is affected by lycanthropy as if it were a secret and obscene disease. His transformation into the hairy beast disqualifies him from the female attention he obviously desires; additionally, though, since Gwen's fiancé is the Talbots' estate gamekeeper, it buries him below his rival (and employee) in social station.

Talbot's injured social status also explicitly overlaps with the stigma of mental illness. His father (Claude Rains) refers early on to lycanthropy as a disease of the mind, and the discrepancies in his son's story (was he attacked by a wolf or by a gypsy?), along with his anxious behavior, lead the local doctor and constable to doubt his sanity. "They're treating me like I was crazy!" he cries after the men question him. The once confident, outgoing man-about-town has become enfeebled, fearful, racked with self-doubt, and ejected from a social hierarchy in which he was previously impressively integrated.

The psychological subtext is amplified in the film's loose 2010 remake through a deliberate Freudian influence focused on childhood trauma.[24] In this version, Larry Talbot (Benicio Del Toro) is initially bitten (we discover later) by his own father (Anthony Hopkins), who thereby passes on the curse of his hyper-aggressive masculinity. The film opens with Talbot playing Hamlet (the exemplary oedipal character) in the West End, where he receives news that his brother has been killed in an animal attack. Talbot reluctantly agrees to return upon the request of Gwen (Emily Blunt), his brother's widow in this telling of the tale. Talbot is haunted by his mother's death when he was a child: in dreams he recalls finding mom lying with a slashed throat and a straight-razor in her hand. But eventually the true memory rises to conscious awareness: his father the werewolf killed her, and little Larry saw it. The memory is a version of the "primal scene" described by Freud, in which the child witnesses a sexual act between his parents, and in his confusion interprets it as an act of violence toward the mother.[25] For the unwed and childless Talbot, sexuality is lethal and traumatic. At one point he finds himself gazing deeply at the exposed skin above where Gwen's dress is buttoned—then entranced by her lips as she speaks to him—and the werewolf infection begins to exert its power over him, the curse suffusing sexuality with danger.

Unlike its predecessor, the remake doesn't shy away from the pleasures of bestial violence. Straight-jacketed and sedated in an asylum, Talbot is run through a battery of Victorian psychiatric tortures by doctors who assume he's simply disturbed. But he soon transforms before a crowd of these smug medical spectators (Fig. 9.6), escaping captivity to smash his way around the city much in the manner of King Kong before him (albeit on a smaller scale). Social destruction feels good, but ultimately the recognition of one's power demands that it be directed toward restoring order rather than demolishing it: Talbot must confront his monstrous werewolf dad. Sir John Talbot has been completely out of control: not only did he infect his son, but it was also he who killed the brother, over his own desire for Gwen. Father and son fight in werewolf form, as Sir John barks, "Finally you're the man I always wanted you to be." Sir John represents a by-now familiar brand of intolerably violent and oversexed masculinity that cannot endure. But also, given the film's overtly Freudian schema, he's intended to symbolize the Id, the aggression his son contains but must conquer.

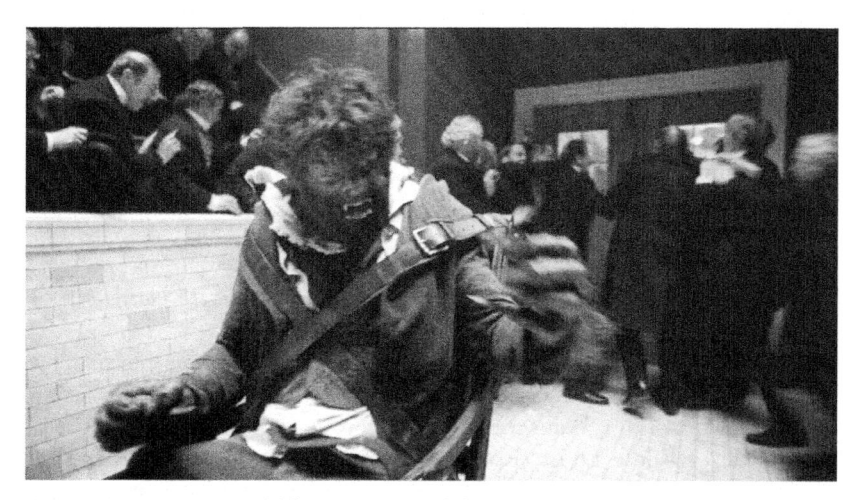

Figure 9.6. Lawrence Talbot (Benicio del Toro) begins busting through his restraints as terrified doctors flee the lecture theater in Joe Johnston's *The Wolfman* (Universal, 2010). Digital frame enlargement.

Bestial Desires: *The Curse of the Werewolf*

In Hammer's *The Curse of the Werewolf* (1961), lycanthropy is also strongly inflected by sexual transgression, although within a more moralistic framework. After a mute servant girl (Yvonne Romain) resists the advances of the cruel and decrepit Spanish marquis (Anthony Dawson) for whom she works, she's imprisoned in his castle dungeon. She rejects one predator only to fall into the den of another—being raped by a prisoner (Richard Wordsworth) at least as revolting as her employer. Her grubby attacker has been locked up so long his humanity is obviously in retreat, his arms grotesquely bristling with white hair. She escapes and gives birth to a boy but dies soon afterward, and the infant, Leon, is adopted, baptized, and raised by an affluent Spanish couple. One day he sweetly tries to kiss and make better a squirrel shot by his uncle, but the taste of its blood triggers some latent impulse: from now on he will sneak out by night to savage local livestock. The boy's wolfish impulses are tamed by the love of his concerned mother and father, but shortly after he leaves home (as a fully grown Oliver Reed), old hungers re-emerge.

Curse is one of the most conservative treatments of the werewolf myth. Leon is quite fine until he strays into a brothel one night and finds himself lured upstairs. The moon is full as the young man, sulky and sweaty, tries and fails to resist transformation. This moral subtext is supported by the film's consistently grotesque depiction of sexuality generally, through the mother's victimization by the vile Marquis and then the foul dungeon-lurker who rapes and impregnates her. As an adult, Leon also gets a chiding from his employer after his visit to the brothel. In the world of the film, male sexuality outside of marriage seems to invite moral corruption and, in Leon's case, risks irreversible animal transformation.

Sexual Awakenings in *The Howling* and *An American Werewolf in London*

The turmoil of repressed and stifled sexuality returns in *The Howling* and *An American Werewolf in London*, both released in 1981. In *The Howling*, reporter Karen (Dee Wallace) takes dangerous steps investigating serial sex-murderer Eddie Quist (Robert Picardo) for a television special, following Quist's instructions to meet him in a seedy LA porno theater. She takes a seat as a rough group-sex scene plays out on the screen, a bound and gagged woman writhing on a bed. Eddie sits behind Karen, whispering his obsession with her as she faces the front, where a forceful version of male sexual aggression plays out. At Eddie's request, she turns to look at him. We don't get to see him ourselves (his visage cloaked in darkness), but his supernaturally lowered voice, and Karen's reverse-shot reaction, tells us that some disturbing transformation has taken place and what she sees is now not a figurative but instead a literal monster. Karen flees the theater, and the police shoot the killer dead. But the trauma has made its mark, and after a run of dreams and flashbacks, Karen and her husband Bill (Christopher Stone) are sent on a therapeutic retreat by psychiatrist Dr. Waggner (Patrick Macnee),[26] where further terror, not healing, follows.

Karen's traumatic werewolf experience is obviously matched to transgressive sexual desire. The grimy neon cityscape she navigates on her way to the porno theater suggests both danger and desire, as does what she sees on the movie screen there. The psychiatrist Waggner also links suppressed sexuality and violence: he's brought in initially as a talking head for a documentary on serial killers, but the theme is "the beast in all of us," and he advocates a sort of Freudian hedonism in which repressed desires are safely expressed. The experience with Eddie Quist stuns Karen out of the world of domesticated sexual normalcy, and she cannot bring herself to agree to sex with her husband—seemingly too dangerous after her alarming encounter. At Waggner's therapy retreat, Bill begins indulging his own repressed desires by ditching his vegetarian diet and falling under the spell of the nymphomaniac Marsha (Elisabeth Brooks); there's only so much polite civility, the film seems to suggest, that we can comfortably take. Marsha is of course a werewolf, transforming her new lover: the two sprout fangs during sex in a symbolic fusion of danger and illicit desire (Fig. 9.7).

As it turns out, the therapeutic retreat, a parody of the utopian free-love communes of the hippie era, is really a camouflaged werewolf enclave. The getaway here is designed to help them channel their powers, to realize Waggner's philosophy of properly channeled impulses. Eddie Quist, also a retreat member, comes back to life and stalks around the grounds after Karen. Chaos breaks out among these ravenous residents, making clear that the experiment is a failure—the condition cannot be tamed. The idealistic Waggner doesn't grasp the fundamentally anarchic nature of sexuality: sex in *The Howling*, like the wolf, is forever unpredictable. Through sex-murderer Eddie Quist the film seems to imply that freeing repressed desires might have the allure of liberation, but it's also on a continuum that sometimes goes very far indeed.

The Howling twice notes that Karen didn't adopt her husband's surname: it may be that the film intends to comment conservatively on feminism's resistance to tradition, suggesting that marriage offers safeguards against sexual vulnerability. In any case, the ambivalence of sexual transgression seems to be flattened into a traditional good/evil paradigm by the film's conclusion. Karen escapes the retreat, and broadcasts the existence of werewolves on live television, attempting to warn the outside

Figure 9.7. Bill Neill (Christopher Stone) sprouts fangs during a moonlight tryst with werewolf Marsha (Elisabeth Brooks, out of frame) in *The Howling* (Joe Dante, Universal, 1981). Digital frame enlargement.

world. In doing so, she lectures on the struggle between cruelty and kindness "that separates us from the animals," and turns into a werewolf on camera to prove her sensational claims, before a colleague shoots her dead in a prearranged act of euthanasia. Once one is contaminated, there is no way back to normalcy. In a comic twist, her TV-viewing audience dismisses what they've seen as just a lurid special-effects stunt. *The Howling* as a whole contains several semi-comic moments, but this response from the audience marks a definitive turn into comedy. We see that she-wolf Marsha has escaped the camp: she orders a rare hamburger in a bar, a jokey prelude to a more taboo kind of treat. This conclusion relieves the tension accumulated around Karen's dramatic death, but it also suggests that the film's vision of sexuality-as-werewolfism is so fundamentally volatile that the narrative can resolve only by diffusing chaos into comedy.

More overtly comic, John Landis's hit *An American Werewolf in London* focuses on the transformation of David (David Naughton), an American teen abroad in England with his pal Jack (Griffin Dunne). On a grim Yorkshire moor by night, Jack is killed and David mauled by the mythical beast, after which the survivor is bombarded by peculiar dreams that herald his upcoming metamorphosis. A nostalgic take on the genre that reaches a clawed hand back to the past, the film signals its ironic tone early as Bobby Vinton's "Blue Moon" plays over the opening credits. When Jack notices a pentagram on the wall of a pub before his death, he recognizes it only because "Lon Chaney Jr. and Universal Studios maintain that's the mark of the wolf man!" After his death, Jack continues to chat to his buddy, a steadily putrefying comic presence that only David can see—but who's still able to mooch his hospital food.

After his attack, David is improbably seduced by a lovely nurse (Jenny Agutter) while recovering: it's then that his lycanthropy rises to the surface, stymying his almost dreamlike sexual success. The film's celebrated transformation scene shows David's naked body, recently wrapped up in a lot of blissfully erotic scenarios, now subject to alarming malfunction (Fig. 9.8). As in *The Wolf Man*, werewolfism equates to an alarming disqualification from the stratum of sexual success. In a "behind the scenes"–style interview, director John Landis speaks of the transformation as a sort of straining erection, as David's hand painfully extends into a wolfish paw,[27] although it's difficult to gauge the habitually jovial director's level of seriousness here. David's a little old for werewolfism to be a metaphor for puberty—and he's already (gloriously) sexually active. The transformation seems more suggestive of the corruption of erotic opportunities, a grotesque parodying of sexual prowess rather than an expression of it.

Figure 9.8. Bodily dysfunction: the naked David (David Naughton) begins to transform in *An American Werewolf in London* (John Landis, Universal, 1981). Digital frame enlargement.

Old Dog: *Wolf*

Mike Nichols's *Wolf* (1994) links ejection from social currency to a decline of robust sexual masculinity associated with increasing age. Will Randall (Jack Nicholson) is an aging senior editor at a New York publishing house (Fig. 9.9). The company has recently been acquired by a billionaire interested in

Figure 9.9. Jack Nicholson as the (almost) obsolete literary editor Will Randall in Mike Nichols's *Wolf* (Columbia, 1994). Digital frame enlargement.

pushing his new acquisition in a different direction, and pushing Will out of his job. Replacing Will is his handsome young protégé, Stewart (James Spader). The rival wows Will's colleagues and clients with a practiced, smarmy charm, and the primal conflict between the two is compounded when Stewart is found sleeping with Will's wife. Having taken Will's resources, purpose, and position, Stewart takes his woman as well.

All is not lost: a bite from a wolf on a snowy rural road has initiated some curious symptoms, supercharging Will's senses. His hearing and sense of smell improve radically; he edits the work of his authors at superhuman speed without his reading glasses, and his sex drive comes back in spades. In short, his contamination actually infuses him with an exaggerated youthful vigor. After discovering his wife with Stewart, the mild-mannered Will decides that it's time to bite back: he courts a stable of authors to his side and railroads the boss into giving him his job back, allowing him to fire his rival. Stewart confronts Will in the men's room, where Will nonchalantly pisses on his younger competitor's shoes: "I'm just marking my territory," he smirks. He also commences a relationship with a younger woman, Laura (Michelle Pfeiffer), the defiant daughter of his boss. Will's transformation exemplifies what Sally Chivers has suggested is a standard theme in many movies focused on aging men: "The older male figure . . . whose masculinity is perceived to be fading [is transformed into] a man whose masculinity is exaggerated and compensatory."[28] The wolf bite is essentially a dark blessing for Will in that it puts him back in touch with a virile masculinity that helps him survive and thrive in a cut-throat corporate world threatening to leave him behind.

Yet Will remains troubled by dreams in which he chases down a deer, and he's naturally curious about the consequences of his strange condition. His wife being found dead casts him under suspicion and evokes the male honor violence of earlier werewolf films. It turns out it wasn't Will who killed her, but rather Stewart, whom Will bit on the hand in a scuffle and who now carries the werewolf curse himself. Stewart's transformation into a werewolf underlines the primal threat he poses, allowing the film to climax with a confrontation between the two male wolves (Fig 9.10), now over Will's new lover, Laura. Adapting the themes of previous werewolf films, *Wolf* establishes a world in which the status of the aging male is in jeopardy: if the threat of werewolves isn't literally real, the threat of rising same-sex rivals certainly is.

Wolves in Every Guise—or, Guys: *The Company of Wolves* and *Bad Moon*

Neil Jordan's *The Company of Wolves* (1984), co-written by Angela Carter, reorients the genre to a female perspective on the wolf as a metaphor for

Figure 9.10. Will Randall (Jack Nicholson), bloodied but unbowed, faces his younger challenger in *Wolf* (Mike Nichols, Columbia, 1994). Digital frame enlargement.

male sexuality as both fearsome and fascinating. Teenage girl Rosaleen (Sarah Patterson), bright-red lipstick smeared over her mouth as if in experimental foray into sexual self-presentation, is in bed suffering from a stomach ache (presumably the cramps of first menstruation) upstairs in her family's Edwardian stately home. She falls into a dream world of kaleidoscopic fairytale motifs, their oscillation centering around the tale of "Little Red Riding Hood," its heroine interpreted as a girl approaching sexual maturity. In Rosaleen's dream, her no-nonsense grandmother (Angela Lansbury), filled with canny and hard-won wisdom, advises her that wolves wear many disguises, and the worst kind are "hairy on the inside." Clearly these wolves are more symbolic than literal. The film comprises a series of vignettes around this theme, implicating aggressive and hypocritical men. In one episode, a husband (Stephen Rea) absconds on his wedding night to join his wolfish brethren, only to return many years later. Absurdly enraged that his wife (Kathryn Pogson) has not remained faithful, he gorily transforms into a wolf in an analogue of domestic abuse.

Jordan's film builds a vision of men who, like wolves, may be darkly beautiful yet also deadly; who will lie and cheat and conceal their true selves; and who tend to reveal themselves only after they've gotten what they want from their female lovers. Yet the film is careful to resist sinking its heroine into the resigned despair of victimhood. The girl's mother in her dream advises, "If there's a beast in men, it meets its match in women too," in appreciation of female agency and canniness.

Bad Moon (1996) also emphasizes a female's perspective of male volatility. Intrepid filmmaker Ted (Michael Paré) is mauled deep in the Amazon jungle, and his girlfriend is killed by an eight-foot, silver-haired, snarling lupine terror. Back in the United States, he looks up his sister, Janet (Mariel Hemingway), who lives with her young son, Brett (Mason Gamble) and the family dog, a gallant German Shepherd named Thor (canine actor Primo). After hearing of a series of gory attacks in the woodland area where Ted lives, Janet invites her brother to stay with her. The faithful Thor, however, knows a bad dog when he smells one, and keeps an eye on the intruder, observing his transformation and defending the family against his eventual attack (Fig. 9.11).

The family depicted in *Bad Moon* is notably without a father, although hardly "lacking": as a tough-talking lawyer, Janet repels a threatening male huckster early in the film, demonstrating that she isn't as vulnerable as he expected. Additionally, Thor dotes on his human companions, an additionally protective guardian for young Brett. Ted's secrecy and escalating volatility is reminiscent of one concealing a drug addiction that gradually strips away the family fabric. Privately, Ted hopes that a return to the nourishing family environment might be the only thing that could cure him, a notion unfamiliar from werewolf lore but suggestive of a drug detox. More generally, like *The Company of Wolves*, *Bad Moon* fosters suspicion around a predatory maleness that intrudes to rupture domestic stability. That stability is eventually restored, not through the

Figure 9.11. Thor the Alsatian (canine performer Primo) warily surveils the werewolf Ted (Michael Paré) as he steps from his trailer in *Bad Moon* (Eric Red, Warner Bros., 1996). Digital frame enlargement.

restoration of a (human) male within the family, but instead through the heroics of the family dog, Thor.

Girls Gone Wild: *Cat People* and *Ginger Snaps*

While the werewolf genre is traditionally male-centric, a few wild femmes fatale have nevertheless reared their hairy heads. In Italian B-grade erotic-horror *Werewolf Woman* (1976), Daniella (Annik Borel) believes herself to be the reincarnation of an oversexed occult ancestor who became a grunting wolf woman and murdered the men she seduced. Daniella advertises her sexual intent with nymphomaniac energy, then replaces it with fatal violence—she's a tantalizing yet terrible trap. We later learn that her aggression arises from the trauma of being raped when she was thirteen: as in the more metaphorical animal transformations of *Black Swan* (2010) or Selina Kyle/Catwoman in *Batman Returns* (1992), "animalized" female sexual aggression is the result of abused innocence. A female werewolf is also featured toward the conclusion of *The Company of Wolves*, wounded by a gunshot. A timid, vulnerable creature, the wolf girl arises (in human form) to seek care after her injury, another figure characterized through her victimization by a man.

Not quite a werewolf film but very closely related is Jacques Tourneur's *Cat People* (1942): Serbian immigrant Irena (Simone Simon) is descended from an ancient tribal witch cult whose members transform into panthers when their blood runs too hot, either in intimacy or anger (Fig. 9.12). She meets a nice fellow, Oliver (Kent Smith), who marries

Figure 9.12. Oliver (Kent Smith) tries to comfort his reluctant lover, Irena (Simone Simon), who's sexually hindered by knowledge of her occult werecat lineage in Jacques Tourneur's *Cat People* (RKO, 1942). Digital frame enlargement.

her and urges her into therapy for her anxiety. But Oliver is also a nice fellow to his assistant, Alice (Jane Randolph), with whom he eventually falls in love, provoking Irena's "cattiness." As in the male werewolf tale, passion and betrayal are centralized as the trigger for transformation. Irena's fear of amorous contact is clearly indicative of sexual repression (the fear that sex will degrade her to an "animal") but more interestingly, as in *Werewolf of London* or "Bisclavret," the focus on infidelity means bestial transformation is used to metaphorize jealous rage.

Although it's sometimes stereotyped this way, extreme jealousy isn't experienced only by men.[29] However, studies have demonstrated important average differences in the nature of jealousy in the minds of men and women. While jealousy's value as a mate-guarding impulse is equally applicable, the threat of cuckoldry cannot be an underlying adaptive driver for women, hence women tend not to be fixated on sexual infidelity particularly to the extent that men are.[30] As we discussed much earlier, during the period in which our brains were reaching their modern state, important to a male's mate-value was his ability to provision offspring and provide resources and assistance during a long and metabolically expensive pregnancy. Accordingly, on average, women consider emotional infidelity more serious than sexual infidelity.[31] Buss recounts how male study participants reported that they would find sexual infidelity harder to forgive than emotional infidelity; for women, the opposite is true.[32] These self-report results have been confirmed through experiments in which electrodes measure subjects' stress levels. When asked to imagine their partners having sex with someone else, men experience greater physiological distress than women do; women are more distressed to imagine their partner forming deep emotional bonds—falling in love with someone else.[33] These patterns have been shown to hold across a wide range of cultures, including those that contrast considerably in terms of how sexually liberal they are, such as China and Sweden.[34] Sexual infidelity is hardly irrelevant to women, since men often become emotionally involved with the women they have sex with,[35] but emotional infidelity is more directly unsettling. While mate-murder as an extreme form of jealousy is more commonly committed by men, extreme romantic jealousy is certainly not sex-specific per se.

Irena and Oliver never consummate their marriage; their relationship is entirely an emotional one. This is a threatening arrangement from the outset, since Irena is highly emotionally dependent, and she knows the relationship is vulnerable to interlopers who might offer Oliver something more sexually fulfilling. In the film's most memorable scene, Irena in feline form stalks her rival Alice as she wades alone at night in an indoor swimming pool. As she screams for help, Alice can hear Irena's enraged panther-roar around her, but can see only the undulating shadow of her predator (Fig. 9.13). While Irena's fear of transformation is linked to her sexual apprehension, the film also uses it to powerfully manifest her antagonism toward the competition.

In Paul Schrader's loose, erotically amplified, and nearly hallucinatory *Cat People* remake (1982), the cat condition is more explicitly linked to sexual repression. The virginal Irena (Nastassja Kinski) is here also harassed by a long-lost brother, Paul (Malcolm McDowell), with whom she stays while visiting New Orleans. The tribe from which she's descended are incestuous, Paul explains to her, and sex with outsiders triggers transformation—so she should give it up to him. Despite his creepy come-ons, Paul's warning is legitimate: having no luck with his sister, he finds a casual fling, but makes a bloody mess of her afterward. But Paul also seems to transform from lack of sex. Early in the film he waits on a prostitute, but transforms before she can offer him the relief he craves: transformation arises seemingly from sexual over-anticipation and indulgence both.

Irena falls for Oliver (John Heard), a local zookeeper; and, as in the original film, she's scared of sex. Oliver's colleague Alice (Annette O'Toole) is again waiting in the wings, and again subject to Irena's feline stalking.

Figure 9.13. Alice (Jane Randolph), all alone in the pool, flounders and shrieks as her mate-rival, Irena—in the form of a snarling black panther—stalks the room around her in *Cat People* (Jacques Tourneur, RKO, 1942). Digital frame enlargement.

Oliver compels Irena to ignore her brother's incestuous sexual prescription. As Paul predicted, she transforms and kills after sex—but manages to hold off killing Oliver himself. The situation seems impossible, so she resigns to flee and live with her own kind. Before she leaves, however, she's captured by the zoo, where she's held as one of Oliver's exhibits, with Oliver now left to Irena's human rival, Alice. With Irena effectively imprisoned by her volatile desire, in Schrader's film there seems to be no repairing the problems of repression and jealousy. For Irena, sexuality is either irretrievably volatile or coercively incestuous, able to exist only at extremes of unhealthy introversion or murderous aggression.

Returning to the theme of lupine lasses, John Fawcett's *Ginger Snaps* (2000) offers a developed treatment of the werewolf theme linked to female social and sexual life. The eponymous Ginger (Katharine Isabelle) fantasizes about suicide in her basement bedroom, along with her equally sulky sister, Bridget (Emily Perkins). They vaguely envision their deaths as an act of vengeance against the banal high school hierarchy from which they feel excluded. But once Ginger is bitten by a werewolf, her problems acquire a more serious edge. Her process of transformation is used to symbolically overlay and express the trials of female adolescence. Prior to the attack, male students begin erotically appraising her, and she has her first period virtually simultaneous with the attack—what Ginger calls "the curse" becomes the literal "curse" of lycanthropy. Afterward, she worries over a turf of pale hairs sprouting from a scratch-wound in a reaction that doubles for the anxiety of any ordinary bodily change. Ginger throws herself into sexual activity, now enthralled by the urges of her changing body, although this exposes her to reputational damage in the status-focused culture of high school. Her new sexual energy increases attention from male admirers (Fig. 9.14), but it also stokes the rivalry of less sexually precocious female peers, including her sister.

Ginger's reckless—and eventually murderous—behavior alienates her increasingly from her friends and challenges our sympathy as viewers. Once she turns fully werewolf, things aren't so sexy: her social climbing is over, forever. Now she's consigned to the same position of irretrievable isolation as a whole tradition of male werewolves. Bianca Nielsen suggests that through the double-edged sword of werewolfism, the film "portrays the double-binds teenage girls face"; Ginger is "an embodiment of . . . impossible binaries: she is at once sexually attractive and monstrous, 'natural' and 'supernatural,' human and animal, 'feminine' and transgressive, a sister and a rival."[36] In the world of the film, female sexual assertiveness is empowering but also degrading; social success brings admiration from some and ire from others; and one's changing body is both exciting and monstrous. While the majority of werewolf films focus on male characters, *Ginger Snaps* demonstrates the ability of

Figure 9.14. Animal magnetism: Ginger Fitzgerald (Katharine Isabelle) enjoys her newfound allure as she strides down the high-school corridor in John Fawcett's *Ginger Snaps* (Motion, 2000). Digital frame enlargement.

the tradition to be transposed onto the challenges of female social and sexual belonging.

Wolves have long been understood as possessed of dreadful ferocity in their interactions with their prey; and for many years, and in many regions, we counted ourselves among their potential victims. Cinematic werewolfism, as a general theme, depicts disturbing human traits and tendencies as more characteristic of nonhuman than of human nature. In doing so, it disowns those traits as part of humanity—it can be only an "animal curse" that causes such behavior. Werewolves manifest frightening expressions of transgressive and criminal impulses that threaten to undermine both social cohesion and human self-worth. At the same time, the narratives that surround these figures tip us off to their true (human) nature. The sympathy many werewolves elicit indicates our fascination with the motives of the monster, and the terror of what we too may be capable. Our horror is also not unmixed with admiration: the assertiveness of the predator is on liberating display in *Ginger Snaps* and *Wolf*, in which (as we know from other animal horror films) at least a touch of the animal is necessary to deal with the human predators around us. But as we also know, a touch is one thing; an excess is another and rarely ends well.

Aftermath

We humans inflict an astonishing toll on our animal cousins. Data calculated in 2008 by the United Nations Food and Agricultural Organization indicates that the number of farmed land animals killed for food is around fifty-six billion per year worldwide[1] (the number of marine creatures is more difficult to estimate, although certainly higher); and this number is projected to double by 2050.[2] Obviously, we are now predators of a magnitude that is wildly unprecedented in the history of the planet. And yet, as the enduring popularity of animal horror well into that period of staggering dominance attests, we are still thrilled and haunted by the knowledge of a more uncertain time, haunted by the possibilities that our prey-status might yet be revived.

Upon the release of *The Shallows* in 2016, film critic Noah Gittell suggested that it was time to "retire" animal horror: battling animals for dominance not only fails to reflect our current reality, he pointed out, but the destruction of the environment and rates of species extinction for which we're responsible demonstrate that the shoe is well and truly on the other foot.[3] Similarly, essayist Barbara Ehrenreich has written that "ten thousand years after our collective ascent to the status of global alpha predator, we are still obsessed with nonhuman predators and in ways that are not particularly productive or healthy," as paying to see movies in which we are "torn limb from limb" indicates.[4] It may be the case that animal horror maintains a now false narrative of danger that obscures the systematic violence we perpetrate against animals for food, clothing, medical science, and sport. We know this violence happens, but especially in the case of food production it's often kept tastefully out of sight. Carol Adams describes the animals we consume as "absent-referents": they are all around us, yet also—through death and commoditization—absent or invisible.[5] Perhaps the hostile incursions of onscreen animals consolidate our dominance by legitimizing our power over real ones. If we see gripping visions of animal violence, we don't feel so bad about our own species' far more prolific brutality. More subtly, perhaps the symbolic role of animals in films such as *The Shallows* and *The Grey*—lurking obstacles that developing protagonists must overcome—also overwrites the moral question of our much more routine power over real creatures.

These are speculative questions, and I leave them for the reader to consider. We can say that an ideological program of maintaining animal exploitation is not necessary to account for the popularity of animal horror, given its deeper origins. However, it's still possible that animal horror is one way that exploitation finds implicit support. I'm sympathetic to the concerns of those who regard animal horror with ethical suspicion for the way it depicts animals. Still, as this book has argued, animal horror is woven into who we are. I agree with Paul Trout, who speculates that there "there will be no end to the phantom of the predator haunting the human imagination."[6] Our ancestral prey-status means these stories, whether "healthy" or not, will never disappear, at least not until the glacial process of adaptation has caught up (and for some humans living in regional areas today, anti-predator adaptations remain important to survival). It's a tall order to just "switch off" a million-year habit: calling for the subgenre to be retired is a bit like calling for a retirement of fear of the dark.[7]

While I share these ethical concerns, my own view is more optimistic. These films may not be the most "productive" way we engage with animals; they may not be the most flattering portrayals (I'm sure that the sharks and spiders and lions of the world would have a thing or two to say, if they could, about how they're represented). Nevertheless, it's not clear to me that these films necessarily work to justify the killing of real-life animals, nor that we are so easily programmed by them to embrace anti-animal agendas. What is clear to me is that they find root in our interest in animals—and fearful interest is not itself unethical. Edward O. Wilson suggests that because we evolved within the infinite symphony of biological life, its ungrasped limits are a source of endless wonder. The scale of what is around us, he suggests, is

> the natural domain of the most restless and paradoxical part of the human spirit. Our sense of wonder grows exponentially: the greater the knowledge, the deeper the mystery and the more we seek knowledge to create new mystery. This catalytic reaction, seemingly an inborn human trait, draws us perpetually forward in search for new places and new life. Nature is to be mastered, but (we hope) never completely. A quiet passion burns, not for total control but for the sensation of constant advance.[8]

We exist on this planet with creatures entrancing in their variety, and we look at them in astonishment, admiration, curiosity, and fear. Animal horror is one form through which we marvel at the natural world around us and, I hope, promote contemplation of our role within it. The tremendous public and educational shark interest following the release of *Jaws* should indicate that even the most defamatory depictions of animals may promote curiosity and regard rather than blind hostility.

Animals have been cinematic subjects since the medium's inception, and fierce animals have been the focus of artistic fascination as far back as we can trace.[9] As I hope this book has gone some way toward demonstrating, we can see in these films our continuing attempts to countenance and explore, to mythologize, and to weave stories about the diversity and magic of the creatures around us. In many of these movies, we thrillingly brush up against the limits of our worldview, our comfort, our ethics, and our sense of dominance. And perhaps through this fascination we are also, in one way or another, drawn into curious and challenging contemplation of our own animal selves.

Notes

Introduction

1. Donna Hart and Robert W. Sussman, *Man the Hunted: Primates, Predators, and Human Evolution* (New York: Westview Press, 2005) 2.

2. Barbara Ehrenreich, *Blood Rites: Origins and History of the Passions of War* (New York: Henry Holt and Company, 1997) 46.

3. Hans Kruuk, *Hunter and Hunted: Relationships between Carnivores and People* (Cambridge, UK: Cambridge University Press, 2002) 108.

4. Kruuk 112.

5. Kruuk 28.

6. Hart and Sussman 5, 27–28.

7. Hart and Sussman 68.

8. Kruuk 103.

9. Hart and Sussman 119.

10. Hart and Sussman 115.

11. Hart and Sussman 119.

12. *Extinct Short-faced Bear*, 2017, North American Bear Center. 1 Nov 2017 www.bear.org/website/bear-pages/extinct-short-faced-bear.html

13. Bryan G. Fry et al., "A Central Role for Venom in Predation by *Varanus Komodoensis* (Komodo Dragon) and the Extinct Giant *Varanus* (*Megalania*) *priscus*." *Proceedings of the National Academy of Sciences of the United States of America* 106.22 (2009): 8969–8974. www.ncbi.nlm.nih.gov/pmc/articles/PMC2690028

14. Hart and Sussman 65–66.

15. Michael Fuchs, "'They are a fact of life out here': The Ecocritical Subtexts of Three Early-Twenty-First-Century Aussie Animal Horror Movies," *Animal Horror Cinema: Genre, History and Criticism*, eds. Katarina Gregersdotter, Johan Höglund, and Nicklas Hållén (London: Palgrave Macmillan, 2015) 39–40.

16. Kruuk 58–59.

17. Hart and Sussman 3.

18. Hart and Sussman 3–4.

19. Kruuk 60.

20. Kruuk 59–60.

21. Hart and Sussman 85.

22. Kim Hill and A. Magdalena Hurtado, *Ache Life History: The Ecology and Demography of a Foraging People* (New York: Routledge, 1996) 162.

23. Brian Handwerk, "Crocodiles Have Strongest Bite Ever Measured, Hands-on Tests Show," *National Geographic* 15 Mar 2012. news.nationalgeographic.com/news/2012/03/120315-crocodiles-bite-force-erickson-science-plos-one-strongest

24. Fuchs 39.

25. Jeffrey A. Lockwood, *The Infested Mind: Why Humans Fear, Loathe, and Love Insects* (New York: Oxford University Press, 2013) 21.

26. Ian Tattersall, "Foreword," Hart and Sussman xiii.

27. The reader might be wondering whether we've not continued to evolve since this period. We have, but relatively little. Lactase persistence (the ability in some populations to continue to digest milk into adulthood) is an example of a more modern adaptation. However, evolution obviously occurs extremely slowly, leaving little time for complex adaptations. The Pleistocene is identified as a key approximate period for evolutionary psychologists because many of our characteristics, if they didn't emerge during this period (and naturally many did not, since mammals go back much further), underwent stabilization then. This means that adaptions are refined, and variation is reduced through consistency of environmental selection pressures over a long period of time (a process known as "stabilizing selection"). Consequently, as Hagen explains, "the Pleistocene—which (almost) encompasses the origins of our genus, but excludes the recent period of dramatic change—is conveniently identified as the epoch which shaped human physiology and psychology." Edward Hagen, "Why is the EEA equated with the Pleistocene," *Evolutionary Psychology FAQ*. University of California, Santa Barbara, Department of Anthropology, 2004. www.anth.ucsb.edu/projects/human/evpsychfaq.html. For a more comprehensive and up-to-date introduction, see David M. Buss, *Evolutionary Psychology: The New Science of the Mind*, 5th ed. (London and New York: Routledge, 2016).

28. Joshua M. Tybur, Debra Lieberman, Robert Kurzban, and Peter DeScioli, "Disgust: Evolved Function and Structure," *Psychological Review* 120.1 (2013): 65–84. psycnet.apa.org/doiLanding?doi=10.1037%2Fa0030778; Val Curtis, Robert Auger, and Tamer Rabie, "Evidence that Disgust Evolved to Protect from Risk of Disease," *Proceedings of the Royal Society B: Biological Sciences* 271.4 (2004): S131–S133. rspb.royalsocietypublishing.org/content/271/Suppl_4/S131; Diana Fleischman, "Sex-Differences in Disease Avoidance," *Encyclopedia of Evolutionary Psychological Science*, eds. T. K. Shackelford and V. A. Weekes-Shackelford (Cham, Switzerland: Springer, 2018): 1–3. link.springer.com/10.1007/978-3-319-16999-6

29. Kruuk 166.

30. H. Clark Barrett, "Adaptations to Predators and Prey," *The Handbook of Evolutionary Psychology*, 2nd ed., ed. David M. Buss (Hoboken, NJ: John Wiley & Sons, 2016) 246.

31. Barrett 246.

32. Craig Packer, Alexandra Swanson, Dennis Ikanda, and Hadas Kushnir, "Fear of Darkness, the Full Moon, and the Nocturnal Ecology of African Lions," *PLoS ONE* 6.7 (2011): 1–2. doi.org/10.1371/journal.pone.0022285

33. Barrett 251.

34. Ottmar V. Lipp and Nazanin Derakshan, "Attentional Bias to Pictures of Fear-Relevant Animals in a Dot Probe Task," *Emotion* 5.2 (2005): 365–369; Stefanie Hoehl, Kahl Hellmer, Maria Johansson, and Gustaf Gredebäck, "Itsy Bitsy Spider . . . : Infants React with Increased Arousal to Spiders and Snakes," *Frontiers in Psychology* 18 Oct 2017. doi.org/10.3389/fpsyg.2017.01710

35. Isaac Marks, *Fears, Phobias and Rituals: Panic, Anxiety, and Their Disorders* (New York and Oxford: Oxford University Press, 1987) 58–69.

36. Kruuk 168.

37. Kruuk 168–169.

38. Kruuk 171.

39. Kruuk 177.

40. Kruuk 176.

41. Arne Öhman and Susan Mineka, "Fears, Phobias, and Preparedness: Toward an Evolved Module of Fear and Fear Learning," *Psychological Review* 108.3 (2001): 483.

42. Edward O. Wilson, *In Search of Nature* (Washington, DC and Covelo, CA: Inland Press / Shearwater Books, 1996) 7.

43. Wilson 8–9.

44. Barbara Ehrenreich, Foreword, *Deadly Powers: Animal Predators and the Mythic Imagination*, by Paul Trout (Amherst, NY: Prometheus Books, 2011) 15.

45. Paul Trout, *Deadly Powers: Animal Predators and the Mythic Imagination* (Amherst, NY: Prometheus Books, 2011) 21.

46. Trout 26.

47. Qtd. in David G. E. Caldicott, Ravi Mahajani, and Marie Kuhn, "The Anatomy of a Shark Attack: A Case Report and Review of Literature," *Injury: International Journal of the Care of the Injured* 32 (2001): 445.

48. Pinker, among other evolutionary thinkers, has influentially theorized that wrapped up in the allure of fiction is not simply that it entertains, but that, within or behind that, we sense something to be learned: "Fictional narratives supply us with a mental catalogue of the fatal conundrums we might face someday and the outcomes of strategies we could display in them" (543). Steven Pinker, *How the Mind Works* (St. Ives, Cornwall: Penguin, 2009). See also Brian Boyd, *On the Origin of Stories: Evolution, Cognition, and Fiction* (Cambridge, MA: Harvard UP, 2009).

49. For a cinematic overview, I would recommend Katarina Gregersdotter, Johan Högland, and Nicklas Hållán, "A History of Animal Horror Cinema," *Animal Horror Cinema: Genre, History and Criticism*, eds. Gregersdotter, Högland, and Hållén (London: Palgrave Macmillan, 2015): 19–35.

50. Dan Whitehead, *Tooth and Claw: A Field Guide to "Nature Run Amok" Horror Movies* (n.p.: The Zebra Partnership, 2012) 7.

51. Barbara Ehrenreich, "Foreword," Trout 16.

52. Lynne A. Isbell, *The Fruit, The Tree, and the Serpent: Why We See So Well* (Cambridge, MA and London: Harvard University Press, 2009).

53. Katarina Gregersdotter, Johan Högland, and Nicklas Hållén, "Introduction," *Animal Horror Cinema: Genre History and Criticism*, eds. Gregersdotter, Högland, and Hållén (London: Palgrave Macmillan, 2015) 5.

54. Gregersdotter, Högland, and Hållén, "Introduction" 5.

55. Belinda Smaill, *Regarding Life: Animals and the Documentary Moving Image* (Albany: State University of New York Press, 2016) 6; Gregersdotter, Högland, and Hållén, "Introduction" 10–11.

56. Cary Wolfe, *Animal Rites: American Culture, the Discourse of Species, and Posthumanist Theory* (Chicago and London: University of Chicago Press, 2003) 8; Pramod K. Nayar, *Posthumanism* (Cambridge, MA: Polity Press) 8–9.

57. The idea that human's perceptions and treatment of animals is interlocked with other oppressive ideologies is also foundational to the field typically described as Critical Animal Studies.

58. Nayar 28–29.

59. David Bordwell, "Contemporary Film Studies and the Vicissitudes of Grand Theory," *Post-Theory: Reconstructing Film Studies*, eds. David Bordwell and Noël Carroll (Madison: University of Wisconsin Press, 1996). Kindle edition.

60. Bordwell n.p.

61. Francesca Ferrando, "Posthumanism, Transhumanism, Antihumanism, Metahumanism, and New Materialisms," *Existenz: An International Journal of Philosophy, Religion, Politics, and the Arts* 8.2 (2013) 29; Nayar 12; Bordwell n.p.

62. Brian Boyd, Joseph Carroll, and Jonathan Gottschall, "Introduction," *Evolution, Literature, and Film: A Reader*, eds. Boyd, Carroll, and Gottschall (New York: Columbia University Press, 2010) 1.

63. Steven Pinker, *The Blank Slate: The Modern Denial of Human Nature* (2002; New York: Penguin, 2007).

64. Pinker 51–52.

65. Pinker 54.

66. Boyd, Carroll, and Gottschall 3.

67. Boyd, Carroll, and Gottschall 3.

68. David Bordwell and Noël Carroll, eds. *Post-Theory: Reconstructing Film Studies* (Madison: University of Wisconsin Press, 1996). Kindle edition.

69. David Bordwell, "What Snakes, Eagles, and Rhesus Macaques Can Teach Us," *Evolution, Literature, and Film: A Reader*, eds. Brian Boyd, Joseph Carroll, and Jonathan Gottschall (New York: Columbia University Press, 2010) 270–285.

70. Boyd, Carroll, and Gottschall 3.

71. Joseph Carroll, "Human Nature and Literary Meaning," Julie Rivkin and Michael Ryan, eds. *Literary Theory: An Anthology*, 3rd ed. (Malden, MA: Wiley Blackwell, 2017) 1329–1359.

72. Boyd, Carroll, and Gottschall 3.

73. Brian Boyd, Joseph Carroll, and Jonathan Gottschall, "Introduction," *Evolution, Literature, and Film: A Reader*, eds. Boyd, Carroll, and Gottschall (New York: Columbia University Press, 2010) 3.

74. Gregersdotter, Högland, and Hållén, "Introduction" 6.

75. Qtd. in Stefan Lovgren, "'Jaws' at 30: Film Stoked Fear, Study of Great White Sharks," *National Geographic News* 15 June 2005. news.nationalgeographic.com/news/2005/06/0615_050615_jawssharks.html

76. E.g. Christopher J. Ferguson, "Does Sexy Media Promote Teen Sex? A Meta-Analytic and Methodological Review," *Psychiatric Quarterly* 88.2 (2017):

449–358; Ferguson, "Does Media Violence Predict Societal Violence? It Depends on What You Look at and When," *Journal of Communication* 65.1 (2015): E1–E22; Christopher J. Ferguson and Eugene Beresin, "Social Science's Curious War with Pop Culture and How it was Lost: The Media Violence Debate and the Risks it Holds for Social Science," *Preventative Medicine* 99 (2017): 69–76.

77. Gregory Mitchell and Philip E. Tetlock, "Popularity as a Poor Proxy for Utility: The Case of Implicit Prejudice," *Psychological Science under Scrutiny*, eds. Scott O. Lilienfeld and Irwin D. Waldman (Malden, MA, Wiley-Blackwell, 2017) 164–195; Sarah Teige-Mocigemba, Manuel Becker, Jeffrey W. Sherman, Regina Rechardht, and Karl Christoph Klauer, "The Affect Misattribution Procedure: In Search of Prejudice Effects," *Experimental Psychology* 64 (2017): 215–230. econtent.hogrefe.com/doi/abs/10.1027/1618-3169/a000364

78. William T. L. Cox and Patricia G. Devine, "Experimental Research on Shooter Bias: Ready (or Relevant) for Application in the Courtroom?" *Journal of Applied Research in Memory and Cognition* 5 (2016): 236–238. www.sciencedirect.com/science/article/pii/S2211368116300754

79. For the closest thing, with brief summaries of a large number of films, see Whitehead's *Tooth and Claw*, as well as Lee Gambin's wide-ranging *Massacred by Mother Nature: Exploring the Natural Horror Film* (Baltimore, MD: Midnight Marquee Press, 2012).

80. A note on terminology: although I'm well aware that humans are themselves animals, throughout this book I'll often refer to nonhuman animals as simply "animals" for the sake of readability.

Chapter 1

1. Cynthia Erb, *Tracking King Kong: A Hollywood Icon in Global Culture*. 2nd ed. (Detroit: Wayne State University Press, 2009) 59–120.

2. Qtd. in Katarina Gregersdotter, Johan Höglund, and Nicklas Hållén, "A History of Animal Horror Cinema," *Animal Horror Cinema: Genre History and Criticism*, eds. Gregersdotter, Höglund, and Hållén (London: Palgrave Macmillan, 2015) 19.

3. Ted Gott and Kathryn Weir, *Gorilla* (London: Reaktion, 2013) 127–132.

4. Edgar Rice Burroughs, *Tarzan of the Apes & Other Tales*, Centenary ed. (London: Gollancz, 2012) 118.

5. John C. Wright, "'Twas Beauty Killed the Beast': King Kong and the American Character," *King Kong is Back!: An Unauthorized Look at One Humongous Ape*, eds. David Brin and Leah Wilson (Dallas, TX: Benbella, 2005) 197.

6. David N. Rosen, "King Kong: Race, Sex, and Rebellion," *Jump Cut* 6 (1975), 1 Nov, 2017. www.ejumpcut.org/archive/onlinessays/JC06folder/KingKong.html; Fatimah Tobing Rony, *The Third Eye: Race, Cinema, and Ethnographic Spectacle* (Durham, NC: Duke University Press, 2001) 157–191; Phillip Atiba Goff, Jennifer L. Eberhardt, Melissa J. Williams, and Matthew Christian Jackson, "Not Yet Human: Implicit Knowledge, Historical Dehumanization, and Contemporary Consequences," *Journal of Personality and Social Psychology* 94.2 (2008): 293.

7. Noël Carroll, "*King Kong*: Ape and Essence," *Planks of Reason: Essays on the Horror Film*, Rev. ed., eds. Barry Keith Grant and Christopher Sharrett (Lanham, MA: The Scarecrow Press, 2004): 215.

8. Carroll 213.

9. Carroll 126.

10. Carroll 230.

11. Jerome Barkow, "Introduction," *Missing the Revolution: Darwinism for Social Scientists*, ed. Barkow (New York: Oxford University Press, 2005) 5.

12. For a wealth of examples see David M. Buss, ed., *The Handbook of Evolutionary Psychology* (Hoboken, NJ: John Wiley & Sons, 2016).

13. John Alcock, *The Triumph of Sociobiology* (Oxford and New York: Oxford University Press, 2001) 129–137; Steven Pinker, *The Blank Slate: The Modern Denial of Human Nature* (2002; New York: Penguin, 2007).

14. Barkow, "Introduction" 4.

15. Richard Dawkins, *The Selfish Gene*. 40th Anniversary ed. (Oxford: Oxford University Press, 2016).

16. Similarly, the problem with so-called "Social Darwinism" wasn't its attempt to apply Darwinist thinking to social behavior per se (since society necessarily has some biological basis); it was its bastardization of that thinking to justify social inequality and racism. Latching onto the idea of "survival of the fittest" as a kind of ethical principle, Social Darwinism assumed that the "fittest" advanced naturally in society through genetic determinism, and that therefore those left behind were thrust downward only by their own genetics, and shouldn't be assisted. Such ideas simplistically assumed that one's social success/failure was owed to individual genetic predestination to the exclusion of other factors. Moreover, atop this radically reductionist thesis was added the naturalistic fallacy: the idea that what is "natural" is also "right" or desirable. (Incidentally, we might also clarify here that "the fittest" in Darwinian theory does not mean "the strongest" but rather that which leads to higher reproductive success.)

17. Noël Carroll, "Ape and Essence" 228.

18. Barbara Creed, *Darwin's Screens: Evolutionary Aesthetics, Time and Sexual Display in the Cinema* (South Australia: Melbourne University Press, 2009) 180.

19. David M. Buss, *The Evolution of Desire: Strategies of Human Mating*. Revised and updated edition (New York: Basic Books, 2016) 9–10.

20. David M. Buss, *Evolutionary Psychology: The New Science of the Mind*, 5th ed. (London and New York: Routledge, 2016) 105–111; Geoffrey F. Miller, *The Mating Mind: How Sexual Choice Shaped the Evolution of Human Nature* (New York: Random House, 2000). See index entries under "female choice"; Peter K. Jonason, Norman P. Li, and Laura Madson, "It Is Not All About the Benjamins: Understanding Preferences for Mates with Resources," *Personality and Individual Differences* 52.3 (2012): 306.

21. Buss, *Evolutionary Psychology* 107; David P. Schmitt, "Yes, but . . .": Answers to Ten Common Criticisms of Evolutionary Psychology," *The Evolution Institute*, 1 Nov 2017. evolution-institute.org/article/on-common-criticisms-of-evolutionary-psychology

22. Buss, *Evolutionary Psychology* 110; Todd K. Shackelford, David P. Schmitt, and David M. Buss, "Universal Dimensions of Human Mate Preferences," *Personality and Individual Differences* 39 (2005): 447–458, 1 Nov 2017. labs.la.utexas.edu/buss/files/2015/09/universal-dimensions-of-mate-prefs-Shackelford-Schmitt-Buss-PAID-2005.pdf; Christopher Von Rueden, Michael Gurven, and Hillard Kaplan, "Why Do Men Seek Status: Fitness Payoffs to Dominance and Prestige," *Proceedings of the Royal Society B: Biological Sciences* (2010): rspb20102145, 1 Nov 2017. rspb.royalsocietypublishing.org/content/early/2010/12/04/rspb.2010.2145; Miller, The *Mating Mind* 210–211.

23. Buss, *Evolutionary Psychology* 110–111; von Rueden et al.

24. Buss, *Evolutionary Psychology* 115.

25. Sarah Blaffer Hrdy also notes that "[i]n every well-studied species of group-living primates, males have been reported to offer some form of care or protection to infants." *The Woman That Never Evolved* (Cambridge, MA & London: Harvard University Press, 1999) 72.

26. Kong's antiheroism is thus remarkably close to that of Erik (Lon Chaney), the hideously disfigured Opera Ghost in *The Phantom of the Opera* (dir. Rupert Julian, 1925), who works to bring all manner of benefits to his beloved Christine (Mary Philbin), but whose horrendous appearance means that, really, he was always disqualified from her love.

27. Wright 198.

28. Buss, *Evolutionary Psychology* 115–118; Alcock 136–143; Joanna E. Scheib, Steven W. Gangestad, and Randy Thornhill, "Facial Attractiveness, Symmetry and Cues of Good Genes," *Proceedings of the Royal Society B: Biological Sciences* 266.1431 (1999): 1913–1917; Jason Grotuss and Sarah Jane Beard, "Appearance/Beauty in Girls," *Encyclopedia of Evolutionary Psychological Science*, eds. Todd K. Shackelford and Viviana Weekes-Shackelford (Cham, Switzerland: Springer, 2018). dx.doi.org/10.1007/978-3-319-16999-6_2406-1

29. Robert L. Trivers, "Parental Investment and Sexual Selection," *Sexual Selection and the Descent of Man, 1871–1971*, ed. Bernard G. Campbell (Chicago: Aldine) 136–179.

30. Sarah Blaffer Hrdy, *The Woman That Never Evolved* (Cambridge, MA & London: Harvard University Press, 1999) 18. For an introduction to sexual selection theory, see David M. Buss, "Human Mating Strategies," *Samfundsokonomen* 4 (2002): 47–58, 1 Nov 2017. labs.la.utexas.edu/buss/files/2015/10/Buss-2002-human-mating-strategies.pdf

31. Carroll 230.

32. Charles Derry, *Dark Dreams 2.0: A Psychological History of the Modern Horror Film from the 1950s to the 21st Century* (Jefferson, NC and London: McFarland, 2009) 22.

33. David P. Barash, "Biology Lurks Beneath: Bioliterary Explorations of the Individual versus Society," *Evolutionary Psychology* 2.1 (2004): 201. journals.sagepub.com/doi/full/10.1177/147470490400200125

34. Barash 201. This conflict between individual desires and the social expectation is likely related to the tremendous over-representation of *crime* in

film and literature. Crime texts may engage us in a sympathetic criminal's alluring transgression against the social forces to which we are all otherwise beholden. Alternatively, they may play on the human proclivity toward "detecting cheaters"—those who violate social contracts. The human interest in cheater detection has been observed across all studied cultures and is theorized to be an adaptation to facilitate advantageous social exchange. See Leda Cosmides and John Tooby, "Cognitive Adaptations for Social Exchange," *The Adapted Mind: Evolutionary Psychology and the Generation of Culture*, eds. Jerome Barkow, Leda Cosmides, and John Tooby (Oxford: Oxford University Press, 1992) 163–228.

35. René Girard, *The Scapegoat*, trans. Yvonne Freccero (Baltimore: Johns Hopkins UP, 1986) 21.

36. Carroll 232–233.

37. Martin Rubin, "1933: Movies and the New Deal in Entertainment," *American Cinema of the 1930s: Themes and Variations*, ed. Ina Rae Hark (Newark, NJ: Rutgers University Press) 104.

38. Rubin 104.

39. Gott and Weir 45–69.

Chapter 2

1. Aidan R. Martin, "Biology of Sharks and Rays," *ReefQuest Centre for Shark Research*, 10 Nov 2017. www.elasmo-research.org/education/topics/p_shark_speed.htm

2. Qtd. in Stefan Lovgren, "'Jaws' at 30: Film Stoked Fear, Study of Great White Sharks," *National Geographic News* 15 June 2005. news.nationalgeographic.com/news/2005/06/0615_050615_jawssharks.html

3. Samuel Taylor Coleridge, "The Rime of the Ancient Mariner," 1798. www.gutenberg.org/ebooks/151

4. Georg Glaeser and Hannes F. Paulus, *The Evolution of the Eye* (Berlin: Springer, 2015) 93.

5. American Museum of Natural History, "Sharks and Rays: Myth and Reality," Seminars on Science 2001. www.amnh.org/learn/pd/sharks_rays/rfl_myth/myth_page5.html

6. Antonia Quirke, *Jaws: BFI Modern Classics* (London: British Film Institute/Palgrave Macmillan, 2002) 82–83.

7. Quirke 11.

8. Quirke 44.

9. Nigel Morris, *The Cinema of Steven Spielberg: Empire of Light* (New York: Wallflower Press, 2007) 52.

10. Morris 44.

11. Peter Biskind, "*Jaws*: Between the Teeth," *Jump Cut: A Review of Contemporary Media* 9 (1975): 1–26. www.ejumpcut.org/archive/onlinessays/JC09folder/Jaws.html

12. Barbara Creed, *The Monstrous-Feminine: Film, Feminism, Psychoanalysis* (London and New York: Routledge, 1994) 27, 107; Jane Caputi, *Goddesses and*

Monsters: Women, Myth, Power, and Popular Culture (London: University of Wisconsin Press, 2004) 23–37.

13. Robert Torry, *Velvet Light Trap* (March 22, Spring 1993): 27–38.

14. See Morris, chapter 4, for a useful summary of critical perspectives.

15. Morris 53.

16. The characters' foolish wild/domestic category error is repeated in the later film *Deep Blue Sea* (1999), in which a converted Navy base in the middle of the ocean is used to keep sharks in aquatic pens for the purpose of experimentation. The scientists will find out as the film progresses, but we know from the outset, that keeping sharks in holding pens befitting domestic animals is a recipe for chaos. The cinematic shark is fundamentally anarchic and unpredictable—beyond presumptuous human wrangling or routine.

17. H. Clark Barrett, "Adaptations to Predators and Prey," *Handbook of Evolutionary Psychology*, 2nd ed., ed. David M. Buss (Hoboken, NJ: John Wiley & Sons, 2016) 246.

18. Aside from his thorough nastiness, this character's inability to be redeemed may be compounded by his offense. *Bait* was is a Singaporean co-production, and the city-state is known for its severe penalties for drug-related offenses, which at the time the film was made still included a mandatory death penalty for all trafficking offenses.

19. Although the absurdity of *Sharknado*'s premise is part of its novel interest value, after Cyclone Debbie lashed the east coast of Australia in 2017, a five-foot bull shark was found lying (dead) on a country road, prompting numerous news reports referencing the film.

20. As Fuchs highlights, Australian killer croc films *Rogue* and *Black Water* both "utilize a style and production ethos similar to *Jaws*" (42).

21. Adam Britton and Andrew Campbell, "Croc Attacks: A New Website with Bite," *The Conversation* 3 Dec 2013. theconversation.com/croc-attacks-a-new-website-with-bite-20671

22. Plumwood, Val. "Being Prey." *Terra Nova* 1.3 (Summer 1996): 43.

23. Plumwood 42.

24. Michael Fuchs, "'They are a fact of life out here': The Ecocritical Subtexts of Three Early-Twenty-First-Century Aussie Animal Horror Movies," *Animal Horror Cinema: Genre, History and Criticism*, eds. Katarina Gregersdotter, Johan Högland, and Nicklas Hållén (London: Palgrave Macmillan, 2015) 45.

Chapter 3

1. Val Plumwood, *Feminism and the Mastery of Nature* (London and New York: Routledge, 1993) 42.

2. Plumwood 43.

3. Plumwood 43.

4. Dan Whitehead, *Tooth and Claw: A Field Guide to "Nature Run Amok" Horror Movies* (N.p.: The Zebra Partnership, 2012) 100.

5. Robert E. Bieder, *Bear* (London: Reaktion, 2005). Kindle edition.

6. While resources afford the men who hold them higher mate-value (as Bob cruelly reminds his older rival), it isn't just having the money that matters, but also being seen to have acquired it through legitimate ability. Research suggests that women tend to prefer mates who *earn* their money over acquiring it through other means, such as inheritance. See Peter K. Jonason, Norman P. Li, and Laura Madson, "It Is Not All About the Benjamins: Understanding Preferences for Mates with Resources," *Personality and Individual Differences* 52.3 (2012): 306–310. By withholding how Charles attained his massive wealth, *The Edge* better sets up the opportunity for him to prove himself.

7. Katarina Gregersdotter and Nicklas Hållán, "Anthropomorphism and the Representation of Animals as Adversaries," *Animal Horror Cinema: Genre, History and Criticism*, eds. Katarina Gregersdotter, Johan Högland, and Nicklas Hållán (New York: Palgrave Macmillan, 2015). 208.

8. Dawn Keetley, "*Frozen, The Grey*, and the Possibilities of Posthumanist Horror," *Animal Horror Cinema: Genre, History and Criticism*, eds. Katarina Gregersdotter, Johan Högland, and Nicklas Hållán (New York: Palgrave Macmillan, 2015) 197.

9. Keetley 199.

10. Keetley 202.

Chapter 4

1. Smithsonian Institution, "BugInfo: Number of Insects (Species and Individuals)," *Encyclopedia Smithsonian*, 18 Nov 2017. www.si.edu/Encyclopedia_SI/nmnh/buginfo/bugnos.htm

2. Cited in E. L. Bouvier, *The Psychic Life of Insects* (New York: The Century Company, 1922) xiv.

3. Jeffrey A. Lockwood, *The Infested Mind: Why Humans Fear, Loathe, and Love Insects* (New York: Oxford University Press, 2013) 11.

4. "The Making of Indiana Jones and the Temple of Doom." *Empire* 227, 9 Oct 2012. www.empireonline.com/movies/features/indiana-jones-making-temple-doom

5. Arachnids also stroll leggily beyond horror, appearing in the form of spider titan Shelob in Tolkien's *Return of the King* and its 2003 cinematic adaptation, and Aragog the human-eating "Acromantula" of J. K. Rowling's *Harry Potter and the Chamber of Secrets* and the 2002 film of the same name. The military adventurers of *Kong: Skull Island* also find themselves underneath a towering spider-like brute that begins shooting tethers of spidery goo down onto its human prey.

6. Diana Fleischman, "Sex Differences in Disease Avoidance," *Encyclopedia of Evolutionary Psychological Science*, eds. T. K. Shackelford and V. A. Weekes-Shackelford (Cham: Switzerland, Springer, 2018). dx.doi.org/10.1007/978-3-319-16999-6_2976-1

7. Fleischman, "Sex Differences in Disease Avoidance" 2.

8. Graham C. L. Davey, "The 'Disgusting' Spider: The Role of Disease and Illness in the Perpetuation of Fear of Spiders," *Society and Animals* 2.1 (1994): 20; Diana Fleischman, "Women's Disgust Adaptations," *Evolutionary Perspectives*

on Human Sexual Psychology and Behaviour, eds. V. A. Weekes-Shackelford and T. K. Shackelford (New York: Springer, 2014): 227. dianafleischman.com/DisgustChapter2014.pdf

9. Lockwood 16.

10. Lockwood 60.

11. Martin Nyffeler and Klaus Birkhofer, "An estimated 400 to 800 million tons of prey are annually killed by the global spider community," *The Science of Nature* 104.30 (2017). rdcu.be/vodK

12. Christopher Ingraham, "Spiders could theoretically eat every human on Earth in one year," *The Washington Post* 28 Mar 2017. www.washingtonpost.com/news/wonk/wp/2017/03/28/spiders-could-theoretically-eat-every-human-on-earth-in-one-year/?utm_term=.fd418eae8a6a

13. Davey 18.

14. Lockwood 9.

15. Antje B. M. Gerdes, Gabriele Uhl, and Georg W. Alpers, "Spiders are Special: Fear and Disgust Evoked by Pictures of Arthropods," *Evolution and Human Behavior* 30.1 (2009): 70.

16. Joshua J. New and Tamsin C. German, "Spiders at the Cocktail Party: An Ancestral Threat that Surmounts Inattentional Blindness," *Evolution and Human Behavior* 36 (2015): 170.

17. New and German 171.

18. Stefanie Hoehl, Kahl Hellmer, Maria Johansson, and Gustaf Gredebäck, "Itsy bitsy spider . . . : Infants react with increased arousal to spiders and snakes," *Frontiers in Psychology* 8.1710 (2017). www.cbs.mpg.de/Fear-of-spiders-and-snakes-is-deeply-embedded-in-us

19. Katarzyna Michalski and Sergiusz Michalski, *Spider* (London: Reaktion, 2010) 46.

20. Jeffrey Ross Suchard, "'Spider Bite' Lesions are Usually Diagnosed as Skin and Soft Tissue Lesions," *Journal of Emergency Medicine* 41.5 (2011): 473–481. www.sciencedirect.com/science/article/pii/S0736467909007926; Richard S. Vetter and Geoffrey K. Isbister, "Medical Aspects of Spider Bites," *Annual Review of Entomology* 53 (2008): 409–429. www.annualreviews.org/doi/abs/10.1146/annurev.ento.53.103106.093503

21. For example, Gerdes, Uhl, and Alpers offer an explanation of why our inherited prejudice against spiders does not extend significantly toward bees, given that while only some spiders are harmful to humans, all bees have the ability to sting—sometimes fatally in the case of allergic responses. Bees offer a benefit in terms of honey to offset the cost of interaction, with our harvesting of this food stemming right back to hunter-gatherer cultures. Because of honey, humans have had more experience being stung by bees without fatal consequences, and of gaining a net benefit from this interspecies interaction, which may have hindered the development and transmission of a pre-prepared aversion to bees (70).

22. Gerdes, Uhl, and Alpers; Sandra A. N. Mulkins, Peter J. de Jong, and Harald Merckelbach, "Disgust and Spider Phobia," *Journal of Abnormal Psychology* 105.3 (1996): 464–468. www.ncbi.nlm.nih.gov/pubmed/8772018; Sheila

R. Woody, Carmen McLean, and Tammy Klassen, "Disgust as a Motivator of Avoidance of Spiders," *Anxiety Disorders* 19 (2005): 461–475. www.ncbi.nlm.nih.gov/pubmed/15721575

23. For further assurances see Irena Lobato-Villa, "Size Matters (for Insects)!" *All You Need is Biology* 18 Jan 2016. allyouneedisbiology.wordpress.com/tag/giant-insects-are-impossible

24. Lockwood 11.

25. Gwendolyn Audrey Foster, "Monstrosity and the Bad-White-Body Film," *BAD: Infamy, Darkness, Evil, and Slime on Screen*, ed. Murray Pomerance (Albany: State University of New York Press) 50.

26. In reality, the majority of creatures used in production are flat huntsman spiders (*Delena cancerides*), a reasonably common sight in Australia, to which they are native. They do not spin webs, and while fast moving are not considered harmful to humans. The original South American spider in the film is a Goliath birdeater tarantula (*Theraphosa blondi*), native to the region's rainforests, which may bite but not to any significant medical effect. The hulking "General" spider against which Ross will finally prove himself is (thankfully) animatronic. Despite all the swatting and stamping depicted onscreen, no real arachnids were harmed in the making of the film.

27. Gerdes, Uhl, and Alpers; Lockwood also suggests that the discomfort provoked by insects may also be related to their rapid movement, "which leads to retinal images similar to those involved in falling—and this causes a startle response that we then interpret as fright" (23).

28. Robin L. Murray and Joseph K. Heumann, *Ecology and Popular Film: Cinema on the Edge* (Albany: State University of New York Press, 2009) 111.

29. Lockwood 40.

Chapter 5

1. Cary Funk and Lee Rainie, "Opinion about the Use of Animals in Research," *Internet and Technology* 1 July 2016, *Pew Research Center*, 13 November 2017. www.pewinternet.org/2015/07/01/chapter-7-opinion-about-the-use-of-animals-in-research

2. David J. Skal, *The Monster Show: A Cultural History of Horror* (New York: Faber & Faber, 1993) 247.

3. Cyndy Hendershot, *Paranoia, the Bomb, and 1950s Science Fiction Films* (Bowling Green, OH: Bowling Green State University Popular Press, 1999) 77.

4. Hendershot 88.

5. Skal 248.

6. Skal 248.

7. Readers may recognize this theme from James Cameron's *Terminator II: Judgment Day* (1992), in which the cyborg killing-machine (Arnold Schwarzenegger) voluntarily allows himself to be lowered into a vat of molten steel. Not only must the plans for the technology of devastation be destroyed, but the chip within his own head must also never be accessed.

8. Godzilla has continued to be associated with nuclear fears, but also possibilities. In his latest appearance, *Shin Godzilla* (2016), Godzilla is energized by radiation, and many critics linked the film to the Fukushima Daiichi nuclear disaster of 2011. However, his strange element-converting anatomy also holds the secret of an unknown isotope. As Deputy Chief Cabinet Secretary (Hiroki Hasegawa) summarizes, "Godzilla is both a threat to mankind, and also poses a revelation of limitless potential."

9. Kate Wheeling and Max Ufberg, "The Ocean is Boiling: The Complete Oral History of the 1969 Santa Barbara Oil Spill," *Pacific Standard* 18 April, 2017. psmag.com/news/the-ocean-is-boiling-the-complete-oral-history-of-the-1969-santa-barbara-oil-spill

10. Wheeling and Ufberg.

11. For a timeline of ozone depletion observations, see David W. Fahey and Michaela I. Hegglin, *Twenty Questions and Answers about the Ozone Layer: 2010 Update*. Scientific Assessment of Ozone Depletion: 2010, World Meteorological Organization Global Ozone Research and Monitoring Project, Report No. 52. U.S. Department of Commerce; National Oceanic & Atmospheric Administration. www.esrl.noaa.gov/csd/assessments/ozone/2010/twentyquestions/booklet.pdf

12. Toads are not particularly frightening villains, but what effect they do elicit is probably owed to a disgust response triggered by their warty appearance. Despite the rumor, touching toads does not cause warts, but warts themselves are contagious, so it's easy to see how this bit of folklore would have arisen.

13. Jennifer Schell, "Polluting and Perverting Nature: The Vengeful Animals of *Frogs*," *Animal Horror Cinema: Genre, History and Criticism*, eds. Katarina Gregersgotter, Johan Högland, and Nicklas Hållén (London: Palgrave Macmillan, 2015) 60.

14. Schell points out that the family's surname "Crockett" is likely intended to evoke iconic American historical personality Davy Crockett, underscoring their allegorical role (68).

15. Ina Rae Hark, "Crazy Like a Prof: Mad Science and the Transgressions of the Rational," *Bad: Infamy, Darkness, Evil and Slime on* Screen, ed. Murray Pomerance (Albany: State University of New York Press, 2004) 302.

16. Hark 308.

17. Christopher P Tourney, "The Moral Character of Mad Scientists: A Cultural Critique of Science," *Science, Technology, & Human Values* 17.4 (1992): 434. www.jstor.org/stable/689735

18. H. Clark Barrett, Adaptations to Predators and Prey. *Handbook of Evolutionary Psychology*. 2nd ed., ed. David M. Buss (Wiley & Sons, 2016) 247.

Chapter 6

1. Thomas Nagel, "What Is It Like to Be a Bat?" *The Philosophical Review* 83.4 (1974): 439. www.jstor.org/stable/2183914

2. Katarina Gregersdotter and Nicklas Hållén, "Anthropomorphism and the Representation of Animals as Adversaries," *Animal Horror Cinema: Genre, History*

and Criticism, eds. Katarina Gregersdotter, Nicklas Hållén, and Johan Höglund (New York: Palgrave Macmillan) 215.

3. John Berger, *Why Look at Animals?* (London: Penguin, 2009) 27.

4. For an extended discussion of this point, see chapter 1 of Jonathan Burt, *Animals in Film* (Wiltshire, England: Reaktion Books, 2002).

5. Randy Malamud suggests that the visual positioning of animals in our culture "keenly parallels" (73) feminist film theory's notion of the "male gaze" postulated by Laura Mulvey, in which an active male viewer expects a passive and objectified onscreen female: "[i]t is a smooth extrapolation to characterize Mulvey's male gaze (upon the filmed female creature) as a human gaze (upon the filmed animal creature)" (74). Accordingly, women under the male gaze are objectified and subject to male regimes of interest, becoming "two-dimensionally caricatured in a good girl/bad girl dichotomy, angel/whore" (Malamud 74). For Malamud, animals are subject to a similarly narrow grid of meaning: those that contradict our power are "earn our scorn, and . . . serve the purpose of allowing people to satiate our sadistic drives toward animals by hating or destroying these creatures" (74). The symmetry might be pleasing, but this is certainly too reductive: criticisms of Mulvey's psychoanalytic theory itself aside, the phenomenon of humans looking at animals involves far more conceptual variables (if only because animals are an extremely varied group) than heterosexual men women looking at women. For instance, lions or bears are suggestive of real danger; the idea that these only appear onscreen to satiate a sadistic desire to dominate them is obviously too cynical. With Mulvey's theory of a male/active and female/passive cinematic dichotomy in hand, Malamud states, "I simply transpose this to characterize the image of the animal as passive raw material for the active gaze of the human" (74). Indeed, but the problem is we do not see as "simply" as that. See Randy Malamud, *An Introduction to Animals and Visual Culture* (Great Britain: Palgrave Macmillan, 2012) 73–74.

6. Katarina Gregersdotter, Nicklas Hållén, and Johan Höglund, "Introduction," *Animal Horror Cinema: Genre, History and Criticism*, eds. Katarina Gregersdotter, Nicklas Hållén, and Johan Höglund (New York: Palgrave Macmillan) 16–17.

7. H. Clark Barrett, "Adaptations to Predators and Prey," *Handbook of Evolutionary Psychology*, 2nd ed., ed. David M. Buss (Hoboken, NJ: John Wiley & Sons, 2016) 252.

8. Hans Kruuk, *Hunter and Hunted: Relationships between Carnivores and People* (Cambridge, UK: Cambridge University Press, 2002) 176.

9. Donna Hart and Robert W. Sussman, *Man the Hunted: Predators, Primates, and Human Evolution* (New York: Westview, 2005) 3.

10. Barrett 256.

11. Hart and Sussman 7.

12. Cited in Hart and Sussman 159.

13. Mary Ellen Bellanca, "The Monstrosity of Predation in Daphne du Maurier's "The Birds," *Interdisciplinary Studies in Literature and Environment* 18.1 (2011) 38.

14. Bellanca 38.

15. Slavoj Žižek, *Looking Awry: An Introduction to Jacques Lacan through Popular Culture* (Cambridge, MA: MIT Press, 1992) 93.
16. Qtd. in Richard Allen, "Avian Metaphor in *The Birds*," *Framing Hitchcock: Selected Essays from the Hitchcock Annual*, eds. Sidney Gottlieb and Christopher Brookhouse (Detroit, MI: Wayne State University Press, 2002) 281.
17. Zizek 99.
18. Slavoj Žižek, *The Pervert's Guide to Cinema*, dir. Sophie Fiennes, perf. Slavoj Žižek (Mischief Films & Amoeba Films, 2006).
19. Žižek, *Looking Awry* 93–94.
20. Murray Pomerance, "Thirteen Ways of Looking at *The Birds*," *Hitchcock at the Source: The Auteur as Adaptor*, eds. R. Barton Palmer and David Boyd (Albany: State University of New York Press, 2011) 271.
21. Pomerance 272.
22. Bellanca 38.
23. Jacques Derrida, *The Animal That Therefore I Am*, ed. Marie-Louise Mallet, trans. David Willis (New York: Fordham University Press, 2008) 4.
24. Derrida 5.

Chapter 7

1. Edward O. Wilson, *In Search of Nature* (Washington, DC: Island Press, 1996) 18.
2. J. Polák, K. Sedláčková, D. Nácar, E. Landová, and D. S. Frynta, "Fear the Serpent: A Psychometric Study of Snake Phobia," *Psychiatry Research* 242 (2016): 163. www.ncbi.nlm.nih.gov/pubmed/27280527
3. Arne Öhman and Susan Mineka, "The Malicious Serpent: Snakes as a Prototypical Stimulus for an Evolved Module of Fear," *Current Directions in Psychological Science* 12.1 (2003): 5–9. www.jstor.org/stable/20182821; Wilson, *In Search of Nature* 6, 18–21.
4. Kim Hill and A. Magdalena Hurtado, *Ache Life History: The Ecology and Demography of a Foraging People* (New York: Routledge, 1996) 162.
5. Öhman and Mineka 6.
6. Stefanie Hoehl, Kahl Hellmer, Maria Johansson, and Gustaf Gredebäck, "Itsy bitsy spider . . . : Infants react with increased arousal to spiders and snakes," *Frontiers in Psychology* 8.1710 (2017). www.cbs.mpg.de/Fear-of-spiders-and-snakes-is-deeply-embedded-in-us
7. Ottmar V Lipp and Nazanin Derakshan, "Attentional Bias to Pictures of Fear-Relevant Animals in a Dot Probe Task," *Emotion* 5.3 (2005): 368. psycnet.apa.org/doiLanding?doi=10.1037%2F1528-3542.5.3.365; Jan W. Van Strien and Lynne A. Isbell, "Snake scales, partial exposure, and the Snake Detection Theory: A Human-Related Potentials Study." *Scientific Reports* 7.46331 (2017): 2. www.nature.com/articles/srep46331
8. Van Strien and Isbell 2.
9. Öhman and Mineka 5.
10. Wilson, *In Search of Nature* 18.

11. There obviously remains some differences in the extent to which people fear snakes. Although the fears may of course be overcome, Öhman and Mineka suggest that genetic variability may account for differences in snake-fear and the ease with which one learns snake-fear (6).

12. Edward O. Wilson, *Biophilia: The Human Bond with Other Species* (Cambridge, MA and London: Harvard University Press) 85.

13. Drake Stutesman, *Snake* (London: Reaktion, 2005) 55.

14. Stutesman 56.

15. Stutesman 66.

16. Sune Borkfelt, "Colonial Animals and Literary Analysis: The Example of Kipling's Animal Stories," *English Studies* 90.5 (2009): 557. www.tandfonline.com/doi/abs/10.1080/00138380903181023

17. Sigmund Freud, "Medusa's Head," *The Standard Edition of the Complete Psychological Works of Sigmund Freud*, vol. XVIII (London: Hogarth, 1955) 273.

18. Stutesman 153.

19. Stutesman 153.

20. Robin Wood, *Hollywood: From Vietnam to Reagan . . . and Beyond*, Rev. and exp. ed. (New York: Columbia University Press, 2003) 152.

21. *BoxOfficeMojo*, "Anaconda." www.boxofficemojo.com/movies/?id=anaconda.htm

Chapter 8

1. Edward O. Wilson, *Biophilia: The Human Bond with Other Species* (Cambridge MA and London: Harvard University Press, 1984) 125–126.

2. "A dog's life," *Brewer's Dictionary of Phrase and Fable*, 18th ed. (London: Brewer's, 2009) 386.

3. Adrienne McLean, "Introduction: Wonder Dogs," *Cinematic Canines: Dogs and Their Work in the Feature Film*, ed. McLean (Newark, NJ: Rutgers University Press, 2014) 14.

4. Murray Pomerance, "Hitchcock's Canine Uncanny," *Cinematic Canines: Dogs and Their Work in the Feature Film*, ed. Adrienne McLean (Newark, NJ: Rutgers University Press, 2014) 215.

5. Pomerance 213.

6. George M. Strain, "How Well Do Dogs and Other Animals Hear?" Louisiana State University. www.lsu.edu/deafness/HearingRange.html

7. Peter Singer, *Animal Liberation*, 1975 (London: Pimlico, 1995) 191–192.

8. Rowena Loverance, *Christian Art* (Cambridge, MA: Harvard University Press, 2007) 141–142.

9. Val Plumwood, "Being Prey," *Terra Nova* 1.3 (Summer 1996): 41–42.

10. Elizabeth Leane and Guinevere Narraway, "Things from Another World: Dogs, Aliens, and Antarctic Cinema," *Cinematic Canines: Dogs and Their Work in the Feature Film*, ed. Adrienne McLean (Newark, NJ: Rutgers University Press, 2014) 181.

11. Leane and Narraway, 184.

12. Noël Carroll, *The Philosophy of Horror: Or, Paradoxes of the Heart* (London: Routledge, 1990) 34.

13. Emphasizing violence in "wild" female characters is also probably a less intuitive choice than it is for male characters given that (taken as a group) men have a greater tendency toward "uncivilized" aggression than women. See Marco Del Giudice, "Gender Differences in Personality and Behavior," *International Encyclopedia of the Social and Behavioral Sciences*, 2nd ed., ed. James D. Wright (Amsterdam: Elsevier, 2015) 750–756.

Chapter 9

1. Donna Hart and Robert W. Sussman, *Man the Hunted: Primates, Predators, and Human Evolution* (New York: Westview Press, 2005) 94–95.

2. Charlotte F. Otten, ed., *A Lycanthropy Reader: Werewolves in Western Culture* (Syracuse, NY: Syracuse University Press, 1986) 21–47.

3. Leslie A. Sconduto, *Metamorphoses of the Werewolf: A Literary Study from Antiquity through the Renaissance* (Jefferson, NC and London: McFarland & Company, 2008). Kindle edition.

4. Otten 51–53.

5. David M. Buss, *The Dangerous Passion: Why Jealousy is as Necessary as Love or Sex* (London: Bloomsbury, 2001) 31–33; David M. Buss, Randy J. Larsen, Drew Westen, and Jennifer Semmelroth, "Sex Differences in Jealousy: Evolution, Physiology, and Psychology," *Psychological Science* 3.4 (1992): 255.

6. Buss, *The Dangerous Passion* 3–6, 52–53; Buss, Larsen, Westen, and Semmelroth note that anti-cuckoldry behavior has been observed in a wide variety of other species, although since humans show greater paternal investment than other primate species, we would expect selection pressures against paternity uncertainty to be more intense (251).

7. Buss, *The Dangerous Passion* 52–53; David M. Buss, *The Murderer Next Door: Why the Mind is Designed to Kill* (New York: Penguin, 2005) 85.

8. Buss, *The Dangerous Passion* 55–57; Buss, Larsen, and Westen 251–255; Edlund et al., "Sex Differences in Jealousy: The (Lack of) Influence of Researcher Theoretical Perspective," *The Journal of Social Psychology* 16.1 (2017): 67–78. doi.org/10.1080/00224545.2017.1365686

9. Buss, *The Dangerous Passion* 122. This is certainly not to imply that murder under some circumstances is *determined* by our inherited psychology (and that the murderer is therefore somehow blameless), only that inherited tendencies or predispositions toward it exist under a limited set of circumstances.

10. Buss, *The Murderer* 85–88.

11. Buss, *The Murderer* 87.

12. Buss, *The Murderer* 88.

13. Buss, *The Dangerous Passion* 122.

14. Buss, *The Dangerous Passion* 122. As Shackelford et al. point out, "Since selection is the result of the relative reproductive fitness of competing designs, damaging an intrasexual rival's fitness effectively increases one's own." Todd K.

Shackelford, David M. Buss, and Viviana A. Weekes-Shackelford, in "Wife Killings Committed in the Context of a Lover's Triangle," *Basic and Applied Social Psychology* 25.2 (2003): 138. The authors also note, in support of the anti-cuckoldry theory, that a woman's likelihood of being murdered by her husband in a love-triangle scenario is related to her youth and thus closeness to reproductive age. Their study shows that risk "decreases precipitously as a function of the woman's age," exactly as would be expected if mate-murder in such circumstances is linked to defenses against paternity uncertainty (141).

15. Buss, *The Murderer* 88.
16. Buss, *The Murderer* 88.
17. Buss, *The Dangerous Passion* 8.
18. Buss, *The Dangerous Passion* 125.
19. Buss, *The Dangerous Passion* 124–125.
20. Marie de France, "Bisclavret," *The Lais of Marie de France*, 2nd ed., with Two Further Lais in the Original Old French, trans. Glyn S. Burgess and Keith Busby (England: Penguin, 1999) 68.
21. de France 71.
22. Sconduto.
23. de France 68.
24. Joe Johnston's remake styles the title as two words—*The Wolfman* instead of *The Wolf Man*.
25. Freud wrote of this theory in his study of "Little Hans," a case he referred to as "the wolfman," because he believed the boy's dream of a tree filled with wolves was a deflected manifestation of the trauma of the primal scene. Sigmund Freud, "From the History of an Infantile Neurosis" (1918), reprinted in Peter Gay, *The Freud Reader* (London: Vintage, 1995) 400–426.
26. The therapist is named in tribute to the director of *The Wolf Man* (1941), George Waggner.
27. "Interview with John Landis," dir. Adam Simon, perf. John Landis, *An American Werewolf in London*: Extras (Universal, 2003) DVD.
28. Sally Chivers, *The Silvering Screen: Old Age and Disability in Cinema* (Toronto: University of Toronto Press, 2011) 99.
29. Buss, *The Dangerous Passion* 50–51.
30. "The discovery [of sex differences in jealousy] has inspired many attempted counter-demonstrations, perhaps driven by distaste for the idea that women and men are in any way psychologically dissimilar, but the evidence is consistent and abundant. . . . It is also unsurprising when we consider that cuckoldry risk is sexually asymmetrical." Margo Wilson and Martin Daly, "Coercive Violence by Human Males against Their Female Partners," *Sexual Coercion in Primates and Humans: An Evolutionary Perspective on Male Aggression against Females*, eds. Martin N. Muller and Richard W. Wrangham (Cambridge, MA and London: Harvard University Press, 2009) 275.
31. Buss, *The Dangerous Passion* 55–57; Buss, Larsen and Westen; Edlund et al.
32. Buss, *The Dangerous Passion* 56.
33. Buss, *The Dangerous Passion* 56–57; Buss, Larsen, and Westen 252.
34. Buss, *The Dangerous Passion* 60.

35. Buss, *The Dangerous Passion* 55.

36. Bianca Nielsen, "'Something's Wrong, Like More Than You Being Female': Transgressive Sexuality and Discourses of Reproduction in *Ginger Snaps*," *ThirdSpace: A Journal of Feminist Theory and Culture* 3.2 (2004). journals.sfu.ca/thirdspace/index.php/journal/article/view/nielsen/176

Aftermath

1. Gowri Koneswaran and Danielle Nierenberg, "Global Farm Animal Production and Global Warming: Impacting and Mitigating Climate Change," *Environmental Health Perspectives* 116.5 (2008): 578. 27 Nov 2017. www.ncbi.nlm.nih.gov/pmc/articles/PMC2367646

2. To better put this in perspective, it has been estimated that only about 100 billion humans have ever lived on this planet (since the emergence of homo sapiens). Wesley Stephenson, "Do the dead outnumber the living?" *BBC News: Magazine* 4 Feb 2012. www.bbc.com/news/magazine-16870579

3. Noah Gittell, "It's Time to Retire the Man vs. Animal Movie," *Splice Today* 30 June 2016. www.splicetoday.com/moving-pictures/it-s-time-to-retire-the-man-vs-animal-movie

4. Barbara Ehrenreich, "Foreword." Paul Trout, *Deadly Powers: Animal Predators and the Mythic Imagination* (Amherst, NY: Prometheus Books, 2011) 16.

5. Carol J. Adams, *The Sexual Politics of Meat: A Feminist-Vegetarian Critical Theory*, 20th Anniversary ed. (New York: Bloomsbury, 2010) 66–67.

6. Paul Trout, *Deadly Powers: Animal Predators and the Mythic Imagination* (Amherst, NY: Prometheus Books, 2011) 26.

7. Indeed, as noted earlier, fear of the dark is itself thought to be an antipredator adaptation, given that big cats (which have superb night vision) hunt primarily at night. See Craig Packer, Alexandra Swanson, Dennis Ikanda, and Hadas Kushnir, "Fear of Darkness, the Full Moon, and the Nocturnal Ecology of African Lions," *PLoS ONE* 6.7 (2011): 1–2. doi.org/10.1371/journal.pone.0022285

8. Edward O. Wilson, *Biophilia: The Human Bond with Other Species* (Cambridge, MA and London: Harvard University Press, 1984) 9.

9. Trout 35.

Works Cited

Adams, Carol J. *The Sexual Politics of Meat: A Feminist-Vegetarian Critical Theory*. 20th Anniversary ed. New York: Bloomsbury, 2010.
Alcock, John. *The Triumph of Sociobiology*. Oxford and New York: Oxford University Press, 2001.
Allen, Richard. "Avian Metaphor in The Birds." *Framing Hitchcock: Selected Essays from the Hitchcock Annual*. Eds. Sidney Gottlieb and Christopher Brookhous. Detroit: Wayne State University Press, 2002. 281–309.
American Museum of Natural History. "Sharks and Rays: Myth and Reality." Seminars on Science. 2001 www.amnh.org/learn/pd/sharks_rays/rfl_myth/myth_page5.html
Barash, David P. "Biology Lurks Beneath: Bioliterary Explorations of the Individual versus Society." *Evolutionary Psychology* 2.1 (2004): 200–219. journals.sagepub.com/doi/full/10.1177/147470490400200125
Barkow, Jerome, ed. *Missing the Revolution: Darwinism for Social Scientists*. New York: Oxford University Press, 2005.
Barrett, H. Clark. "Adaptations to Predators and Prey." *Handbook of Evolutionary Psychology*. 2nd ed. Ed. David M. Buss. Hoboken, NJ: John Wiley & Sons, 2016. 246–263.
Bieder, Robert E. *Bear*. London: Reaktion, 2005. Kindle edition.
Bellanca, Mary Ellen. "The Monstrosity of Predation in Daphne du Maurier's "The Birds," *Interdisciplinary Studies in Literature and Environment* 18.1 (2011): 26–46. doi.org/10.1093/isle/isq123
Berger, John. *Why Look at Animals?* London: Penguin, 2009.
Biskind, Peter. "Jaws: Between the Teeth." *Jump Cut: A Review of Contemporary Media* 9 (1975): 1–26. www.ejumpcut.org/archive/onlinessays/JC09folder/Jaws.html
Bordwell, David. "Contemporary Film Studies and the Vicissitudes of Grand Theory." *Post-Theory: Reconstructing Film Studies*, eds. David Bordwell and Noël Carroll. Madison: University of Wisconsin Press, 1996. Kindle edition.
———. "What Snakes, Eagles, and Rhesus Macaques Can Teach Us." Boyd, Carroll, and Gottschall 270–285.
Borkfelt, Sune. "Colonial Animals and Literary Analysis: The Example of Kipling's Animal Stories." *English Studies* 90.5 (2009): 557–568. www.tandfonline.com/doi/abs/10.1080/00138380903181023

Bouvier, E. L. *The Psychic Life of Insects*. New York: The Century Company, 1922.
BoxOfficeMojo. "Anaconda." www.boxofficemojo.com/movies/?id=anaconda.htm
Boyd, Brian. *On the Origin of Stories: Evolution, Cognition, and Fiction*. Cambridge, MA: Harvard UP, 2009.
Boyd, Brian, Joseph Carroll, and Jonathan Gottschall, eds. *Evolution, Literature, and Film: A Reader*. New York: Columbia University Press, 2010.
———. "Introduction." Boyd, Carroll, and Gottschall 1–17.
Britton, Adam, and Andrew Campbell. "Croc Attacks: A New Website with Bite." *The Conversation* 3 Dec 2013. theconversation.com/croc-attacks-a-new-website-with-bite-20671
Burroughs, Edgar Rice. *Tarzan of the Apes & Other Tales*. Centenary ed. London: Gollancz, 2012.
Buss, David M. *The Dangerous Passion: Why Jealousy is as Necessary as Love or Sex*. London: Bloomsbury, 2001.
———. *The Evolution of Desire: Strategies of Human Mating*. Revised and updated ed. New York: Basic Books, 2016.
———. *Evolutionary Psychology: The New Science of the Mind*. 5th ed. London and New York: Routledge, 2016.
———. *The Murderer Next Door: Why the Mind is Designed to Kill*. New York: Penguin, 2005.
———. "Human Mating Strategies." *Samfundsokonomen* 4 (2002): 47–58. labs.la.utexas.edu/buss/files/2015/10/Buss-2002-human-mating-strategies.pdf
———, ed. *The Handbook of Evolutionary Psychology*. Hoboken, NJ: John Wiley & Sons, 2016.
———, Randy J. Larsen, Drew Westen, and Jennifer Semmelroth, "Sex Differences in Jealousy: Evolution, Physiology, and Psychology," *Psychological Science* 3.4 (1992): 251–255.
Burt, Jonathan. *Animals in Film*. Wiltshire, England: Reaktion Books, 2002.
Caldicott, David G. E., Ravi Mahajani, and Marie Kuhn. "The Anatomy of a Shark Attack: A Case Report and Review of the Literature." *Injury: International Journal of the Care for the Injured* 32 (2001): 445–453.
Caputi, Jane. *Goddesses and Monsters: Women, Myth, Power, and Popular Culture*. London: University of Wisconsin Press, 2004.
Carroll, Joseph. "Human Nature and Literary Meaning." Rivkin and Ryan 1329–1359.
———. *Reading Human Nature: Literary Darwinism in Theory and Practice*. Albany: State University of New York Press, 2011.
———, Dan P. McAdams, and Edward O. Wilson. *Darwin's Bridge: Uniting the Humanities and Sciences*. New York: Oxford University Press, 2016.
Carroll, Noël. "King Kong: Ape and Essence." *Planks of Reason: Essays on the Horror Film*. Rev. ed. Eds. Barry Keith Grant and Christopher Sharrett. Lanham, MA: The Scarecrow Press, 2004. 212–239.
———. *The Philosophy of Horror: Or, Paradoxes of the Heart*. London: Routledge, 1990.

Chivers, Sally. *The Silvering Screen: Old Age and Disability in Cinema.* Toronto: University of Toronto Press, 2011.

Coleridge, Samuel Taylor. "The Rime of the Ancient Mariner." 1798 www.gutenberg.org/ebooks/151

Cosmides, Leda, and John Tooby. "Cognitive Adaptations for Social Exchange." *The Adapted Mind: Evolutionary Psychology and the Generation of Culture.* Eds. Jerome Barkow, Leda Cosmides, and John Tooby. Oxford: Oxford University Press, 1992.

Cox, William T. L., and Patricia G. Devine. "Experimental Research on Shooter Bias: Ready (or Relevant) for Application in the Courtroom?" *Journal of Applied Research in Memory and Cognition* 5 (2016): 236–238.

Creed, Barbara. *Darwin's Screens: Evolutionary Aesthetics, Time and Sexual Display in the Cinema.* South Australia: Melbourne University Press, 2009.

———. *The Monstrous-Feminine: Film, Feminism, Psychoanalysis.* London and New York: Routledge, 1994.

Curtis, Val, Robert Auger, and Tamer Rabie. "Evidence that Disgust Evolved to Protect from Risk of Disease." *Proceedings of the Royal Society B: Biological Sciences* 271.4 (2004): S131–S133. rspb.royalsocietypublishing.org/content/271/Suppl_4/S131

Davey, Graham C. L. "The 'Disgusting' Spider: The Role of Disease and Illness in the Perpetuation of Fear of Spiders." *Society and Animals* 2.1 (1994): 17–24.

Dawkins, Richard. *The Selfish Gene.* 40th anniversary ed. (Oxford Landmark Science). Oxford: Oxford University Press, 2016.

de France, Marie. "Bisclavret." *The Lais of Marie de France.* 2nd ed., with Two Further Lais in the Original Old French. Trans. Glyn S. Burgess and Keith Busby. England: Penguin, 1999. 68–72.

Del Giudice, Marco. "Gender Differences in Personality and Behavior," *International Encyclopedia of the Social and Behavioral Sciences*, 2nd ed. Ed. James D. Wright (Amsterdam: Elsevier, 2015) 750–756.

Derrida, Jacques. *The Animal That Therefore I Am.* Ed. Marie-Louise Mallet. Trans. David Willis. New York: Fordham University Press, 2008. 4.

Derry, Charles. *Dark Dreams 2.0: A Psychological History of the Modern Horror Film from the 1950s to the 21st Century.* Jefferson, NC and London: McFarland, 2009.

"A dog's life." *Brewer's Dictionary of Phrase and Fable.* 18th ed. London: Brewer's, 2009.

Edlund, John, Jeremy D. Heider, Austin Lee Nichols, Randy J. McCarthy, Sarah E. Wood, Cory R. Scherer, Jessica L. Hartnett, and Richard Walker. "Sex Differences in Jealousy: The (Lack of) Influence of Researcher Theoretical Perspective," *Journal of Social Psychology* 16.1 (2017): 67–78. doi.org/10.1080/00224545.2017.1365686

Ehrenreich, Barbara. *Blood Rites: Origins and History of the Passions of War.* New York: Henry Holt and Company, 1997.

———. "Foreword." Trout 13–18.

Erb, Cynthia. *Tracking King Kong: A Hollywood Icon in Global Culture*. 2nd ed. Detroit: Wayne State University Press, 2009.
Fahey, David W., and Michaela I. Hegglin. *Twenty Questions and Answers about the Ozone Layer: 2010 Update*. Scientific Assessment of Ozone Depletion: 2010; World Meteorological Organization Global Ozone Research and Monitoring Project, Report No. 52. U.S. Department of Commerce; National Oceanic & Atmospheric Administration. www.esrl.noaa.gov/csd/assessments/ozone/2010/twentyquestions/booklet.pdf
Ferguson, Christopher J. "Does Media Violence Predict Societal Violence? It Depends on What You Look at and When." *Journal of Communication* 65.1 (2015): E1–E22.
———. "Does Sexy Media Promote Teen Sex? A Meta-Analytic and Methodological Review." *Psychiatric Quarterly* 88.2 (2017): 449–358.
———, and Eugene Beresin, "Social Science's Curious War with Pop Culture and How it was Lost: The Media Violence Debate and the Risks it Holds for Social Science." *Preventative Medicine* 99 (2017): 69–76.
Ferrando, Francesca. "Posthumanism, Transhumanism, Antihumanism, Metahumanism, and New Materialisms." *Existenz: An International Journal of Philosophy, Religion, Politics, and the Arts* 8.2 (2013) 26–32.
Fleischman, Diana. "Sex-Differences in Disease Avoidance." Shackelford and Weekes-Shackelford. dx.doi.org/10.1007/978-3-319-16999-6_2976-1
———. "Women's Disgust Adaptations." *Evolutionary Perspectives on Human Sexual Psychology and Behaviour*. Eds. V. A. Weekes-Shackelford and T. K. Shackleford (New York: Springer, 2014): 227–296. dianafleischman.com/DisgustChapter2014.pdf
Foster, Gwendolyn Audrey. "Monstrosity and the Bad-White-Body Film." *BAD: Infamy, Darkness, Evil, and Slime on Screen*. Ed. Murray Pomerance. Albany: State University of New York Press. 39–53.
Freud, Sigmund. "From the History of an Infantile Neurosis." 1918. *The Freud Reader*. Ed. Peter Gay. London: Vintage, 1995. 400–426.
Fry, Bryan G., et al. "A Central Role for Venom in Predation by Varanus Komodoensis (Komodo Dragon) and the Extinct Giant Varanus (Megalania) priscus," *Proceedings of the National Academy of Sciences of the United States of America* 106.22 (2009): 8969–8974. www.ncbi.nlm.nih.gov/pmc/articles/PMC2690028
Fuchs, Michael. "'They are a fact of life out here': The Ecocritical Subtexts of Three Early Twenty-First-Century Aussie Animal Horror Movies." *Animal Horror Cinema: Genre, History and Criticism*. Eds. Karatina Gregersdotter, Johan Höglund, and Nicklas Hållén. New York: Palgrave Macmillan, 2015. 37–57.
Funk, Cary, and Lee Rainie. "Opinion About the Use of Animals in Research." *Internet and Technology* 1 July 2016. Pew Research Center. www.pewinternet.org/2015/07/01/chapter-7-opinion-about-the-use-of-animals-in-research
Gambin, Lee. *Massacred by Mother Nature: Exploring the Natural Horror Film*. Baltimore, MD: Midnight Marquee Press, 2012.
Goff, Phillip Atiba, Jennifer L. Eberhardt, Melissa J. Williams, and Matthew Christian Jackson. "Not Yet Human: Implicit Knowledge, Historical Dehu-

manization, and Contemporary Consequences." *Journal of Personality and Social Psychology* 94.2 (2008): 292–306.
Gott, Ted, and Kathryn Weir. *Gorilla*. London: Reaktion, 2013.
Gerdes, Antje B. M., Gabriele Uhl, and Georg W. Alpers. "Spiders are Special: Fear and Disgust Evoked by Pictures of Arthropods." *Evolution and Human Behavior* 30.1 (2009): 66–73. dx.doi.org/10.1016/j.evolhumbehav.2008.08.005
Girard, René. *The Scapegoat*. Trans. Yvonne Freccero. Baltimore, MD: Johns Hopkins University Press, 1986.
Gittell, Noah. "It's Time to Retire the Man vs. Animal Movie." *Splice Today* 30 June 2016. www.splicetoday.com/moving-pictures/it-s-time-to-retire-the-man-vs-animal-movie
Glaeser, Georg, and Hannes F. Paulus. *The Evolution of the Eye*. Berlin: Springer, 2015.
Gregersdotter, Katarina, Johan Högland, and Nicklas Hållán, eds. *Animal Horror Cinema: Genre, History and Criticism*. New York: Palgrave Macmillan, 2015.
———. "A History of Animal Horror Cinema." Gregersdotter, Högland, and Hållén 19–36.
———. Introduction. Gregersdotter, Högland, and Hållén 1–19.
———, and Nicklas Hållén. "Anthropomorphism and the Representation of Animals as Adversaries." Gregersdotter, Höglund, and Hållén 206–223.
Grotuss, Jason, and Sarah Jane Beard. "Appearance/Beauty in Girls." Shackelford and Weekes-Shackelford. dx.doi.org/10.1007/978-3-319-16999-6_2406-1
Hagen, Edward. "Why is the EEA equated with the Pleistocene," *Evolutionary Psychology FAQ*. University of California, Santa Barbara: Department of Anthropology, 2004. www.anth.ucsb.edu/projects/human/evpsychfaq.html
Handwerk, Brian. "Crocodiles Have Strongest Bite Ever Measured, Hands-on Tests Show." *National Geographic* 15 Mar 2012. news.nationalgeographic.com/news/2012/03/120315-crocodiles-bite-force-erickson-science-plos-one-strongest
Hark, Ina Rae. "Crazy Like a Prof: Mad Science and the Transgressions of the Rational." *Bad: Infamy, Darkness, Evil and Slime on Screen*. Ed. Murray Pomerance. Albany: State University of New York Press, 2004. 302–313.
Hart, Donna, and Robert W. Sussman. *Man the Hunted: Predators, Primates, and Human Evolution*. New York: Westview, 2005.
Hendershot, Cyndy. *Paranoia, the Bomb, and 1950s Science Fiction Films*. Bowling Green, OH: Bowling Green State University Popular Press, 1999.
Hill, Kim, and A. Magdalena Hurtado. *Ache Life History: The Ecology and Demography of a Foraging People*. New York: Routledge, 1996.
Hoehl, Stefanie, Kahl Hellmer, Maria Johansson, and Gustaf Gredebäck. "Itsy bitsy spider . . . : Infants react with increased arousal to spiders and snakes." *Frontiers in Psychology* 8.1710 (2017). doi.org/10.3389/fpsyg.2017.01710
Hrdy, Sarah Blaffer. *The Woman That Never Evolved*. Rev. ed. Cambridge, MA & London: Harvard University Press, 1999.
Ingraham, Christopher. "Spiders could theoretically eat every human on Earth in one year." *The Washington Post*, 28 Mar. 2017. www.washingtonpost.com/

news/wonk/wp/2017/03/28/spiders-could-theoretically-eat-every-human-on-earth-in-one-year/?utm_term=.fd418eae8a6a

Isbell, Lynne A. *The Fruit, the Tree, and the Serpent: Why We See So Well*. Cambridge, MA and London: Harvard University Press, 2009.

"Interview with John Landis." Dir. Adam Simon. Universal, 2001.

Jonason, Peter K., Li, Norman P., and Laura Madson. "It Is Not All About the Benjamins: Understanding Preferences for Mates with Resources." *Personality and Individual Differences* 52.3 (2012): 306–310.

Keetley, Dawn. "Frozen, The Grey, and the Possibilities of Posthumanist Horror." *Animal Horror Cinema: Genre, History and Criticism*. Gregersdotter, Högland, and Hållán 187–205.

Koneswaran, Gowri, and Danielle Nierenberg. "Global Farm Animal Production and Global Warming: Impacting and Mitigating Climate Change." *Environmental Health Perspectives* 116.5 (2008): 578–582. www.ncbi.nlm.nih.gov/pmc/articles/PMC2367646

Leane, Elizabeth, and Guinevere Narraway. "Things from Another World: Dogs, Aliens, and Antarctic Cinema." McLean 181–195.

Lipp, Ottmar V., and Nazanin Derakshan. "Attentional Bias to Pictures of Fear-Relevant Animals in a Dot Probe Task." *Emotion* 5.3 (2005): 365–369. psycnet.apa.org/doiLanding?doi=10.1037%2F1528-3542.5.3.365

Lobato-Villa, Irena. "Size Matters (For Insects)!" *All You Need is Biology*. 18 Jan. 2016 allyouneedisbiology.wordpress.com/tag/giant-insects-are-impossible

Lockwood, Jeffrey A. *The Infested Mind: Why Humans Fear, Loathe, and Love Insects*. New York: Oxford University Press, 2013.

Loverance, Rowena. *Christian Art*. Cambridge, MA: Harvard University Press, 2007.

Lovgren, Stefan. "'Jaws' at 30: Film Stoked Fear, Study of Great White Sharks." *National Geographic News* 15 June 2005. news.nationalgeographic.com/news/2005/06/0615_050615_jawssharks.html

"The Making of Indiana Jones and the Temple of Doom." *Empire* 227, 9 Oct. 2012. www.empireonline.com/movies/features/indiana-jones-making-temple-doom

Malamud, Randy. *An Introduction to Animals and Visual Culture*. Great Britain: Palgrave Macmillan, 2012.

Marks, Isaac. *Fears, Phobias and Rituals: Panic, Anxiety, and Their Disorders*. New York and Oxford: Oxford University Press, 1987.

Martin, Aidan R. "Biology of Sharks and Rays." ReefQuest Centre for Shark Research. www.elasmo-research.org/education/topics/p_shark_speed.htm

McLean, Adrienne, ed. *Cinematic Canines: Dogs and Their Work in the Feature Film*. Newark, NJ: Rutgers University Press, 2014.

———. "Introduction: Wonder Dogs." McLean 1–29.

Michalski, Katarzyna, and Sergiusz Michalski. *Spider*. London: Reaktion, 2010.

Miller, Geoffrey F. "How Mate Choice Shaped Human Nature: A Review of Sexual Selection and Human Evolution." *Handbook of Evolutionary Psychology: Ideas, Issues, and Applications*. Eds. Charles Crawford and Dennis L. Krebs. Mahwah, NJ: Lawrence Erlbaum Associates, 1998. 87–130.

———. *The Mating Mind: How Sexual Choice Shaped the Evolution of Human Nature*. New York: Random House, 2000.

Mitchell, Gregory, and Philip E. Tetlock. "Popularity as a Poor Proxy for Utility: The Case of Implicit Prejudice." *Psychological Science Under Scrutiny*. Eds. Scott O. Lilienfeld and Irwin D. Waldman. Malden, MA: Wiley-Blackwell, 2017. 164–195.
Morris, Nigel. *The Cinema of Steven Spielberg: Empire of Light*. New York: Wallflower Press, 2007.
Mulkins, Sandra A. N., Peter J. de Jong, and Harald Merckelbach. "Disgust and Spider Phobia." *Journal of Abnormal Psychology* 105.3 (1996): 464–468. www.ncbi.nlm.nih.gov/pubmed/8772018
Mulvey, Laura. "Visual Pleasure and Narrative Cinema." *Screen* 16.3 (1975): 6–28.
Murray, Robin L., and Joseph K. Heumann. *Ecology and Popular Film: Cinema on the Edge*. Albany: State University of New York Press, 2009.
Nagel, Thomas. "What Is It Like to Be a Bat?" *The Philosophical Review* 83.4 (1974): 435–450. www.jstor.org/stable/2183914
Nayar, Pramod K. *Posthumanism*. Cambridge, MA: Polity Press.
New, Joshua J., and Tamsin C. German. "Spiders at the Cocktail Party: An Ancestral Threat that Surmounts Inattentional Blindness." *Evolution and Human Behavior* 36 (2015): 165–173.
Nielsen, Bianca. "'Something's Wrong, Like More Than You Being Female': Transgressive Sexuality and Discourses of Reproduction in Ginger Snaps." *ThirdSpace: A Journal of Feminist Theory and Culture* 3.2 (2004). journals.sfu.ca/thirdspace/index.php/journal/article/view/nielsen/176
Nyffeler, Martin, and Klaus Birkhofer. "An estimated 400–800 million tons of prey are annually killed by the global spider community." *The Science of Nature* 104.30 (2017). rdcu.be/vodK
Öhman, Arne, and Susan Mineka. "The Malicious Serpent: Snakes as a Prototypical Stimulus for an Evolved Module of Fear." *Current Directions in Psychological Science* 12.1 (2003): 5–9. www.jstor.org/stable/20182821
———. "Fears, Phobias, and Preparedness: Toward an Evolved Module of Fear and Fear Learning." *Psychological Review* 108.3 (2001): 483–522.
Otten, Charlotte F., ed. *A Lycanthropy Reader: Werewolves in Western Culture*. Syracuse, NY: Syracuse University Press, 1986.
Packer, Craig, Alexandra Swanson, Dennis Ikanda, and Hadas Kushnir. "Fear of Darkness, the Full Moon, and the Nocturnal Ecology of African Lions." *PLoS ONE* 6.7 (2011): 1–2. doi.org/10.1371/journal.pone.0022285
Pinker, Steven. *The Blank Slate: The Modern Denial of Human Nature*. New York: Penguin, 2007.
———. *How the Mind Works*. St. Ives, Cornwall: Penguin, 2009.
Plumwood, Val. "Being Prey." *Terra Nova* 1.3 (1996): 32–44.
———. *Feminism and the Mastery of Nature*. London and New York: Routledge, 1993.
Poe, Edgar Allan. "The Murders in the Rue Morgue." *The Fall of the House of Usher and Other Writings*. Ed. David Galloway. London: Penguin, 2003. 141–176.
Polák, J., K. Sedláčková, D. Nácar, E. Landová, and D. S. Frynta. "Fear the Serpent: A Psychometric Study of Snake Phobia." *Psychiatry Research* 242 (2016): 163–168. www.ncbi.nlm.nih.gov/pubmed/27280527

Pomerance, Murray. "Hitchcock's Canine Uncanny." McLean 199–218.
———. "Thirteen Ways of Looking at The Birds." *Hitchcock at the Source: The Auteur as Adaptor*. Eds. R. Barton Palmer and David Boyd. Albany: State University of New York Press, 2011. 267–293.
Quirke, Antonia. *Jaws*. London: BFI: Palgrave Macmillan, 2002.
Rivkin, Julie, and Michael Ryan, eds. *Literary Theory: An Anthology*. 3rd ed. Malden, MA: Wiley Blackwell, 2017.
Rony, Fatimah Tobing. *The Third Eye: Race, Cinema, and Ethnographic Spectacle*. Durham, NC: Duke University Press, 2001.
Rosen, David N. "King Kong: Race, Sex, and Rebellion." *Jump Cut* 6 (1975): 7–10. www.ejumpcut.org/archive/onlinessays/JC06folder/KingKong.html
Rubin, Martin. "1933: Movies and the New Deal in Entertainment." *American Cinema of the 1930s: Themes and Variations*. Ed. Ina Rae Hark. Newark, NJ: Rutgers University Press, 92–116.
Sconduto, Leslie A. *Metamorphoses of the Werewolf: A Literary Study from Antiquity through the Renaissance*. Jefferson, NC and London: McFarland & Company, 2008. Kindle edition.
Schell, Jennifer. "Polluting and Perverting Nature: The Vengeful Animals of Frogs." *Animal Horror Cinema: Genre, History and Criticism*. Gregersgotter, Högland, and Hållén 58–75.
Schieb, Joanna E., Steven W. Gangestad, and Randy Thornhill. "Facial Attractiveness, Symmetry and Cues of Good Genes." *Proceedings of the Royal Society B: Biological Sciences* 266.1431 (1999): 1913–1917.
Schmitt, David P. "'Yes, but . . .': Answers to Ten Common Criticisms of Evolutionary Psychology." The Evolution Institute, 1 Nov 2017. evolution-institute.org/article/on-common-criticisms-of-evolutionary-psychology
Shackelford, Todd K., David M. Buss, and Viviana A. Weekes-Shackelford. "Wife Killings Committed in the Context of a Lover's Triangle." *Basic and Applied Social Psychology* 25.2 (2003): 137–143. labs.la.utexas.edu/buss/files/2015/09/wk_basp_2003.pdf
———, David P. Schmitt, and David M. Buss. "Universal Dimensions of Human Mate Preferences." *Personality and Individual Differences* 39 (2005): 447–458. labs.la.utexas.edu/buss/files/2015/09/universal-dimensions-of-mate-prefs-Shackelford-Schmitt-Buss-PAID-2005.pdf
———, and Viviana A. Weekes-Shackelford, eds. *Encyclopedia of Evolutionary Psychological Science*. Cham, Switzerland: Springer, 2018 dx.doi.org/10.1007/978-3-319-16999-6
Singer, Peter. *Animal Liberation*. London: Pimlico, 1995.
Skal, David J. *The Monster Show: A Cultural History of Horror*. New York: Faber & Faber, 1993.
Smaill, Belinda. *Regarding Life: Animals and the Documentary Moving Image*. Albany: State University of New York Press, 2016.
Smithsonian Institution. "BugInfo: Number of Insects (Species and Individuals)." *Encyclopedia Smithsonian*. Smithsonian Institution. www.si.edu/Encyclopedia_SI/nmnh/buginfo/bugnos.htm

Stephenson, Wesley. "Do the dead outnumber the living?" *BBC News Magazine* 4 Feb 2012. www.bbc.com/news/magazine-16870579

Strain, George M. "How Well Do Dogs and Other Animals Hear?" Louisiana State University. www.lsu.edu/deafness/HearingRange.html

Studlar, Gaylyn. "Masochism and the Perverse Pleasures of the Cinema." *Quarterly Review of Film Studies* 9.4 (1984): 267–282. dx.doi.org/10.1080/10509 208409361219

Stutesman, Drake. *Snake*. London: Reaktion, 2005.

Suchard, Jeffrey Ross. "'Spider Bite' Lesions are Usually Diagnosed as Skin and Soft Tissue Lesions." *Journal of Emergency Medicine* 41.5 (2011): 473–481. www.sciencedirect.com/science/article/pii/S0736467909007926

Tattersall, Ian. "Foreword." Hart and Sussman xiii.

Teige-Mocigemba, Sarah, Manuel Becker, Jeffrey W. Sherman, Regina Rechardht, and Karl Christoph Klauer. "The Affect Misattribution Procedure: In Search of Prejudice Effects." *Experimental Psychology* 64 (2017): 215–230. econtent.hogrefe.com/doi/abs/10.1027/1618-3169/a000364

Tourney, Christopher P. "The Moral Character of Mad Scientists: A Cultural Critique of Science." *Science, Technology, & Human Values* 17.4 (1992): 411–437. www.jstor.org/stable/689735

Torry, Robert. "Therapeutic Narrative: The Wild Bunch, Jaws, and Vietnam." *Velvet Light Trap* 31 (1993): 27–38.

Trivers, Robert L. "Parental Investment and Sexual Selection." *Sexual Selection and the Descent of Man, 1871–1971*. Ed. Bernard G. Campbell. Chicago: Aldine, 136–179.

Trout, Paul. *Deadly Powers: Animal Predators and the Mythic Imagination*. Amherst, NY: Prometheus Books, 2011.

Tybur, Joshua M., Debra Lieberman, Robert Kurzban, and Peter DeScioli. "Disgust: Evolved Function and Structure." *Psychological Review* 120.1 (2013): 65–84. psycnet.apa.org/doiLanding?doi=10.1037%2Fa0030778

Van Strien, Jan W., and Lynne A. Isbell. "Snake Scales, Partial Exposure, and the Snake Detection Theory: A Human-Related Potentials Study." *Scientific Reports* 7.46331 (2017): 1–9. www.nature.com/articles/srep46331

Vetter, Richard S., and Geoffrey K. Isbister. "Medical Aspects of Spider Bites." *Annual Review of Entomology* 53 (2008): 409–429. www.annualreviews.org/doi/abs/10.1146/annurev.ento.53.103106.093503

Von Rueden, Christopher, Michael Gurven, and Hillard Kaplan. "Why Do Men Seek Status: Fitness Payoffs to Dominance and Prestige." *Proceedings of the Royal Society B: Biological Sciences* (2010): rspb20102145. rspb.royalsocietypublishing.org/content/early/2010/12/04/rspb.2010.2145

Wilson, Edward O. *Biophilia: The Human Bond with Other Species*. Cambridge, MA, and London: Harvard University Press, 1984.

———. *In Search of Nature*. Washington, DC and Covelo, CA: Inland Press/Shearwater Books, 1996.

Wilson, Margo, and Martin Daly. "Coercive Violence by Human Males against Their Female Partners." *Sexual Coercion in Primates and Humans: An*

Evolutionary Perspective on Male Aggression against Females. Eds. Martin N. Muller and Richard W. Wrangham. Cambridge, MA and London: Harvard University Press, 2009. 271–291.

Wheeling, Katie, and Max Ufberg. "The Ocean is Boiling: The Complete Oral History of the 1969 Santa Barbara Oil Spill." *Pacific Standard*. 18 April 2017. psmag.com/news/the-ocean-is-boiling-the-complete-oral-history-of-the-1969-santa-barbara-oil-spill

Whitehead, Dan. *Tooth and Claw: A Field Guide to "Nature Run Amok" Horror Movies*. The Zebra Partnership, 2012.

Wolfe, Cary. *Animal Rites: American Culture, the Discourse of Species, and Posthumanist Theory*. Chicago and London: University of Chicago Press, 2003.

Wood, Robin. *Hollywood: From Vietnam to Reagan . . . and Beyond*. Revised and expanded ed. New York: Columbia University Press, 2003.

Woody, Sheila R., Carmen McLean and Tammy Klassen. "Disgust as a Motivator of Avoidance of Spiders." *Anxiety Disorders* 19 (2005): 461–475. www.ncbi.nlm.nih.gov/pubmed/15721575

Workman, Lance, and Will Reader. *Evolutionary Psychology: An Introduction*. Cambridge: Cambridge University Press, 2004.

Wright, John C. "'Twas Beauty Killed the Beast': King Kong and the American Character." *King Kong is Back! An Unauthorized Look at One Humongous Ape*. Eds. David Brin and Leah Wilson. Dallas: Benbella, 2005. 197–211.

Žižek, Slavoj. *Looking Awry: An Introduction to Jacques Lacan through Popular Culture*. Cambridge, MA: MIT Press, 1992.

———. *The Pervert's Guide to Cinema*. Dir. Sophie Fiennes. Perf. Slavoj Žižek. Mischief Films & Amoeba Films, 2006.

Index

Adams, Carol J., 213, 235n5
Adventures of Tintin, The (Steven Spielberg, 2011), 171
Agar, John, 95
Air Bud (film series, 1997–2013), 171
Alcock, John, 222n13, 223n28
Alien film series, 91, 166
Alien (Ridley Scott, 1979), 92
Allen, Richard, 231n16
Alligator (Lewis Teague, 1980), 59
American Museum of Natural History, 224n5
American Werewolf in London, An (John Landis, 1981), 200–3
Anaconda (Luis Llosa, 1997), 1, 3, 139, 154, 155, 159–63, 164, 167
Anacondas: The Hunt for the Blood Orchid (Dwight H. Little, 2004), 159, 162–63, 164, 167
Anderson, Michael, 51, 52
Anderson, Mitchell, 51
Ankers, Evelyn, 196, 197
Ansara, Michael, 73
Ape, The (William Nigh, 1940), 23
Apocalypse Now (Francis Ford Coppola, 1979), 40, 110
Arachnophobia (Frank Marshall, 1990), 1, 103–7, 109
Armstrong, Robert, 24
Arnold, Jack, 95, 96, 97, 98, 99, 117, 120, 121
Arquette, David, 107
Attenborough, Richard, 129, 132

Backlinie, Susan, 45

Bad Moon (Eric Red, 1996), 206
Bait 3D (Kimble Rendall, 2012), 55–57, 62, 225n18
Baldwin, Alec, 80
Banks, Leslie, 32, 174
Barash, David P., 33, 223n33, 223n34
Barkow, Jerome, 27, 222n11, 222n14
Barrett, H. Clark, 6, 7, 57, 141–42, 218–31, 218n33, 225n17, 229n18, 230n7, 230n10
Bartlett, Jeanne, 194
Bart the Bear (animal performer), 81
Bass, Saul, 101
Batman Returns (Tim Burton, 1992), 207
Beast from 20,000 Fathoms, The (Eugène Lourié, 1953), 114–15, 117, 118
Beethoven (Brian Levant, 1992), 171
Beethoven film series (1992–2014), 171
Beham, Sebald, 10
Bellanca, Mary Ellen, 142, 145–46, 230n13, 230n14, 231n22
Benedict, Dirk, 157
Benji (Joe Camp, 1974), 171
Berger, John, 141, 230n3
Bergman, Sandahl, 157
Bieder, Robert, 81, 225n5
Bingo (Matthew Robbins, 1991), 172
Birds, The (Alfred Hitchcock, 1963), 12, 142–46
"Bisclavret" (Marie de France), 195–96, 208
Biskind, Peter, 147, 224n11
Bitonti, James, 86

Bitonti, Jonathan, 86
Black, Jack, 40
Black Scorpion, The (Edward Ludwig, 1957), 94, 95–97, 117
Black Swan (Darren Aronofsky, 2010), 207
Black Water (David Nerlich & Andrew Traucki, 2007), 59, 62, 225n20
Blade Runner (Ridley Scott, 1982), 156
Blair, Linda, 177
Blob, The (Irvin S. Yeaworth, 1958), 173
Blunt, Emily, 198
Bordwell, David, 14, 16, 220nn59–61, 220nn68–69
Borel, Annik, 207
Borkfelt, Sune, 155, 232n16
Bouvier, E. L., 226n2
Boyd, Brian, 14, 15, 16, 219n48, 220n62, 220nn66–70, 220nn72–73
Brand, Neville, 61
Brando, Marlon, 40
Brazier, Caroline, 64
Bride of the Gorilla (Curt Siodmak, 1951), 24
Bridges, Jeff, 35, 37
Britton, Adam, 225n21
Brooks, Elisabeth, 200, 201
Brown, Leslie Hilton, 142
Brown, Reb, 158
Bucci, Flavio, 175
Bug (William Friedkin, 2006), 109–12
Burgess, George, 17
Burr, Raymond, 117, 172
Burroughs, Edgar Rice, 22, 221n4
Burrows, Saffron, 123
Burt, Jonathan, 230n4
Buss, David M., 191–93, 208, 218n27, 222n12, 222n19, 222nn20–21, 223nn22–24, 223n28, 223n30, 233nn5–14 (chap. 9), 234nn15–20, 234n29, 234nn31–34, 235n35

Cabot, Bruce, 25, 28, 138
Caldicott, David G. E., 219n47

Campbell, Joseph, 157
Capshaw, Kate, 90
Carnahan, Joe, 83, 84, 86
Carroll, Joseph, 16, 220n62, 220nn66–67, 220nn70–73
Carroll, Leo G., 120, 121
Carroll, Noël, 16, 26, 28, 33, 34, 182, 222nn8–10, 222n17, 223n31, 224n36, 233n12 (chap. 8)
Carter, Angela, 204
Cartwright, Veronica, 143
Cassidy, Joanna, 156
Cat People (Jacques Tourneur, 1942), 207–9
Cat People (Paul Schrader, 1982), 209–10
Chaney, Lon, 223n26
Chaney Jr., Lon, 196, 197, 202
Chivers, Sally, 234n28
Coleridge, Samuel Taylor, 44, 224n3
Collet-Serra, Jaume, 65, 67
Collins, Lynn, 110
Company of Wolves, The (Neil Jordan, 1984), 204–6
Conan the Barbarian (John Milius, 1982), 155, 157, 167
Congo (Frank Marshall, 1995), 41
Conjuring, The (James Wan, 2013), 174
Connick Jr., Harry, 110
Cool J., LL, 123
Cooper, Merian C., 21, 25, 27, 28, 31, 32–33, 34, 38
Copycat (Jon Amiel, 1995), 90
Corsaut, Aneta, 173
Cosmides, Leda, 223–24n34
Cox, William T. L., 221n78
Cranach, Lucas, 188
Creed, Barbara, 222n18, 224n12
Croc (Stewart Raffill, 2007), 59
Crocodile (Tobe Hooper, 2000), 59, 61–62
Crocodile Dundee (Peter Faiman, 1986), 60, 147
Cronenberg, David, 123, 124, 126, 128

Cujo (Lewis Teague, 1983), 169, 170, 182–86
Curse of the Werewolf, The (Terence Fisher, 1961), 199–200
Curtis, Jamie Lee, 24

Daniels, Jeff, 103, 107
Dante, Joe, 68, 108, 201
Darcy-Smith, Kieran, 54
Dark Age (Arch Nicholson, 1987), 59, 60–61, 63, 64
Darwin, Charles, 6, 12, 13, 15, 16, 26–28, 32, 34, 38, 222n16
Davenport, Nigel, 101
Davey, Graham C. L., 226n8 (chap. 4), 227n13
Davis, Geena, 126, 127, 128
Dawkins, Richard, 222n15
Dawson, Anthony, 199
Day of the Animals (William Girdler, 1977), 70, 71, 73–75, 119, 139
Deadly Mantis, The (Nathan Juran, 1957), 117
Deep Blue Sea (Renny Harlin, 1999), 123, 225n16
Deep Red (Dario Argento, 1975), 140
de France, Marie, 195, 234nn20–21, 234n23
De Laurentiis, Dino, 35
Del Giudice, Marco, 233n13
Del Toro, Benicio, 198, 199
DeMille, Cecil B., 23
Dermody, Maeve, 62
Dern, Laura, 131
Derry, Charles, 223n32
Derakshan, Nazanin, 219n34
Derrida, Jacques, 146–47, 231nn23–24
Devine, Patricia G., 221n78
DiCaprio, Leonardo, 70
Dogs (Burt Brinckerhoff, 1976), 169
Donner, Richard, 174
Douglas, Gordon, 94, 95
Douglas, Kirk, 78
Douglas, Michael, 77, 78
Doyle, Arthur Conan, 155

du Maurier, Daphne, 142
Dunne, Griffin, 202

Eaten Alive (Tobe Hooper, 1977), 59, 61
Edge, The (Lee Tamahori, 1997), 70, 71, 79–83, 84, 87
Ehrenreich, Barbara, 2, 11, 213, 217n2, 219n44, 219n51
Eight Legged Freaks (Ellory Elkayem, 2002), 107–9
Elliott, Sam, 119
Ellis, David R., 163, 165
Erb, Cynthia, 221n1
Exorcist, The (William Friedkin, 1973)
Exorcist III, The (William Peter Blatty, 1990), 154, 155, 169, 177–79, 185

Fahey, David W., 229n11
Fawcett, John, 210, 211
Ferguson, Christopher J., 220n76
Ferrando, Francesca, 220n61
Fierce Creatures (Robert Young & Red Schepisi, 1997), 24
Fierro, Lee, 47
Finney, Albert, 148
Fleischman, Diana, 218n28, 226nn6–8 (chap. 4)
Florey, Robert, 22
Fly, The (Kurt Neumann, 1958), 118, 123–26, 127
Fly, The (David Cronenberg, 1986), 123, 126–29
Ford, Harrison, 7
Foster, Gwendolyn Audrey, 97
Four Feathers, The (Merian C. Cooper, Lothar Mendes & Ernest B. Schoedsack, 1929), 32
Franco, James, 123
Frankenstein (Mary Shelley), 120
Frederick, Lynne, 101
Frémiet, Emmanuel, 21, 22, 23, 24
Freud, Sigmund, 145, 156, 198, 200, 232n17, 234n25
Friday the 13th (Sean S. Cunningham, 1980), 140

250 Index

Friedkin, William, 109, 110, 112, 177, 178, 179
Fry, Brian G et al., 217n13
Fuchs, Michael, 217n15, 218n24, 225n20, 225n24
Fuller, Sam, 175
Funk, Cary, 228n1
Funny Games (Michael Haneke, 1997 & 2007), 174

Gambin, Lee, 221n79
Gamble, Mason, 206
Garland, Judy, 172
George, Christopher, 71, 73
George, Susan, 158
Gerdes, Antje, B. M., 227n15, 227nn21–22, 228n27
German, Tamsin C., 92, 227nn16–17
Getz, John, 127
Ghost and the Darkness, The (Stephen Hopkins, 1996), 75–79, 87, 140
Ginger Snaps (John Fawcett, 2000), 207, 210—211
Girard, René, 34, 224n35
Girdler, William, 71, 73, 74, 75
Gittell, Noah, 213, 235n3
Glaeser, Georg, 224n4
Gleeson, Brendan, 62
Glenn, Diana, 62
Godzilla (Ishirō Honda, 1954), 18, 21, 115–17, 229n8
Godzilla (Gareth Edwards, 2014), 40
Godzilla: King of the Monsters! (Ishirō Honda & Terry O. Morse, 1956), 116–17
Goldblum, Jeff, 126, 128, 130
Goodman, John, 103
Gott, Ted, 221n3, 224n39
Gottschall, Jonathan, 220n62
Grantley, Gyton, 53
Gray, Lorraine, 47
Gregersdotter, Katarina, 12–13, 17, 84, 139, 141, 219n49, 219nn53–55, 220n74, 221n2, 226n7, 229n2, 230n6
Gremlins (Joe Dante, 1984), 108

Grey, The (Joe Carnahan, 2011), 7, 71, 83–87, 138, 178, 214
Grillo, Frank, 85
Grizzly (William Girdler, 1976), 70, 71–73, 75
Grizzly Rage (David DeCoteau, 2007), 70
Grodin, Charles, 35
Grotuss, Jason, 223n28
Guest, Lance, 51
Guillermin, John, 35, 36, 37, 38
Gwenn, Edmund, 94, 117

Hagen, Edward, 218n27
Hållán, Nicklas, 84, 219n49, 219n53, 220n54, 226n7
Halloween (John Carpenter, 1978), 140
Hamilton, Margaret, 172
Handwerk, Brian, 218n23
Handy, James, 105
Hark, Ina Rae, 120, 122, 229nn15–16
Harris, Richard, 51
Harryhausen, Ray, 114
Hart, Donna, 1, 2, 4, 187, 217n1, 217n6, 217n7, 217nn9–11, 217n14, 217nn17–18, 217n21, 230n9, 230nn11–12, 233n1
Hayden, Sterling, 158
Heard, John, 209
Hedison, David, 124, 125
Hedren, Tippi, 142, 143
Heine, Cariba, 55
Heithaus, Mike, 44
Hellmer, Kahl, 219n34, 227n18, 231n6
Helm, Fay, 196
Hemingway, Mariel, 206
Hendershot, Cyndy, 114, 115, 117, 228n3, 228n4
Henriksen, Lance, 121
Herbert, Charles, 124
Heumann, Joseph K., 108, 228n28
Hill, Kim, 217n22, 231n4
Hirata, Akihiko, 116
Hobson, Valerie, 189, 191
Hoehl, Stefanie, 219n34, 227n18, 231n6

Index

Hogan, Paul, 60
Högland, Johan, 219n49, 219n53, 220n54, 220n74, 221n2
Holcomb, Lance, 158
Homeward Bound: The Incredible Journey (Duwayne Dunham, 1993), 172
Honey, I Shrunk the Kids (Joe Johnston, 1989), 97–101
Hooper, Tobe, 61
Hopkins, Anthony, 79, 80, 198
Hopkins, Stephen, 75, 76, 77, 140
Horowitz, Margaret, 145
Hostel: Part III (Scott Spiegel, 2011), 90
Hound of the Baskervilles, The (Terence Fisher, 1959), 174
Howard, Bryce Dallas, 133
Howling, The (Joe Dante, 1981), 200–2
Hrdy, Sarah Blaffer, 32, 223n25, 223n30
Hull, Henry, 122, 190, 191, 194
Hurtado, A. Magdalena 217n22, 231n4

Incredible Shrinking Man, The (Jack Arnold, 1957), 97–100, 102, 103, 117
Indiana Jones and the Temple of Doom (Steven Spielberg, 1984), 90
Ingagi (William Campbell, 1930), 21
Ingraham, Christopher, 227n12
Inspector Rex (TV, 1994–2004), 171
Into the Grizzly Maze (David Hackl, 2015), 70
Isabelle, Katharine, 210, 211
Isbell, Lynne A., 12, 154, 219n52, 231n7–8
Island of Doctor Moreau, The (Don Taylor, 1977), 120–21

Jackson, Peter, 38, 39, 40
Jackson, Samuel L., 40, 164
Jaeckel, Richard, 71
Jaenada, Óscar, 65
Jarratt, John, 60, 64
Jaws (Steven Spielberg, 1975), 1, 7, 12, 17, 43, 44–49, 51, 52, 55, 57, 66, 68, 72, 78, 87, 120, 137, 138, 139, 146–48, 149, 160, 162, 166, 175, 185, 215
Jaws of Satan (Bob Claver, 1981), 155
Jaws 2 (Jeannot Szwarc, 1978), 49, 51
Jaws: The Revenge (Joseph Sargent, 1987), 51
Jaws 3-D (Joe Alves, 1983), 49–51
Jed (animal performer), 180, 181
Johansson, Maria, 219n34, 227n18, 231n6
Johansson, Scarlett, 109
Johnson, Victoria, 72
Jonason, Peter K., 222n20, 226n6
Jones, James Earl, 157
Jones, L. Q., 80
Jordan, Neil, 204, 205
Judd, Ashley, 109, 110
Jurassic Park (Steven Spielberg, 1993), 1, 4, 8, 9, 114, 129–32, 149–51
Jurassic Park III (Joe Johnston, 2001), 133
Jurassic World (Colin Trevorrow, 2015), 133–35

Kafka, Franz, 124
Kani, John, 76
Keetley, Dawn, 84, 85, 86, 226nn8–10 (chap. 3)
Kelly, Daniel Hugh, 183
Khan, Irrfan, 133
Killer Crocodile (Fabrizio De Angelis, 1989), 59
Kilmer, Val, 75, 140
King Cobra (David Hillenbrand, 1999), 154
King Kong (Merian C. Cooper & Ernest B. Schoedsack, 1933), 1, 12, 19, 21–35, 96, 115, 138, 147, 149, 156, 198
King Kong (John Guillermin, 1976), 35–38
King Kong (Peter Jackson, 2005), 38–40

Kinski, Klaus, 158
Kinski, Nastassja, 209
Kipling, Rudyard, 155
Kirk, Tommy, 184
Kitsch, Taylor, 165, 165
Kline, Kevin, 24
Knight, Wayne, 151
Koneswaran, Gowri, 235n1
Kong Island (Roberto Mauri, 1968), 24
Kong: Skull Island (Jordan Vogt-Roberts, 2017), 40–41
Kosak, Harley Jane, 103
Kozlowski, Linda, 60
Kruuk, Hans, 2, 8, 9, 217nn3–5, 217n8, 217n16, 217nn19–20, 218n29, 219nn36–40, 230n8
Kubrick, Stanley, 101
Kurzban, Robert, 218n28
Kushnir, Hadas, 218n32, 235n7

Ladd, Alan, 79
Lake Placid (Steve Miner, 1999), 59, 62
Lancaster, Burt, 120
Landis, John, 202, 203
Lange, Jessica, 35, 36, 37
Lansbury, Angela, 205
Lassie (TV, 1954–1973), 171
Lassie Come Home (Fred M. Wilcox, 1943), 171
Last Temptation of Christ, The (Martin Scorsese, 1988), 155
Lauter, Ed, 184
Lawson, Byron, 163
Lawson, Henry, 155
Leane, Elizabeth, 181–2, 232nn10–11
Lee, Christopher, 174
Letts, Tracy, 109
Lewis, Lincoln, 55
Lieberman, Debra, 218n28
Lipp, Ottmar V., 219n34, 231n7
Little, Dwight H., 162
"Little Red Riding Hood," 187, 205
Lively, Blake, 65, 67
Llosa, Luis, 3, 159, 160, 161, 162, 163

Lobato-Villa, Irena, 228n23
Lockjaw (Amir Valinia, 2008), 155
Lockwood, Jeffrey A., 5, 91, 112, 218n25, 226n3, 227nn9–10, 227n14, 228n24, 228n27, 228n29
Lopez, Jennifer, 159, 161
Lost World: Jurassic Park, The (Steven Spielberg, 1997), 132
Lourié, Eugène, 114, 115
Loverance, Rowena, 177–8, 232n8
Lovgren, Stefan, 220n75, 224n2
Ludwig, Edward, 25, 26
Lugosi, Bela, 23, 196

Macnee, Patrick, 200
Macpherson, Elle, 79
Maeterlinck, Maurice, 89
Malamud, Randy, 230n5
Maloney, Peter, 179
Mamet, David, 79
Man's Best Friend (John Lafia, 1993), 121–2
Marks, Isaac, 219n35
Marsden, Matthew, 163
Marshall, Frank, 90, 104, 105, 107
Marshall, Neil, 189
Martin, Aidan R., 224n1
Martin, Strother, 120, 157
Mason, James, 68
Masur, Richard, 180
Matthews, Lester, 189
Mazzello, Joseph, 9
McCall, Joan, 72
McCardie, Brian, 76
McCrea, Joel, 32
McDowell, Malcolm, 209
McLean, Adrienne, 172, 232n3
McLeod, Samantha, 164, 165
McMahon, Julian, 56
McNab, Mercedes, 156
McQueen, Steve, 173
Meagher, Ray, 60
Menzies, Heather, 158
Messner, Johnny, 163
Michalski, Katarzyna, 92, 227n19
Michalski, Sergiusz, 92, 227n19

Milland, Ray, 119
Miller, Geoffrey F., 222n20, 223n22
Miller, Jason, 177
Mimic (Guillermo del Toro, 1997), 90
Mineka, Susan, 219n41, 231n3, 231n5, 231n9, 232n11 (chap. 7)
Mitchell, Gregory, 221n77
Mitchell, Heather, 64
Mitchell, Radha, 63
Moby-Dick (Herman Melville, 1851), 41, 48, 52
Montoro, Edward L., 71
Morricone, Ennio, 180
Morris, Nigel, 48, 49, 224nn9–10, 225nn14–15
Mortimer, Emily, 76
Most Dangerous Game, The (Irving Pichel & Ernest Schoedsack, 1932), 32, 174
Murder by Decree (Bob Clark, 1978), 140
Murders in the Rue Morgue (Robert Florey, 1932), 22
Murphy, Michael, 101
Murray, Robin L., 108, 228n28
Muybridge, Eadweard, 141

Nabonga (Sam Newfield, 1944), 24
Nagel, Thomas, 139, 141, 229n1
Narraway, Guinevere, 181–82, 232n10–11
Naughton, David, 202, 203
Nayar, Pramod K., 220n56, 220n58, 220n61
Naylor, Zoe, 53
Neeson, Liam, 83, 84, 85
Neill, Sam, 4, 130
Neumann, Kurt, 118, 123, 125
New, Joshua J., 92, 227nn16–17
Nicholson, Jack, 203, 205
Nielsen, Bianca, 210, 235n36
Nielsen, Leslie, 73, 74
North American Bear Center, 217n12
Nyffeler, Martin, 227n11

O'Brien, Willis, 25, 96

Öhman, Arne, 219n41, 231n3, 231n5, 231n9, 232n11
Old Yeller (Robert Stevenson, 1957), 171–72, 184, 189
Oland, Warner, 189
Olmos, Edward James, 148
Omen, The (Richard Donner, 1976), 174
Open Water (Chris Kentis, 2004), 52–54, 55, 62
Orca: The Killer Whale (Michael Anderson, 1977), 51–52, 55, 120, 139
Otten, Charlotte F., 233n2, 233n4
O'Toole, Annette, 209
Otto, Barry, 63
Owens, Patricia, 124, 125
Oxenbould, Ben, 62

Packer, Craig, 7, 218n32
Pankin, Stuart, 105
Paradise Lost (John Milton), 131
Paré, Michael, 206
Patterson, Sarah, 205
Pearl, Aaron, 156
Peck, Gregory, 175
Perkins, Emily, 210
Pew Research Center, 113, 228n1
Pfeiffer, Michelle, 204
Phase IV (Saul Bass, 1974), 101–3, 109
Philbin, Mary, 223n26
Phillips, Nathan, 163
Picardo, Robert, 200
Pickering, Adrienne, 53
Pinker, Steven, 14, 15, 219n48, 220nn63–65, 222n13
Pintauro, Danny, 183
Piranha (Joe Dante, 1978), 68, 121, 122, 147, 166
Pirreneau, Harold, 80
Plumwood, Val, 59–60, 70, 178, 225nn22–23, 225nn1–3 (chap. 3), 232n9
Poe, Edgar Allan, 21–22
Pogson, Kathryn, 205

Polák, Jakub, 232n2
Pomerance, Murray, 145, 173, 231n20
Preservation (Christopher Denham, 2014), 174
Primeval (Michael Katleman, 2007), 59
Primo (animal performer), 206
Prine, Andrew, 71

Quirke, Antonia, 44, 45, 47, 224nn6–8

Raiders of the Lost Ark (Steven Spielberg, 1981), 7, 155
Rains, Claude, 197
Randolph, Jane, 208, 209
Rattlers (John McCauley, 1976), 154
Rea, Stephen, 205
Rear Window (Alfred Hitchcock, 1954), 172–73
Rechardht, Regina, 221n77
Reed, Oliver, 158, 159, 199
Reef, The (Andrew Traucki, 2010), 44, 52, 53–55
Reid, Tara, 58
Reilly, John C., 40
Revenant, The (Alejandro G. Iñárritu, 2015), 70
Richards, Ariana, 8, 150
Rise of the Planet of the Apes (Rupert Wyatt, 2011), 21, 123, 152
Rivkin, Julie, 16
Rodoreda, Andy, 62
Rogue (Greg McLean, 2007), 7, 59, 62, 63–65
Romain, Yvonne, 199
Rosen, David N., 221n6
Rottweiler (Brian Yuzna, 2004), 169, 174, 175
Rubin, Martin, 34, 224n37
Ryan, Blanchard, 52, 54
Ryan, Michael, 16

Sacks, Martin, 56
Samuel, Xavier, 56
Scagnetti, Franca, 175
Scerbo, Cassie, 57

Scheib, Joanna E., 223n28
Scheider, Roy, 47
Schell, Jennifer, 119, 229n13
Schoedsack, Ernest B., 21, 25, 27, 28, 31, 32–33, 34, 38, 138
Schrader, Paul, 209–10
Schwarzenegger, Arnold, 157, 228n7
Sconduto, Leslie, 188, 195, 233n3, 234n22
Searchers, The (John Ford, 1956), 79
Serkis, Andy, 38
Shackelford, Todd K., 223n22, 233n14
Shakespeare, William, 155
Shallows, The (Jaume Collet-Serra, 2016), 65—68, 70, 87, 178, 213, 214
Shane (George Stevens, 1953), 79
Shannon, Michael, 110
Sharknado (Anthony C. Ferrante, 2013), 55, 57–59, 68, 225n19
Shaw, Robert, 48
Sheedy, Ally, 122
Sherman, Jeffrey W., 221n77
Shimura, Takashi, 116
Sia (musician), 68
Sign of the Cross, The (Cecil B. DeMille, 1932), 23
Simon, Simone, 207
Singer, Peter, 232n7
Skal, David J., 115, 228n2, 228nn5–6
Smaill, Belinda, 220n55
Small, Michael, 137
Smith, Kent, 207
Smithsonian Institution, 226n1
Snake Island (Wayne Crawford, 2002), 154, 155
Snakes on a Plane (David R. Ellis, 2006), 1, 140, 154, 155, 163–67
Solon, Ewen, 174
Son of Kong (Ernest Schoedsack, 1933), 23
Spader, James, 204
Spiders (Gary Jones, 2000), 93
Sssssss (Bernard L. Kowalski, 1973), 120, 123, 130, 155, 156, 157–58

Starship Troopers (Paul Verhoeven, 1997), 91
Steele, Barbara, 122
Stephens, Harvey, 175
Stephenson, Wesley, 235n2
Stevens, Andrew, 74
Stewart, James, 172
Stoltz, Eric, 159
Stone, Christopher, 184, 200, 201
Strain, George M., 232n6
Strickland, KaDee, 163
Strieber, Whitley, 148
Stutesman, Drake, 154, 157, 232nn13–15, 232nn18–19
Suchard, Jeffrey Ross, 227n20
Suspiria (Dario Argento, 1977), 169, 175–177
Sussman, Robert W., 1, 2, 4, 187, 217n1, 217nn6–7, 217nn9–11, 217n14, 217n17, 217n18, 217n21, 218n26, 230n9, 230nn11–12, 233n1
Swanson, Alexandra, 218n32, 235n7

Tamahori, Lee, 79, 80
Tandy, Jessica, 143
Tarantula (Jack Arnold, 1955), 94, 95, 96, 97, 117, 120–21, 122
Tarzan of the Apes (Edgar Rice Burroughs, 1912), 22–23, 30, 31, 221n4
Tattersall, Ian, 6, 218n26
Taylor, Don, 120
Taylor, Robert, 64
Taylor, Rod, 142
Teague, Lewis, 170, 182, 183, 184
Teige-Mocigemba, Sarah, 221n77
Tennyson, Alfred, 30
Tetlock, Philip E., 221n77
Texas Chainsaw Massacre, The (Tobe Hooper, 1974), 61
Them! (Gordon Douglas, 1954), 94–95, 101, 117, 118
Thing, The (John Carpenter, 1983), 169, 179–82
Thomas, Daniel, 52, 54
Thompson, Kenan, 166

Tonkin, Phoebe, 56
Torry, Robert, 225n13
Tourneur, Jacques, 207, 209
Tourney, Christopher, 122, 129n17
Traucki, Andrew, 53
Trevorrow, Colin, 133, 134
Trivers, Robert L., 223n29
Trout, Paul, 11, 214, 219nn45–46, 235n6, 235n9
Turner and Hooch (Roger Spottiswoode, 1989), 171
Twenty Thousand Leagues Under the Sea (Richard Fleischer, 1954), 68
Tybur, Joshua M., 218n28

Ufberg, Max, 118, 229nn9–10
Underworld film series (2002–2016), 189
Unholy Three, The (Tod Browning, 1925), 21
United Nations, The, 118, 213

Valli, Alida, 175
Van Strien, Jan W., 154, 231nn7–8
Vartan, Michael, 63
Venom (Piers Haggard, 1981), 154, 155, 158–59, 167
Vetter, Richard S., 227n20
Vinson, Sharni, 56
Vinton, Bobby, 202
Vipers (Bill Corcoran, 2008), 154, 156
Voight, Jon, 159, 161, 162
von Rueden, Christopher, 223nn22–23
von Sydow, Max, 177, 178
Voorhees, Jeffrey, 47

Walker, Stuart, 190, 191, 194
Wallace, Dee, 183, 200
Walshe-Howling, Damian, 53
Watts, Naomi, 38, 39
Wayne, John, 79
Weaver, Sigourney, 90
Weir, Kathryn, 221n3, 224n39
Weldon, Joan, 94

Wells, H. G., 120
Werewolf of London (Stuart Walker, 1935), 122–23, 130, 189–96, 208
Werewolf Woman (Rino Di Silvestro, 1976), 207
Wheeling, Kate, 118, 229nn9–10
White, Betty, 162
White Dog (Sam Fuller, 1982), 175
Whitehead, Dan, 11, 71, 219n50, 221n79, 225n4
Whitelaw, Billie, 174
Williams, Grant, 97, 98, 99
Williams, John, 137, 149
Wilson, Edward O., 10, 11, 153, 154, 170, 214, 219nn42–43, 231n1, 231n3, 231n10, 232n12, 232n1, 235n8
Wilson, Margo, 234n30
Wilson, Owen, 159
Wizard of Oz, The (Victor Fleming, 1939), 172
Wolf (Mike Nichols, 1994), 203–5, 211
Wolfe, Cary, 220n56

Wolfen (Michael Wadleigh, 1980), 148–49
Wolf Man, The (George Waggner, 1941), 196–98, 202, 234n26
Wolfman, The (Joe Johnston, 2010), 198–99
Wong, BD, 130
Wood, Robin, 232n20
Woody, Sheila R., 227n22
Wordsworth, Richard, 199
Worthington, Sam, 64
Wray, Fay, 24, 28, 32, 138
Wright, John C., 24, 31, 222n5, 223n27
Wuhrer, Kari, 107, 159
Wyllie, Dan, 56

X-Files, The, 90

Yeaworth, Irvin S., 173

Ziering, Ian, 57
Žižek, Slavoj, 144–45, 231n15, 231n17–19

THE SUNY SERIES

HORIZONS OF CINEMA

MURRAY POMERANCE | EDITOR

Also in the series

William Rothman, editor, *Cavell on Film*

J. David Slocum, editor, *Rebel Without a Cause*

Joe McElhaney, *The Death of Classical Cinema*

Kirsten Moana Thompson, *Apocalyptic Dread*

Frances Gateward, editor, *Seoul Searching*

Michael Atkinson, editor, *Exile Cinema*

Paul S. Moore, *Now Playing*

Robin L. Murray and Joseph K. Heumann, *Ecology and Popular Film*

William Rothman, editor, *Three Documentary Filmmakers*

Sean Griffin, editor, *Hetero*

Jean-Michel Frodon, editor, *Cinema and the Shoah*

Carolyn Jess-Cooke and Constantine Verevis, editors, *Second Takes*

Matthew Solomon, editor, *Fantastic Voyages of the Cinematic Imagination*

R. Barton Palmer and David Boyd, editors, *Hitchcock at the Source*

William Rothman, *Hitchcock: The Murderous Gaze, Second Edition*

Joanna Hearne, *Native Recognition*

Marc Raymond, *Hollywood's New Yorker*

Steven Rybin and Will Scheibel, editors, *Lonely Places, Dangerous Ground*

Claire Perkins and Constantine Verevis, editors, *B Is for Bad Cinema*

Dominic Lennard, *Bad Seeds and Holy Terrors*

Rosie Thomas, *Bombay before Bollywood*

Scott M. MacDonald, *Binghamton Babylon*

Sudhir Mahadevan, *A Very Old Machine*

David Greven, *Ghost Faces*

James S. Williams, *Encounters with Godard*

William H. Epstein and R. Barton Palmer, editors, *Invented Lives, Imagined Communities*

Lee Carruthers, *Doing Time*

Rebecca Meyers, William Rothman, and Charles Warren, editors, *Looking with Robert Gardner*

Belinda Smaill, *Regarding Life*

Douglas McFarland and Wesley King, editors, *John Huston as Adaptor*
R. Barton Palmer, Homer B. Pettey, and Steven M. Sanders, editors, *Hitchcock's Moral Gaze*
Nenad Jovanovic, *Brechtian Cinemas*
Will Scheibel, *American Stranger*
Amy Rust, *Passionate Detachments*
Steven Rybin, *Gestures of Love*
Seth Friedman, *Are You Watching Closely?*
Roger Rawlings, *Ripping England!*
Michael DeAngelis, *Rx Hollywood*
Ricardo E. Zulueta, *Queer Art Camp Superstar*
John Caruana and Mark Cauchi, editors, *Immanent Frames*
Nathan Holmes, *Welcome to Fear City*
Homer B. Pettey and R. Barton Palmer, editors, *Rule, Britannia!*
Milo Sweedler, *Rumble and Crash*
Ken Windrum, *From El Dorado to Lost Horizons*
Matthew Lau, *Sounds Like Helicopters*
William Rothman, *Tuitions and Intuitions*